# Instruction

# Instruction
## *A Models Approach*

MARY ALICE GUNTER
*The University of Virginia*

THOMAS H. ESTES
*The University of Virginia*

JAN HASBROUCK SCHWAB
*Charlottesville Public Schools*
*Charlottesville, Virginia*

ALLYN AND BACON
*Boston   London   Sydney   Toronto*

Copyright © 1990 by Allyn and Bacon
A Division of Simon & Schuster, Inc.
160 Gould Street
Needham Heights, Massachusetts 02194-2310

**Credits**

*pp. xviii, 5, 29, 31, 39, 56, 66, 79, 91, 208, 248, 259* Shoe cartoons reprinted by permission of Tribune Media Services. *p. 120* "Fog" from *Chicago Poems* by Carl Sandburg, copyright 1916 by Holt, Rinehart and Winston, Inc., renewed 1944 by Carl Sandburg, reprinted by permission of Harcourt Brace Jovanovich, Inc. *pp. 143–144* Reprinted from an adaptation of "Water Boiling in a Peruvian Village: A Diffusion Campaign that Failed" by Edward Wellin, in *Health, Culture, and Community*, ed. Benjamin D. Paul, © Russell Sage Foundation, 1955. Used with permission of the Russell Sage Foundation. *p. 202* Lines from "Abraham Lincoln Walks at Midnight" are from *Collected Poems* of Vachel Lindsay (New York: Macmillan, 1923).

Series Editor: Sean W. Wakely
Series Editorial Assistant: Carolyn O'Sullivan
Production Administrator: Annette Joseph
Production Coordinator: Susan Freese
Editorial-Production Service: Kailyard Associates
Cover Administrator: Linda K. Dickinson

**Library of Congress Cataloging-in-Publication Data**

Gunter, Mary Alice, 1935–
    Instruction : a models approach / Mary Alice Gunter, Thomas H. Estes, Jan
Hasbrouck Schwab.
        p.    cm.
    ISBN 0-205-12131-4
    1. Teaching.   2. Curriculum planning.   3. Classroom environment.   4. Group work
in education.   5. Teachers–In-service training.   I. Estes, Thomas H., 1940–  .   II.
Schwab, Jan Hasbrouck, 1932–  .   III. Title.
    LB1025.2.G86   1990
    375'.001–dc20                                                                    89-27826
                                                                                     CIP

Printed in the United States of America

10  9  8  7  6  5  4  3  2  1     95  94  93  92  91  90

# Brief Contents

# Contents

# Preface

Teachers today are under unprecedented pressure from all sides. Everyone, it seems, is an expert on teaching. Newspapers and magazines are full of advice about what teachers should do in classrooms, and still more advice comes from sources as varied as legislators and preachers, parents and students, school board members and university professors. Who isn't qualified to speak with authority about schools and teaching? After all, didn't everyone go to school for many years and leave with the full knowledge of how school should have been?

More to the point, perhaps, there is a sense that everyone *is* a teacher. The root meaning of the word *teach* is "to show, to tell, to point out." Parents *tell* their children what to do; doctors *point out* proper procedures to their patients; auto mechanics *show* how to make minor adjustments to a car. Everyone *teaches* others to do things, and so everyone is a teacher, at least in an amateur sense.

Before mistakenly jumping to the conclusion that there really is nothing very special or unique about being a teacher, consider the word *teach* in its professional sense, in relation to the word *instruction*. The meaning of the word *instruct* derives from the root "to build" or "to structure." Professional teachers not only *teach* in the usual sense of the word, they also *instruct*. They *structure* classroom environments and *build* series of experiences for students who have wide ranges of abilities, interests, and needs. Whereas parents, doctors, and auto mechanics usually teach spontaneously by telling, pointing out, or showing, professional educators must carefully design and plan for their teaching.

There is a natural analogy between instruction and building based on the process of structuring environments. The teacher, as an instructor, is comparable to the builder in three ways.

1. *Planning for a specific audience.* The builder and the teacher alike must first determine the needs of their clients. The house required for a family of six with four dogs, three hamsters, and a rabbit will be very different from that for an elderly couple with a parakeet. Similarly, the instructional design for an advanced placement class in physics will be different from the design for a fifth-grade math class. Both the builder and the teacher must consider their clients, and they need to know how to formulate a plan that will be sound, original, and functional.

A good design for teaching grows out of a clear understanding of the needs of learners and the goals of education. Each design that a professional teacher creates is unique because different groups of learners have individual needs, and different types of learning require specific instructional approaches.

2. *Formulating objectives and evaluation procedures.* The needs of their clients will help both the teacher and the builder to specify as clearly as possible the intended outcome of their work. No builder would think of starting a construc-

tion project without having a clear picture of how the final product should look. To get halfway through the project only to realize that what was emerging was not what the client wanted or needed would be professionally embarrassing and very expensive to correct. The teacher who works without a careful design also leaves too much to chance. As a professional, the teacher must plan how to achieve specific intended learning outcomes. Otherwise, valuable instructional time can go to waste, and neither the teacher nor the students find satisfaction.

An essential part of setting objectives is determining effective evaluation procedures that make certain that what was intended is what is taking place. Like the builder who must constantly check on the construction, the teacher must determine whether the instruction is producing the desired results. It would be foolish to wait until a building was completed to check on the workmanship and determine if all was proceeding as planned. Likewise, a teacher must utilize effective evaluation procedures throughout the process of teaching.

Evaluation is continuous, forming the basis of all decisions at every step—determining needs, formulating objectives, and selecting materials and methods. Evaluation is the process of continually asking "Where are we going?" "How do we get there?" and "How far along are we?" The teacher can never stop asking whether the instruction is appropriate and effective. Thus, evaluation showing the intermediate and ultimate results of teaching must be used to reform the process of teaching. Continuous evaluation makes this possible.

**3.** *Selection of materials and procedures.* The builder has available a variety of materials and techniques from which to choose and must decide which combination will produce the structure most nearly like the one intended. Each project must be analyzed to determine the appropriate combinations; for instance, not every house can be built only of brick or wood. Likewise, each student is an individual with special needs, strengths, and interests. Moreover, each class is unique in terms of the dynamics of a particular group. Therefore, the teacher needs to have at hand a variety of approaches and techniques to accomplish specific instructional objectives and to manage problems as they arise.

Unfortunately, classroom environments are sometimes boring and monotonous, for the teacher as well as the students, because there is so little variety in instruction. John Goodlad, in his definitive study of schooling in America, *A Place Called School*, concluded:

> The data from our observations in more than 1,000 classrooms support the popular image of a teacher standing or sitting in front of a class imparting knowledge to a group of students. Explaining and lecturing constituted the most frequent teaching activities. . . . On the whole, teachers at all levels did not know how to vary their instructional procedures, did not want to, or had some kind of difficulty doing so.[1]

Goodlad described an "extraordinary passivity" that is evident in so many classrooms in which children sit, listen, answer questions, and take tests. Discipline problems often arise in such classrooms, and the cause is seldom identified as instructional, even though effective planning and instructional design can resolve many of these problems.

The teacher who repeatedly uses the same instructional technique is like the builder who can build only one house. A repertoire of instructional and management strategies is necessary to meet the varied needs of learners.

## Plan for the Text

The philosophy behind this book is the belief that the process of instruction unites all teachers as professional educators. Our intended audience is teachers of any subject who teach or plan to teach learners of any age. We have tried to address teaching as a challenging, exciting, and demanding profession with great rewards for all who follow it.

This text was written not as a rule book but as an invitation to consider the opportunities for professional decision making that constitute instruction. We have chosen to present some of the intriguing possibilities facing the professional educator who tries to identify procedures appropriate to situations that arise in the classroom.

Progress toward mastery teaching is a continuous process of learning and adapting, modifying, and changing. The difference between last year's class and this year's, between third period and fourth, between one reading group and another, between the child in the front seat in the second row and the child in the last seat in the corner are the challenges that make instruction a process of seeking solutions and making choices.

We have divided this text into three parts. Part One centers on a description of the process of setting goals, writing objectives, designing units, and selecting instructional materials. The teacher must decide *what* is to be learned in the classroom before considering *how* to present the material through instruction. A variety of options may be considered in designing the instructional plan.

Part Two presents a selected group of instructional models along with examples of how these models can be used in the design process. We are indebted to the many individuals whose research formed the basis for these models. We also relied on our own experience and the experience of many classroom teachers in determining what steps make these models most effective. Part Two is enriched by the work of Dr. Phyllis Hotchkiss, a former colleague at the University of Virginia and presently an Associate Professor of Education at Midwestern State University in Wichita Falls, Texas. Dr. Hotchkiss is the author of Chapter 11 on cooperative learning and has worked extensively using these models of instruction.

Part Three contains three chapters—each a case study—that describe how teachers match objectives to instruction in the design process. Part Three concludes with a chapter that suggests ways of creating a positive environment for learning in the classroom.

We have included both exercises and activities throughout the book. Exercises are specific, focusing on the particular subject under discussion, and can be completed as the text is read. Answers are provided immediately following each of the exercises in order that the reader may react to suggestions for how the questions could be answered. Activities, on the other hand, are more general and usually require that the reader complete them outside the classroom. No answers are provided for the activities, as they will require the evaluation of a teacher or a participating group.

## Acknowledgments

Appearing by special invitation in the text is Schuyler, a character in the cartoon creation *Shoe* by Jeff McNelly, reprinted by permission of Tribune Media Services. Schuyler reminds us that one of the most important characteristics of a successful teacher is a good sense of humor.

We would also like to acknowledge those individuals who reviewed this text at various stages: Kent Davis, Purdue University; F. Elizabeth Fridt, Metropolitan State College; Meredith Gall, University of Oregon; Tom Gregory, Indiana University; Howie Jones, University of Houston; Larry Kennedy, Illinois State University; Wayne Mahood, State University of New York–Geneseo; Dennie Smith, Memphis State University; and Patty Wiley, University of Tennessee.

## ◾ NOTE

1. John Goodlad, *A Place Called School* (New York: McGraw-Hill, 1983), 121.

# Part One

# Planning for Instruction

An old farmer was asked how his family happened to settle in a remote section of Arkansas. He replied, "Well, we were heading for California when Pap took a wrong turn at the Mississippi River."

Pity these travelers, crossing a continent with no map and only a vague notion of their destination. Likewise, for many students and teachers traveling across unfamiliar intellectual terrain, there are "wrong turns" in the classroom: too often, they work without a "map" in the form of specific plans and without clearly defined objectives for their "travels." At the end of a poorly planned lesson or unit, teachers often feel let down, that they have not reached their intended destination. In the classroom, careful planning is essential if students are to enjoy a successful journey toward knowledge and understanding.

The planning process we describe in the following chapters is an interdependent process with overlapping steps, though these steps are not a formula to be followed rigidly or even a series to be completed one by one in order. In fact, no exact formula or recipe for good instruction exists, though good instruction is founded in good planning. With these caveats in mind, we have listed, in the most general terms, the steps of instructional planning.

1. Set goals and develop a rationale for instruction.
2. Define objectives.
3. Construct a means of evaluation.
4. Create units of study that will encompass the content of the course of study.
5. Design lessons for instruction.
6. Select instructional materials.

These steps are the major topics of the four chapters that comprise Part One of this text. Step 1 is discussed in Chapter 1, "Describing Educational Goals." Steps 2 and 3 are discussed in Chapter 2, "Determining Learning Outcomes and Evaluation Strategies." Steps 4 and 5 are discussed in Chapter 3, "Organizing Content." Step 6 is discussed in Chapter 4, "Selecting Instructional Tools."

Planning for instruction is a continuous process, and the steps of planning overlap. We present in this first part of the text some procedures for instructional design that can help in this process. It is up to each reader to determine the ways in which he or she will implement these procedures. What is not optional is the incorporation of a serious planning process into every teacher's approach to instruction.

# Chapter 1

# Describing Educational Goals

## The Learner, Society, and the Subject Matter

Overheard in the teacher's lounge: "My short-term goal is Friday and my long-term goal is June." Busy teachers may feel they have no time for thinking about the goals of education. Often, the pressure of just getting the job done seems overwhelming. Teachers and prospective teachers usually ask for techniques or rules regarding *how* to teach before determining *what* students need to be taught. However, effective teaching must begin with a determination of appropriate educational goals. Some goals are *pre*determined for the teacher, and some are left to the teacher to decide.

## Setting Goals

Goals are general statements of intent that reflect (1) the needs of the learner, (2) the societal purpose of schooling, and (3) the subject matter to be learned. The ability to consider, express, and incorporate these goals into a planning process is one of the primary qualities of a professional educator.

### ■ The Needs of Learners

Concern for students must be the foundation of all planning. No matter how interesting or relevant the material may be or how enthusiastic the teacher is about the subject, learners must be able and willing to learn. If teaching does not result in learning, then it fails. But if teaching has the effect of engaging learners in the process of understanding, of bringing learners into close contact with what the teacher wants them to learn, and of giving learners an opportunity to explain what they understand, then learning is likely to occur. These then are the needs of the learner:

1. Meaningful engagement in the process of learning;
2. Direct contact with what is to be learned (to the greatest possible extent); and
3. Opportunity to explain their understandings.

#### *Background Information*

Before establishing the goals of a course or unit of study, it is essential to know about the particular group of students to be taught. In general, it is a good idea to become familiar with their records, to study the average and individual test scores of the students. Though group-normed standardized test results are no more than general indicators for individuals, they do provide an index of past achievement and a barometer of future success. Of more direct use, an informal assessment of the prior knowledge of students in relation to what they are expected to learn can be crucial to good planning and teaching. Successful learning often depends on making a connection between what the learner already knows and what he or she is trying to understand.

The personal and skill needs of learners is a necessary consideration in planning for instruction. We can state these considerations by posing a series of questions:

1. Will the instruction fulfill any personal, social, or occupational goals the students may have?
2. Is the learning process (i.e., how they are asked to learn) appropriate to the students' present skill development? If not, what will they have to be taught or what additional help will they need to insure their successful learning?
3. How much do the students already know about the topic (e.g., food chains, punctuation, the colonial period, addition or subtraction), and how much can they be expected to learn?

There are many ways to get at what students know. One way is to ask them, "If you were going to write a book for this course (in American literature, for example), what are the ideas and readings you would want to include?" Though individual answers to such a question would probably be limited in scope, a group of students brainstorming ideas is often able to reveal an impressive array of understandings, expectations, and background knowledge. When students feel they have some part in the planning of the course or unit they are about to undertake, the instructional goals are likely to be more appropriate and, thus, their instruction more successful.

### Learning Styles

In thinking about the learning needs of individuals, it is important to realize that students learn in different ways and that teachers have different styles of teaching. Research on learning styles[1] indicates that some people are more intuitive than others. Some respond to material delivered in a logical order; others learn better through problem solving. Some students learn better through listening; others by reading or viewing films. Some prefer to learn alone; others learn better in groups. Some students prefer to be given the rule and then examples; others prefer to formulate the rule for themselves after a presentation of examples.

Students with different learning-style preferences require different instructional approaches, yet students need to learn in more than one way. The more the teacher knows about the learning styles of individual students, the more he or she is able to plan a variety of instructional approaches. One thing can be taken for granted—there will be a variety of learning styles present in every classroom. If a teacher cannot vary instruction to account for those differences, some students will be left out of the instructional process.

### Special Needs

In every classroom there are children with special needs. With the advent of mainstreaming and growing emphasis on the least restrictive environment, children with many different kinds of disabilities have entered the regular classroom. Some handicaps are easily identified by observation; others are less obvious. For instance, some children are extremely gifted—a condition that is often handicapping because these children may feel left out and different from the group. Thus, every teacher needs to be something of a special education teacher to meet the needs of all children scheduled into the standard curriculum.

Even among children who are not characterized as having special needs, there are many factors that cause a wide disparity of development in children of the same age. Although there are predictable stages of children's growth and development—physically, intellectually, socially, and morally—one child may be intellectually advanced and physically slow in development, while another may have well-developed social skills and yet have problems in physical coordination.

Boys and girls of the same age obviously have different patterns of development. In a sixth-grade classroom most of the boys still look like little boys, while about half the girls look like young women. Girls are usually taller, stronger, and more verbal. Teachers need to be conscious of the nature of these differences in setting goals for the curriculum.

## ■ Societal Needs

State and federal agencies, local school boards, and individual schools often set broad educational goals applicable to all courses and toward which all teachers are expected to direct their instruction. These might be called the *macrogoals* of education. These statements are usually very general and noncontroversial, outlining the purposes of schooling to which professional and laypersons alike

would presumably assent. They form the basis of a society's justification for its schools. In some abbreviated form, one can almost imagine statements like these posted in the entryway to a school:

Each pupil, consistent with his or her abilities and educational needs, will
- develop competence in the basic learning skills;
- learn to cherish the foundations of a free society;
- develop ethical standards of behavior;
- develop skills necessary to obtain productive employment or to continue to higher education;
- gain respect for his or her body and value good health habits;
- come to value beauty and learn to participate in some form of aesthetic expression; and
- achieve progress commensurate with his or her ability.

From every administrative level—state, district, and school—the teacher is handed prescriptions for education. Notice that all of the goals we have given as examples are so general as to apply to any teacher teaching any subject at any grade level. But are these sorts of goals so general as to have no value to an individual teacher in instructional decision making? On the contrary, we think they provide valuable guidance to the teacher. These macrogoals don't spring out of a vacuum. Rather, they reflect the needs of the community—the state, the city or county, and the neighborhood—and the values and the expectations of the parents. What strengths do the children bring to the school, and what are the needs that should be addressed? Many teachers fail because they lack an understanding of the background and the expectations of their students and their families.

As goals are set, it is important to address the future learning needs of students. Certain trends can be anticipated, such as the importance of computer literacy. Teachers who refuse to develop their own skills in the use of computers or who dismiss claims that the personal computer will have a profound effect on life in the twenty-first century are not being fair to their students.

It is important to remember that the decisions you make as a teacher on how best to teach your students and what subject matter and concepts they can best learn will be made within certain imposed limitations. State legislatures, superintendents of public instruction, parents, school boards, and courts can and do say much about what is and is not to be taught in schools.

### ■ Subject Matter Content

More specific than the goals of education that society demands are the goals relating to subject matter content. Here teachers have relatively more freedom in determining precisely what will be taught, but they are usually provided a starting point.

### State and National Requirements

Most state school administrative bodies provide some statement of broad goals to which all teachers of a particular subject will aspire. There are interesting similarities and differences among localities. Consider, for example, the following list of goals for the content of the social studies curriculum drawn from curriculum documents of several different states.

1. *From the state of Connecticut:* As a result of education in grades K–12, each student should be able to:

- Recognize and analyze events, personalities, trends, and beliefs that have shaped the history and culture of Connecticut, the United States, and the world;
- Demonstrate a knowledge of United States history and government and understand the duties, responsibilities, and rights of United States citizenship;
- Understand the basic concepts of economics;
- Analyze and compare the political and economic beliefs and systems of the United States with those of other nations;
- Apply major concepts drawn from the disciplines of history and the social sciences—anthropology, economics, geography, law and government, philosophy, political science, psychology, and sociology—to hypothetical and real situations;
- Demonstrate basic knowledge of world geography;
- Apply critical thinking skills and knowledge from history and the social sciences to the decision-making process and the analysis of controversial issues in order to understand the present and anticipate the future;
- Understand the roles played by various racial, ethnic, and religious groups in developing the nation's pluralistic society; and
- Appreciate the mutual dependence of all people in the world and understand that our lives are part of a global community joined by economic, social, cultural and civic concerns.[2]

2. *From the state of North Carolina:* The North Carolina social studies curriculum is designed to enable students to:

- Develop concepts and generalizations that will provide insight into the political, economic, and social behavior of people;
- Develop skills and attitudes conducive to the use of rational processes for problem solving, valuing, and decision making;
- Acquire knowledge about (1) the structure and functions of the social, political, and economic institutions in American society; (2) the development and unique characteristics of past and present societies; (3) issues and problems that have persisted throughout history; (4) similarities and differences of past and present societies;

- Develop a system of values consistent with the fundamental tenets of democracy;
- Develop positive attitudes toward other peoples; and
- Develop an understanding of one's self and one's relationship to others and to the environment.[3]

**3.** *From the state of Virginia:*

- To provide experiences that would enable students to participate in society effectively and responsibly;
- To assist students in understanding the basic democratic ideals and values of our society that affect decision making in public and private life; and
- To assist students in acquiring concepts and problem-solving skills in order to foster rational solutions to problems encountered in everyday life.[4]

In addition to the goals that states may set as guidelines for local school districts, the U.S. Department of Education also sets and indirectly enforces goals for instruction in the nation's schools. The National Assessment of Educational Progress (NAEP), *The Nation's Report Card,* is funded by the U.S. Department of Education under a grant to Educational Testing Service. National Assessment is an education research project mandated by Congress to collect and report data over time on the performance of young Americans in various learning areas. It makes available information on assessment procedures (results) to state and local education agencies.[5]

Data on the achievement of students in elementary, middle, and high school levels are made available through this national testing program. The objectives of the testing program embody a strong implication for the instructional programs of local school divisions. To cite an example similar to those cited for the states listed above, the civics objectives of NAEP are described under the title *Civics: United States Government & Politics Objectives.*[6] The contents of this document are divided into three categories: context, cognition, and content. Context includes "home, school, community, nation, and world." Cognition includes (1) "knows" and (2) "understands and applies." Content includes:

**1.** *Democratic Principles and the Purpose of Government.* It is important that students understand the principles underlying the organization and operation of the United States government. It is equally as important that prominent among these democratic principles are the consent of the governed and the basic rights of individuals, which derive from historical precedent, and, to some extent, are set forth in the United States Constitution. Students also should understand that the context within which these principles are to be applied can change and that various political principles have been interpreted differently during different periods of history. Further, some degree of comparative perspective with other countries is necessary for adequate understanding of U.S. political and constitutional values, American social and economic institutions, and patterns of U.S. political, social, intellectual, and economic development.

**2.** *Political Institutions (Structure and Functions).* Students should know the central historical facts related to the development of the United States political system, and its basic organizing principles such as federalism, separation of powers, and checks and balances. They also should understand the structure and operation of the three branches of United States government as well as the policies that are the responsibilities, respectively, of the federal, state, and local governments.

**3.** *Political Processes.* Students need to gain an understanding of the range and importance of the decisions made by government. They should understand the processes involved in government decision making and what influences these processes. An awareness of elections, other forms of political participation, and the roles of interest groups and political parties is also essential.

**4.** *Rights, Responsibilities, and the Law.* Students need to know the specific rights and liberties guaranteed by the U.S. Constitution and the Bill of Rights. They should also understand how judicial decisions are made and how the judicial system operates. Students should understand the purposes of laws and the responsibility of citizens to comply with these laws. Finally, young Americans should recognize that constitutional rights and freedoms extend to all persons and that every individual has a responsibility to promote equal opportunity.

### Activity 1.1

What do you think might account for the difference in emphasis among these goal statements? Are there some goals that you would find difficult to meet? ■

### Matching Content to Needs

In setting educational goals, the challenge is to fit the content of the subject to the needs of the learners. Broadly stated goals for each subject in the school curriculum are a helpful place to start. One immediate problem that teachers face is that everything within a subject cannot be taught to everyone. The teacher must then decide what is appropriate for a particular group and for individuals within that group.

Imagine a young teacher beginning her career in a junior high school armed with a master's degree in English literature and a great enthusiasm for the Romantic poets. As a beginning teacher, she found that she had been assigned remedial classes of ninth-grade boys who had failed at least one year of school and who had marginal reading and writing ability. Needless to say, these ninth-grade boys were not waiting, pencils poised, to learn about the Romantic poets. Her challenge was to find a way to meet the needs of these students; the alternative was to fail as a teacher; the Romantic poets had to wait.

Every teacher must constantly face the challenge of adapting what is taught to the person who is expected to learn it. At the risk of trivializing an important matter, we'd ask every teacher to keep in mind the question, "Am I teaching a subject or am I teaching students?" We hope the answer will always be "both."

### Role of the Teacher in Selecting Content

Each discipline provides a wealth of material from which to select content for the classroom, and each instructional plan may use that content in a variety of ways. Most school divisions prescribe certain content objectives that are to be addressed in each course, but the individual teacher makes many decisions about specific content and material to be used to meet those objectives. For instance, if teachers are required to cover the study of Europe in a particular year, they may have the latitude to determine which individual countries are studied or in what order the countries will be studied. In addition, a teacher may decide to combine the study of European countries with a comparative study of Asia or Africa.

Teachers often complain that they would like to make the content of their courses more interesting but "*They* tell me what I have to teach" or "*They* tell me that I have to use this textbook." But *they* do not and cannot possibly tell teachers everything that must be taught and how it is to be taught. Prescribed goals and objectives for subject-area instruction are part of the support system for teachers; in practice, teachers usually have much more freedom and responsibility than they realize in selecting the content of the subject matter taught in the classroom.

### Exercise 1.1

Label each of the following goal statements with an *L* if the focus is *predominantly* on the learner, an *SO* if the focus is on a societal need, and a *SU* if the focus is on the subject matter.

1. Students will practice sound habits of personal health.
2. Students will recognize major American writers.
3. Students will acquire lifetime learning skills.
4. Students will practice principles of good citizenship.
5. Students will appreciate beauty and participate in aesthetic activities.
6. Students will acquire the basic skills of reading, writing, and computer literacy.
7. Students will increase their sense of personal integrity and self-worth.
8. Students will respect the rights of others.

Answers to Exercise 1.1

Some of the goal statements seem to have more than one focus. For instance, basic skills of reading, writing, and computer literacy are essential as societal goals as well as for the learner. Goal statements 1, 3, 5, and 7, however, seem to focus primarily on the learners; numbers 4 and 8 are essentially societal goals; and 2 and 6 are oriented more toward subject matter.

**Activity 1.2**

In order to avoid the possibility of setting goals for students that are unrealistic or reflect unexamined values, consider (1) the society in which your students live and will live in the future, (2) the conceptual and factual framework of the subject matter you are prepared to teach, and (3) the aspirations you have for the students you will teach.

- If you are in secondary or middle school education, describe a course you would like to teach or one that you are presently teaching. Try to word your course description to account for the interface of society, the subject matter, and learner needs.
- If you are in elementary education, focus on one of the subjects you teach. Explain why you believe this subject is worth knowing. Is it useful to your students? How will it make their lives better, make them more productive, enhance their future? Can all your students benefit from this knowledge?
- As a student preparing to teach, at whatever level, think of the age and ability of the students you are most interested in teaching. What do you believe the world will be like when your students are mature adults? Will the subject matter that you want to teach be important in the future or will it be obsolete? ■

## Developing a Rationale

The preceding activity, which asked you to consider the fundamental reasons for teaching what you want to teach, should help you formulate a statement of justification for any course or subject you want to teach. Such an exposition of the logical basis behind setting particular objectives and teaching specific content is a *rationale*. One method of clarifying teaching goals is to expand the goals into the form of a rationale, which is usually a three- or four-paragraph statement of reasons for the choice of goals, objectives, and subject matter. The rationale incorporates the goals and refines them into a description of the subject or course (see Figure 1.1).

### ■ Examples of Course Rationales

The following example, entitled "Our Window on the World," is an example of an appropriate course rationale written by a teacher for a sixth-grade science class:

> The focus of the science program this year will be on the wonderful world outside our window. From our classroom we can see a field, a stream, and

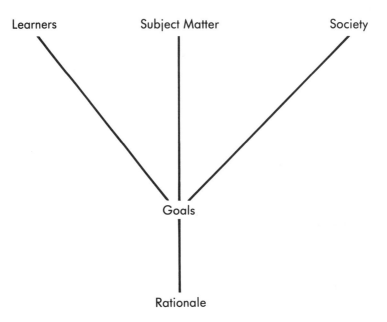

Learners          Subject Matter          Society

Goals

Rationale

**FIGURE 1.1**  Sources for a Rationale

a small stand of trees. Weekly field trips to this area will focus on the study of ecosystems.

Sixth-graders are just beginning to deal with abstractions; such concepts as interdependence and community can best be understood by actually experiencing and observing situations in which they exist. This study will allow the students to spend more time moving about and being outdoors—activities important to these young adolescents.

The skills of data gathering and analysis will be emphasized throughout this course. Each child will maintain a record of the experiments and observations that are conducted. In cooperation with the language arts teacher, the children will be writing about their experiences, drawing from this record of their observations.

Other teachers will also play a part in this instruction. The art teacher has agreed to teach several lessons in sketching natural observations so that artwork can be a part of students' records. Graphs and charts, which they are learning in math, will be incorporated into this study, and the social studies teacher has agreed to utilize this experience in discussing the effects of environment on various parts of our history.

Understanding the world in which we live is essential to our survival, and the world outside our window is the world we can influence the most. Helping the children view that world with wonder, enthusiasm, and concern will be a major goal of this course.

This rationale displays an awareness of the physical, social, and cognitive needs of the learners. There is also a statement of the manner in which interdisciplinary studies will be brought into the course. The importance of learning this material is explained, and the essential concepts and skills are described. As the teacher selects and develops the units of this course and designs the instructional plan, this rationale will serve as a guide.

A similar plan might be written for a seventh-grade social studies class in an urban environment. Consider a unit with the title "Our Window on the World" in the context of a school in one of our nation's large cities.

> The students will use our city as a resource for their social studies this year. Every city is rich in stories about people and events with which students can identify. Walking trips with a camera will enable students to photograph people and places, which will provide rich resource material for reading and writing activities in class.
>
> For instance, near the school is a public park named for a famous Civil War general, which should provide many opportunities for historical research. There are buildings and parks in the city named for outstanding local and national historical figures who will have prominent places in our studies.
>
> Interviews with family members who have lived in the city for many years will provide a basis for historical biographies, which will be assembled as part of a class history project. For those students who have lived in the city only a short time, interviews with long-term residents will be arranged. Ethnic differences will be explored and the students will be encouraged to find out how their families came to this country. Research and reporting techniques will be stressed as a part of this experience.
>
> By concentrating on the world outside the windows of the school building, we will emphasize that history is a real experience that affects the lives of all of us, not something that exists only in books. Urban young people often hear only of the problems of their environment rather than of the rich legacy of people and events that make up their world.

Writing a convincing and appropriate rationale is not an easy task. Following are excerpts from three sample rationales that contain some potential problems. As you read them over, think what each reveals about the values and the beliefs of the writers in regard to the learners, the subject, and society. What problems with instruction do you anticipate for each of the writers? Each of the following excerpts has some positive aspects, but you should spot some problems.

### *Rationale for a Ninth-Grade General English Class in an Urban Area*

I plan to transmit my love for Shakespeare to the students in my class. The Bard continues to gain in significance, and these young people can feel themselves in touch with generations past as they read the immortal words of Hamlet and quake at the evil deeds of Lady Macbeth. There are those who believe Shakespeare is too difficult and too demanding for young people, but I can transcend their reluctance and win them over to the magnificent stories and the fascinating characters. The students will be immersed in the language and in the times of the Elizabethans. What better way to improve the quality and the fluency of today's literarily starved young people?

In this first example, the teacher's love for her subject, particularly Shakespeare, is evident, and such enthusiasm will probably be evident to her students. The question is, can ninth-graders identify as quickly with Hamlet and Macbeth as a person who has spent years studying literature? It is all too easy to forget that novices to a subject need to be introduced gradually. Students asked to plunge in too deeply at first may develop a distaste for the subject that can never be altered. If love for a subject or a particular part of that subject overshadows consideration of the learner, the teacher may be asking for trouble. One way this teacher might have considered introducing Shakespeare is by starting with other plays, such as *Romeo and Juliet,* with its obvious parallels in *West Side Story,* or *A Midsummer Night's Dream,* with its playful fantasy, that are better suited to young adolescents.

### Rationale for a Fifth-Grade Math Program in a Farming Community

The purpose of math instruction for this year will center on understanding mathematical principles and concepts. Math is the key to understanding the universe and the children will develop an appreciation for the subtleties and excitement of the wonderful world of mathematics. Once the principles have been mastered, the children can apply these to problems encountered in the world around them. Since space exploration is such an interesting topic today, problems will be drawn from the space program. Math can be learned and loved by all students; it is simply a matter of dedication and perseverance.

In this second selection, the teacher assumes that fifth-graders are extremely interested in the space program and that the quality of their lives depends on knowing about the program. Fifth-graders in a farming community may be more interested in problems close at hand than with adventures in outer space. What is interesting and fascinating to adults may be less so to children. In addition, an approach to mathematics that is completely oriented toward an understanding of principles may be inappropriate in a community that demands practical application of those principles.

### Rationale for a Social Studies Class in an Affluent Suburb

This course will focus on the inequities that have been a part of our country's history. From the treatment of the native Americans to the pursuit of so-called illegal aliens who cross our borders daily, our nation has ignored or persecuted those outside the power structure. Students will compare other economic systems to determine if a socialistic form of government will contain mechanisms for correcting injustices. The students will be expected to adopt a disenfranchised group and lobby actively for their benefit. The students will leave with an increased awareness of this nation's debt to the underprivileged and of the flaws in our economic system.

This third example does reveal a teacher who cares deeply about inequities in society and wants the students to share those feelings. It is not wrong for a teacher to wish to develop values in students, but it is foolish to do so naively, without carefully weighing the risks ahead of time. Teachers have been dismissed for teaching religious or political beliefs that were contrary to the values of the community; often the dismissed teacher is extremely surprised by the public's reaction. Teachers' opinions and values are almost always evident in their instruction. However, those beliefs and opinions should be identified as such to the class and teachers should endeavor to present all sides of issues. When young people are asked to form their opinions and beliefs based on one side of an issue only, what takes place may be closer to indoctrination than education.

## Activity 1.3

Consider a course you would like to teach or are presently teaching and write a rationale incorporating your goals. Make clear your beliefs about the learners in the class, the importance of this subject to the students' lives, the emphasis and focus of the subject matter, and the skills most needed by these students. Do not try to describe specific instructional techniques or units, but define your overall goals for the course. When you have finished, share your rationale with the class or with a colleague. Analyze the content to see that your goals are compatible with the needs of the learner, the expectations of society, and the demands of subject matter. ■

### ■ Matching Rationales to Learning Environments

The following descriptions are of a variety of learning environments. As you read, analyze each situation described and consider the unique needs of the students—academic, career, and personal. Consider, as well, the community in which the school is located and the impact of social forces within the community on education. Assess how your own subject matter speciality could best be used to meet the varying needs in each situation.

I. Hancock is an inner-city middle school (grades 6–8) in a large eastern city. Located in a once affluent neighborhood, the building is a heavy, gray pile of stone surrounded by decrepit Victorian houses. Half of the students are bused in from a large public housing project and many walk from an old Italian-American neighborhood. The building, once a high school, contains a massive auditorium and gymnasium, both of which are closed to conserve heat. Vandalism in the building is a problem. The rate of teacher turnover is high, but some dedicated staff members have been at the school for years.

Twenty percent of the female students become pregnant during their years at Hancock. Truancy is high, and 30 percent of the young people do not go on to high school. Drug use in the school is a problem, and gang fights are a frequent occurrence. However, many of the families of students at Hancock strongly support the school and their children's education.

II.  Baylor is a small farming community in New Hampshire. Most of the families have lived in New England for generations. There is no movie theater or shopping center in the village. The general store and a local lake are the gathering places for the young. The teenagers often drive to a larger city 30 miles away in search of entertainment.

A small college is in the area and many faculty members send their children to the local school. In addition, the town's economy depends on a local lumber company, farming, and several small businesses. The white frame school buildings are overcrowded and several bond issues to build new ones have failed. In spite of the beauty of the village, most young people choose to leave; opportunities for careers in the community are limited. In general, children of the professors go on to college and the others go to work in factories.

III. Seafarers County on the mid-Atlantic coast has a population of 14,400. Of these, 4,000 are school-aged children. Within this county there are eight distinct localities. All of the localities share commonalities with respect to close family and community bonds, strong religious ties, and an intense pride in their ancestral background. The primary source of income is tourism and marine-oriented occupations.

One part of the county has an island, which has been connected to the mainland by bridge only since the mid-1960s. Of the 2,000 island inhabitants, only 200 are school age. Technological amenities, such as television and electricity, came to this area only after the mainland bridge was built. Income is primarily based on marine occupations, and tourism is not widely accepted or encouraged. An intense sense of community spirit exists; however, it is limited to the existing population of the island, which is totally Caucasian, and does not extend to newcomers perceived to be outsiders.

Of the school-aged population, 40 percent will become high school dropouts; 70 percent will remain on the island after their schooling ends. Sixty percent of the school population are in need of academic special services. Cultural arts, such as music, abound within the school curriculum.

Parental support is limited to those teachers and administrators who are native to the island. Outsiders, which include most of the teachers, are rarely accepted into the community.

IV. Valdez Unified School System is in the desert on a remote Indian reservation. The pay scale for teachers is well below average for the county. Ninety-six percent of the children are eligible for free breakfast and lunch, meaning that the income of their families is below poverty level. In fact, 60 percent of the adult male population is unemployed. Those who are employed commute 65 miles to relatively low-paying jobs, and alcoholism is the major social problem. Most homes have electricity and running water, but few have indoor toilet facilities. The average life span of the people on the reservation is 35 percent lower than that of the general population.

   English is the first language of the children and most of their parents; most grandparents speak only their native language. Few children attend school beyond high school and only two-thirds graduate from high school. Eighth-grade graduation is a very big social event.

   The purpose of school in this setting is a point of debate. Preparing children to leave the reservation and take a place in the major (white) culture is tantamount to cultural genocide. Yet, staying on the reservation, for most people, is a dead-end lifestyle as there is little upward mobility possible there.

V. Jefferson school district is an affluent suburb near a large city. The median family income is high, but there are many non-English-speaking children who have entered the school district in the last 10 years. The school division's interpretation of federal laws is to provide programs for mainstreaming the children as rapidly as possible. Some parents of these children believe their cultural heritage should be preserved; others feel that their children should be absorbed into the majority culture as quickly as possible.

   Language barriers handicap many of the parents seeking employment, and the crime rate in the community is rising. Some white families have moved their children to private schools.

### Activity 1.4

Now, imagine each of these school environments. Bear in mind that the macro-goals of the state department of education could easily be the same for each school district, but specific instructional goals will differ at the school district, building, and classroom levels.

   Select two districts and write goal statements for your subject or main area of teaching based on the information given for each school district. Remember that goals are general statements expressing your philosophical beliefs and values, which also reflect the needs of the students whom you will be teaching, the society in which you will teach, and the application of the subject matter. Consider the need for an examination of your personal values in light of each school's environment and the particular needs of the students. Finally, look at the rationale you wrote for Activity 1.3. Would you make any changes or adjustments if you were a teacher in any one of these school districts? ■

## ■ SUMMARY

In determining instructional goals, the teacher should consider: (1) the needs of the learners, (2) the nature and needs of the society in which the students are presently living and the one(s) in which they will live as adults, and (3) the requirements of the subject matter to be taught. Goals stated in the form of a rationale help teachers to clarify this process and to focus on the essential components of the curriculum. This examination must be ongoing, since the society, the learners, and the subject matter are continually changing, as are the needs and the interests of the teacher.

## ■ NOTES

**1.** Harvey F. Silver and J. Robert Hanson, *Teaching Styles and Strategies* (Moorestown, NJ: The Institute for Cognitive and Behavioral Studies in association with Hanson, Silver and Associates, 1982).

**2.** Connecticut State Board of Education, *Connecticut's Common Core of Learning* (Hartford, CN: Connecticut State Department of Education, January 1987), 14.

**3.** North Carolina Department of Public Instruction, *Course of Study for Elementary and Secondary Schools K–12* (Raleigh, NC: State of North Carolina, 1977), 5.

**4.** Commonwealth of Virginia, *Standards of Learning Objectives for Virginia Public Schools: Social Studies* (Richmond, VA: Commonwealth of Virginia, Department of Education, 1983), vi.

**5.** Educational Testing Service, National Assessment of Educational Progress, *Civics Objectives: 1988 Assessment* (Princeton, NJ: ETS, September 1987), 2.

**6.** Educational Testing Service, *Civics Objectives,* 8–13.

# Chapter 2

# Determining Learning Outcomes and Evaluation Strategies

## Cognitive, Affective, and Psychomotor Objectives

A few years ago we visited a third grade classroom in Appalachia. There were 33 children in the crowded classroom, many of whom had come to school hungry and without adequate clothing. The room was poorly heated and materials were scarce. Covering a part of one wall was an elaborate chart of behavioral objectives, printed on expensive, shiny paper. Every skill conceivable (so it seemed) was broken into miniscule parts. The chart's presence in the room had been mandated by the school district. The weary teacher smiled at an inquiry as to how the chart could be useful to her and said, "At least it adds a little color to the walls."

Many teachers have been disillusioned with educational objectives that seem to have little or nothing to do with the reality of their classrooms. They have been asked to spend precious time mechanically developing objectives to fit a prescribed formula that has little connection to what they really teach. In spite of mindless abuses, however, the writing of objectives can be an exciting and rewarding professional experience.

## Defining Objectives

The goals stated in a rationale are essential to the planning process, but they are too general to serve as organizers for specific lessons or as a basis for evaluation. The next step in the process is to state the intended learning outcomes as objectives in the form of measurable student performance.

Learning objectives are written at different levels of specificity. Objectives for a course are stated in more general terms than objectives for a lesson to be completed in a class period. But whatever the level of generality, objectives provide a framework and a guide for the specific instructional decisions that follow.

Objectives may be defined and written in various ways. For our purposes, we define a learning objective in this way: *A learning objective is a statement of the measurable learning that is intended to take place as a result of instruction.* The following are examples of learning objectives:

As a result of instruction the students will be able to

- *apply* the principles of standard deviation in the solution of word problems.
- *compare* and *contrast* the causes of the French and American Revolutions.
- *discriminate* among vowel sounds.
- *apply* the principles of design in the construction of a birdhouse.
- *appreciate* the humor in the writings of Mark Twain.

Look carefully at the verbs in the examples above. Notice that they are statements of anticipated effects of instruction, they are not merely statements of activities. They describe what the students will be able to do or to feel or to think as a result of instruction. Furthermore, they can be *measured* in some manner.

The following statements are *not* learning objectives. Do you see why?

- The students will go on a field trip to the zoo.
- The students will read the novel *A Tale of Two Cities*.
- The students will keep journals.
- The students will use learning centers.

These are *activities* in which the students will engage, not descriptions of what students will *learn* as a result of instruction. In the first example, "the students will go on a fieldtrip to the zoo," no evaluation is possible other than counting heads to see who showed up and who got left behind. Learning objectives for this activity could be expressed as follows:

As a result of their field trip to the zoo the students will be able to

- name four classes of mammals and compare their living environments.
- collaborate in the process of data gathering.

One must not take statements of such objectives to such extreme specificity that one loses sight of the learners. There are many times when the opportunity to teach an important lesson is unexpected and unintended. We recall the story about the teacher who was escorting her students on a field trip through the zoo. She was overheard to say to the children, who were standing in rapt amazement at the towering necks of giraffes, "Now remember, children, we're here to look at feet." It is equally ridiculous, however, to send children on a field trip to the zoo and have them learn only the location of the refreshment stand.

Stating objectives for learning causes teacher *and students* to focus on what is important in a learning experience. In addition, it helps the teacher clearly identify the type of instruction needed to achieve the objective and evaluate the success of the instruction. In the following exercise, mark the activities with an *A* and the objectives with an *O*.

### Exercise 2.1

1. The students will be able to print legibly the letters of the alphabet.
2. The students will assemble a small motor and use it to operate a simple machine.
3. The students will view a filmstrip.
4. The students will be able to describe three causes of the First World War.
5. The students will read *Huckleberry Finn*.
6. The students will be able to describe the character of Huck in *Huckleberry Finn*.
7. The students will do the exercises in the workbook.
8. The students will participate in a volleyball game, displaying enthusiasm and confidence, as evidenced by videotaped records of the games made periodically.
9. The students will be able to float on their backs for at least two minutes.

Answers to Exercise 2.1

Numbers 3, 5, and 7 are activities; the rest are learning objectives. In number 3, we assume that viewing the filmstrip is a means to some end, not an end in itself. In number 5, the ability to read *Huckleberry Finn* may be the objective, but it is probably an activity required for other learning related to character and plot. Doing the exercises in the workbook in number 7 is an activity to reinforce learning, but not an end of learning.

## Drafting Objectives

There is no magic formula for writing out objectives. But when instructional objectives are clear, it is possible to select effective strategies to bring about the learning desired. In addition, clear objectives make the process of evaluation much easier.

Objectives should be written at every level of the planning process. Course level objectives are more general than unit objectives, and unit objectives are more general than lesson objectives; course objectives should guide the decisions made at each succeeding level.

A rule of thumb for writing a good objective is that students muct act on the material they are learning and, in so doing, connect that material in some way to something else. It is in this process of connecting that students go beyond mere memorization. Write objectives that will enable students to learn by acting on and manipulating ideas.

### Activity 2.1

Consider the following unit-level objectives. Discuss the different classroom activities that would result from each.

1. The students will be able to recite from memory a poem by Wordsworth.
   or
2. The students will interpret through music and dance a poem of their own choosing.

3. The students will be able to label the parts of a flower.
   or
4. The students will analyze the effects of different environmental factors on plants grown in the laboratory.

5. The students will be able to identify the parts of speech.
   or
6. The students will increase their ability to express themselves effectively by editing their own writing in groups and evaluating their progress. ■

## Types of Objectives

There are three basic types of learning objectives to be described in the planning process: (1) cognitive, (2) affective, and (3) psychomotor. Cognitive objectives describe the knowledge that learners are to acquire. Affective objectives describe the attitudes, feelings, and dispositions that learners are expected to develop. Psychomotor objectives relate to the manipulative and motor skills that learners are to master.

Every instructional design needs to include both cognitive and affective objectives. Psychomotor objectives are most prevalent in those classes involving the mastery of physical skills—orchestra, shop, handwriting, computer or typewriter keyboarding, or physical education. However, psychomotor skills should not be overlooked as a basic skill in the performance of other activities. For instance, manual dexterity is essential in working with laboratory equipment or with a compass and protractor in math class.

### ■ Cognitive Objectives

Cognitive objectives relate to the processing of information by the learner. They specify what students will *be able to do* intellectually as a result of instruction; such instructional results range from the memorization of facts to the most complex processes of evaluation and assessment. A committee of college and university examiners, headed by Benjamin S. Bloom of the University of Chicago, placed these cognitive behaviors within a taxonomy,[1] which is the basis of Table 2.1.

It is important to note that Bloom's taxonomy is *not* a statement of educational objectives. Rather, it is a system for *classifying* educational objectives with respect to cognitive categories. Learning objectives should always be written so as to imply the criteria for their own assessment. This aspect is implicit in our definition of learning objectives, which we offered before (see pp. 19–20).

The primary value of Bloom's taxonomy is that it serves to remind teachers that instruction must do more than promote memory. When writing objectives within the cognitive domain, it is important that the objectives of instruction are not all at the lower levels of the taxonomy. There is an interesting relationship between memory and understanding and between understanding and thinking. Put briefly, students will best remember those things that they best understand, and they will understand best those things that they think about. Thus, objectives of instruction should capitalize on the potential for higher order thinking skills. Table 2.1 shows a sample of verbs in the cognitive domain described by Benjamin Bloom and his associates.

For students to be able to process information at higher levels, they must be taught *how* to think, not merely *what* to think. Giving out information is not the most important instructional process, though perhaps it is the most common. The models presented in Part Two of this text describe a variety of instructional approaches that facilitate thinking in the classroom.

### Declarative and Procedural Knowledge

Cognitive objectives specify the knowledge that students will retain as a result of instruction. Actually, cognitive objectives specify two different kinds of knowledge, *declarative* and *procedural*. The more familiar kind of knowledge is declarative knowledge, defined by Gilbert Ryle as "knowledge that."[2] This is knowledge that can be expressed in true (or sometimes false) statements: Columbus discovered America in 1492; water is composed of two molecules of hydrogen and one molecule of oxygen.

Think of declarative knowledge as the tangible result of decades and centu-

**TABLE 2.1    Sample of Verbs in the Cognitive Domain**

| | |
|---|---|
| Knowledge | to recall, to repeat, to recollect, to memorize, to list |
| Comprehension | to identify, to recognize, to select |
| Application | to use, to solve, to practice, to reproduce, to compare, to contrast |
| Analysis | to investigate, to separate, to study, to research, to describe, to distinguish |
| Synthesis | to combine, to formulate, to deduce, to unite, to assemble, to create |
| Evaluation | to appraise, to judge, to assess, to assign value to, to accept, to reject |

ries of scholarly effort. Disciplines of study, and likewise courses of study in school, don't just spontaneously arise. They are the result of accumulated wisdom and understandings. As important as declarative knowledge is to the learning that takes place in school, there is another equally important kind of knowledge cognitive objectives must take into consideration. That is procedural knowledge, defined by Ryle as "knowledge how." This kind of knowledge constitutes knowledge of the *processes of reasoning*. Each discipline of study in school encompasses a way of thinking. Thus, there is a mathematical way of thinking, a scientific way of thinking, an historical way of thinking, an artistic way of thinking, and so on. Virtually every course of study in school, from auto mechanics to integral calculus, is characterized by a manner of thinking in some ways peculiar to the discipline of which it is a part.

Consider the verb *to draw* in relation to the various disciplines. One may draw conclusions, be drawn toward a work of literature, draw a circle, draw a rose, draw out a liquid, end a game in a draw, draw up a proposal, draw out a speech, or draw the curtain. In each instance, the meaning depends on the context in which the action is to take place. Likewise, each discipline defines the thought processes that occur within that discipline.

Since there are two kinds of knowledge to characterize every course of study in school, one might assume that two kinds of cognitive objectives are needed for every course. Not so, however. Look again at the verbs in Table 2.1. *Every objective, except for the objectives at a knowledge level, is a procedural knowledge objective*. A cognitive objective specifies that the learner will *do* something (usually something intellectual) with knowledge. *Knowing what* quickly takes a back seat to *knowing how*. It is not only important to remember the date when Columbus "discovered" America; it is equally important to know the importance of the discovery and to process that knowing with other information.

A teaching demonstration was taking place in a classroom when a 16-year-old student exclaimed aloud, "Oh, wow!" She had just drawn the connection between the age of the Renaissance and the journey of Columbus—which led to an expansion of her understanding of that historical period. Although she knew Columbus discovered America, she had never made a connection to the frame of reference in which that discovery took place. What was once rote information was now set in a meaningful context, and she was excited.

## Exercise 2.2

The following are verbs often used to describe cognitive learning in the classroom. Consider these in relation to the categories listed in Table 2.1. Write an objective using each of these verbs.

| | |
|---|---|
| *design*—Synthesis | *formulate*—Synthesis |
| *solve*—Application | *match*—Comprehension |
| *draw*—Application | *list*—Knowledge |
| *verify*—Analysis | *defend*—Evaluation |

Possible Answers to Exercise 2.2

- The students will be able to *design* an electrical circuit. (Synthesis)
- The students will be able to *solve* problems using square roots. (Application)
- The students will be able to *draw* a circle. (Application)
- The students will be able to *match* words with definitions. (Comprehension)
- The students will be able to *give examples* of proper nouns. (Knowledge)
- The students will be able to *formulate* a hypothesis. (Synthesis)
- The students will be able to *defend* an ethical position. (Evaluation)
- The students will be able to *verify* data. (Analysis)

These words may be placed in more than one category depending on interpretation. A design may be a synthesis of many different procedures in which the designer originates a unique procedure, or it may be merely an application of material that has been previously presented. A drawing by a great artist is certainly a synthesis, whereas the drawing of a line between two given points is the application of a skill. (As we have mentioned before, the context of the discipline usually determines the level of the thought process.) Choosing between alternatives may be comprehension if it requires reiterating what has been taught; however, the process of choice in a situation requiring the assessment of values calls for evaluation.

---

The taxonomic placement of cognitive behaviors depends on what the teacher intends the outcome of instruction to be. Will the learner be expected to give reasons for a new situation based on previous experience or repeat the reasons given by the teacher? In the first case, learning will be at the evaluation level; in the second, it will be at the comprehension level.

Think carefully about the possible levels of cognition in the classroom and guard against keeping learning at the knowledge and application levels. Avoid using vague descriptors like "understand" or "know" to describe what cognitive learning is to take place—precise descriptions will increase the likelihood of effective instruction. Ivor Davies, author of *Objectives in Curriculum Design*, stresses the importance of the action verb in writing objectives, with the emphasis on what the learner is to *do*. "This is the reason for rejecting verbs like 'to understand' and accepting verbs like 'to identify.' "[3]

## Exercise 2.3

What verbs could be used in the following examples to make the objectives more descriptive of a desired instructional outcome? Assume for the moment that these are *cognitive* objectives for specific lessons.

1. The students will *understand* the causes of the Civil War.
2. The students will *study* the Declaration of Independence.
3. The students will *solve* word problems.

Possible answers to Exercise 2.3

**1.** The verb *to understand* is perhaps the most general of all possible descriptors of cognitive behavior. Understanding transcends all the levels of the cognitive domain, and thus there are many different ways in which an objective containing this verb could be rewritten. For example:

- "Students will *list* the causes of the Civil War" puts the objective at the knowledge level.
- "Students will *appraise* the causes of the Civil War as to their relative order of importance" puts the same objective at the level of evaluation.

**2.** The verb *to study* does not refer to cognitive behavior. Studying takes many forms and is generally the activity of students trying to learn independently–by outlining, taking notes, memorizing, gathering information from a variety of sources, etc. One might *study* the Declaration of Independence in any number of ways, each of which might involve different levels of cognition. For example:

- "The students will *state* the major issues in the Declaration of Independence and *describe the relationship* between these issues and events leading to the Revolutionary War." This puts the objective at two related levels of cognition: knowledge and synthesis.

**3.** Every mathematics teacher wants students to be able *to solve* word problems; the error in the objective relates to the generality of the statement. As stated, the objective is appropriate as a course or unit objective, but not as a specific instructional objective. "To solve" is an appropriate verb at the cognitive level of application, but "To solve word problems" subsumes many more specific objectives. For example:

- "The students will *solve* word problems that involve time, distance, and speed of travel" specifies the kind of word problem students will solve.
- "Students will *formulate* word problems in answering questions that involve rates of interest and amortization of loans" puts the objective at the synthesis level.

## ■ Affective Objectives

Following the development of the cognitive objectives in 1956 by Benjamin Bloom and his committee, an affective taxonomy of objectives was developed by

Krathwohl, Bloom, and Masis in 1964.[4] Objectives in this domain concern feelings and attitudes that students are expected to develop as a result of instruction (see Table 2.2). Krathwohl classified these objectives in five parts on a continuum, ranging from willingness to receive to an internalization of the beliefs or values presented. Because teachers believe that affective objectives are difficult to measure, they frequently omit the affective from lists of objectives. However, much teaching is directed toward the development of beliefs, attitudes, and values, and it is important to describe these objectives.

Affective learning is not completely separable from cognitive learning: students often think about their attitudes and feelings, and they will have attitudes and feelings about what they think. So why bother to write objectives that describe attitudes and feelings? Because teachers want students to care about the subject they are learning and to grow from the experience. If the subject is worth learning, it should have some impact on the life of the learner—it should *affect* learners in other than intellectual ways. It should make them more understanding, more caring, more tolerant, more effective, more communicative, and so on. It is possible to overlook this important aspect of learning or to take it for granted unless a conscious effort is made to describe the kind of affective learning outcomes that should result from instruction.

### Exercise 2.4

Consult Table 2.2 and decide in which category to place each of the following verbs. Choose a verb from the list representing each of the categories of the taxonomy and write an objective. Be prepared to justify your decisions in discussion with a colleague or classmate.

> appreciate
> advocate
> participate
> prefer
> attend

Possible answer to Exercise 2.4

- *appreciate*—Valuing: The students will appreciate the importance of good nutritional habits, as evidenced by a food diary kept throughout the semester.

**TABLE 2.2**   **Sample of Verbs in the Affective Domain**

| | |
|---|---|
| Receiving | to take in, to listen, to encounter, to be aware |
| Responding | to react, to reply, to answer, to comply |
| Valuing | to accept, to reject, to esteem, to regard, to desire |
| Organization | to compare, to order, to prioritize |
| Characterization | to internalize, to personalize, to demonstrate |

- *advocate*—Characterization: Students will advocate the preservation of natural resources, as evidenced by their participation in a Clean Water Campaign.
- *participate*—Responding: Students will participate in classroom discussions, as evidenced by data taken periodically by an observer.
- *prefer*—Organization: Students will prefer to read books by authors recommended in class, as evidenced by a survey of the books checked out of the library voluntarily.
- *attend*—Receiving: Students will attend class on a regular basis, as evidenced by attendance records.

## ■ Psychomotor Objectives

In this domain, learning depends on mastery of a physical skill. Learning to hold a pencil, play the piano, throw a baseball, and operate a machine all depend at least in part on manipulative and motor skills. This domain has not, however, received the attention and development of the cognitive and affective domains. Table 2.3 describes one taxonomy in the psychomotor domain.

Too often, psychomotor objectives are considered to be solely the domain of the physical education teacher or the teacher of the very young. Many learning difficulties are associated with an inability to use some part of the body effectively. A person who has difficulty with handwriting may have great difficulty completing essay exams; a person with speech problems will seldom volunteer answers in class.

### Exercise 2.5

Place each of the phrases below into one of the categories described in Table 2.3.

| | |
|---|---|
| get in the water | copy the numbers |
| type by touch | pronounce clearly |
| position the fingers | shows an apptitude for |
| correct the stance | cut on the dotted line |

**TABLE 2.3    Sample of Verbs in the Psychomotor Domain**

| | |
|---|---|
| Readiness | willing, prepared, watches |
| Observation | attends, is interested |
| Perception | senses, has a feel for, is able |
| Response | practices, imitates, replicates |
| Adaptation | masters, develops, changes |

Answers to Exercise 2.5

> get in the water – Readiness
> type by touch – Adaptation
> position the fingers – Response
> correct the stance – Adaptation
> copy the numbers – Response
> pronounce clearly – Adaptation
> cut on the dotted line – Response
> show an aptitude for – Perception
> come to practice – Observation

---

You will notice that the three categories of objectives – cognitive, affective, and psychomotor – are interrelated. One cannot play basketball (psychomotor) without knowing the rules (cognitive) and having the desire (affective) to be a player. The categories serve primarily to assure that a variety of learnings and a range of outcomes are considered in deciding what students will learn from instruction.

### Activity 2.2

At this point, write 10 objectives for the course rationale that you wrote in Chapter 1. Remember, these objectives are the major learnings you want students to acquire by the end of the course. Make sure you have used a range of verbs from the charts and have included affective and skill objectives as well as cognitive objectives. Be sure to check these with a colleague or a class to confirm that your objectives clearly state the intended learning. ■

## Determining Evaluation Strategies

An important test for any objective is to ask the question, "Is there implied in the objective a reasonable means of evaluating whether students learned what was taught?" One way to do this is to write an evaluation method into the objective. For instance:

- The students will be able to apply the principles of long division to the solution of word problems *as evidenced by their ability to solve three out of five word problems correctly.*
- The students will analyze the causes of the Civil War *as evidenced by their solution to problems in a simulated activity.*
- Given a series of musical scales, *90 percent of the students will perform the exercise on the piano with 100 percent accuracy.*

Not all evaluation needs to be or should be conducted by paper and pencil tests. Oral questioning, classroom interviews, student journals and logs, participation in activities and projects are a few of the alternative methods of evaluating learning.

Objectives in the three domains—cognitive, affective, and psychomotor—require different types of evaluation processes. In the following sections, evaluation strategies for each of these three domains are discussed.

### ■ Evaluating Cognitive Objectives

Always keep in mind that evaluation procedures must match learning objectives. For instance, if one's objective is to have students be able to apply the Pythagorean theorem in solving practical problems, then a test of memory of the formula A squared plus B squared equals C squared is inappropriate. Evaluation of the objective should require that the students *apply* the theorem to a new problem.

If the instructional objective is that students *compare* the causes of the Civil War and the causes of the American Revolution, then asking students to list the causes of the Civil War will not test that objective. The evaluation question needs to test students' understanding of causes of the conflict, not simply the facts related to the events. In this case, either the objective or the criterion must be adjusted into closer congruence with the other.

Written examinations are only one of the many possible ways to evaluate cognitive learning. Projects, class discussions, simulated situations in which students are required to utilize their learning are equally effective means. Tape and video recorders are useful tools in maintaining a before and after record of students' comprehension of a subject.

### ■ Evaluating Affective Objectives

Affective objectives are frequently neglected in the design process because teachers feel that they cannot be measured. Measuring attitudes, feelings, and beliefs is not easy, but such measures *are* possible. Affective measures differ significantly

from other kinds of measures in that they are most valid when they are least obtrusive or overt.

If the teacher wants a true measure of students' enthusiasm for a subject, an evaluation system must be designed that allows students to express their feelings anonymously or allows the teacher to make systematic observations without the students' knowledge. Young children may be forthright about their opinions, but as individuals grow older they become more guarded in saying what they really think or believe about a situation. Thus, an unobtrusive checklist of student reactions completed by the teacher may be the best evaluation tool.

An anonymously completed pre- and post-unit questionnaire can serve as part of the teacher's evaluation of a unit of study. A tally of books checked out of the library or a record of the behavior of students on those days when free-reading time is provided in the classroom will serve as measures of interest in reading. If one's objective is to improve the social interactions of the students, then monitoring behavior on the playground when students believe themselves to be unobserved is an appropriate technique for evaluation. Tape recording classroom discussions over a period of time to see if students' interaction has improved can also be effective.

If it is important that students care about and feel positively about experiences in the classroom and the subjects taught, then evaluating their attitudes and feelings is necessary. We once taught a seventh-grade language arts unit on poetry. One of the objectives of the unit was that the students learn to enjoy reading poetry and choose to read it on their own. A pre- and post-unit test was developed that asked the students to check a number of responses regarding their enthusiasm for poetry. After the unit was taught, the students were tested first on their attainment of the cognitive objectives, and most of the students did very well. However, regarding attitudes toward poetry, the students liked it less after the unit than they did before.

This unintended outcome was a shock, but it caused a significant change in the design and delivery of the poetry unit. Inasmuch as the students' feeling about poetry was deemed just as important as what they understood intellectually, instruction that caused them to like it less was an unacceptable outcome.

### ■ Evaluating Psychomotor Objectives

Writing objectives in the psychomotor domain requires a considerable amount of specificity. The psychomotor skill must be broken down into measurable parts and the degree of acceptable performance must be stated. For instance:

- Students will be able to throw a ball with 80 percent accuracy from 3 feet into a 1 foot diameter circle.
- Given two points on a page, students will be able to draw a straight line between the two points with 100 percent accuracy using a ruler and pencil.
- Given a page of text delivered orally, students will be able to type a paragraph with 60 percent accuracy.

Evaluating psychomotor objectives necessitates that a careful record be kept of each student's progress. Psychomotor skills can be broken into steps on a continuum, moving from the simplest step to the most complex. Usually, it is not possible to skip a step and move to one that is higher.

In many cases, learners can keep a record of their own progress on a skill chart, which is regularly monitored by the teacher. Seldom will there be a group in which all students are at the same level of skill development. Thus, it is necessary to pretest the students and start developing each skill at the point at which they are proficient. Progress sheets and skill charts can be useful in learning any type of skill. Reading and math skills can also be kept on skill development charts in order to keep a record of each child's progress.

It is relatively simple to write lists of objectives regarding what students are to learn and how they will respond to the learning experience; it is much more difficult to actually confirm that the desired learning has occurred. In addition, it is important to retest periodically to ensure that the learning has been retained and integrated into the students' knowledge base.

### Exercise 2.6

Describe one evaluation technique for each of the following objectives. (Select a written test as a means of evaluation for no more than two of the objectives.)

1. Students will be able to apply three basic principles of paragraph development in their compositions: topic sentence, supporting detail, and concluding statement.
2. Students will appreciate impressionistic art.
3. Students will individually improve by 30 percent their ability to throw a softball.
4. Students will be able to contrast realism and naturalism in literature.
5. Students will be able to locate the seven continents on a globe.

6. Students will be able to identify the primary colors.
7. Students will be able to place data into categories.
8. Students will be able to locate materials using the card catalog.
9. Students will be able to write their names in cursive.
10. Students will be able to use effective problem-solving techniques in resolving disputes.

Possible Answers to Exercise 2.6

**1.** Use a periodic evaluation through writing samples. Have the students write for five minutes on a particular subject each month, and keep these samples in an individual folder for each student. These writing folders become a record of the students' progress.

**2.** A questionnaire that ensures anonymity would be one technique. Another might be to invite a guidance counselor or another teacher into the class to discuss with the students how they really feel about the subject.

**3.** Videotaped records of student achievement can be invaluable. If this process is too expensive, use written records of a student's progress, taken periodically during the course of study and recorded on a skill chart.

**4.** A written examination could be used effectively here. Another technique would be to have students roleplay the response of characters in first a realistic and then in a naturalistic manner.

**5.** Have each student come to the teacher's desk during a reading period and point out the continents. This should be done several weeks after the unit of study in order to be certain that long-term retention of the information has taken place.

**6. & 7.** Learning centers to which each student can go and complete assigned tasks. The center can be designed so that different students are assigned different levels of difficulty.

**8.** A task that requires students to *use* the card catalog in the library is essential.

**9.** A writing sample kept periodically to track each child's progress.

**10.** Observation on the playground, audio- or videotapes of class discussions, roleplaying, and simulation activities can all measure this objective.

---

Evaluation is a continuing process that allows the teacher to make corrections in order to achieve success. The feedback from evaluation allows the teacher to reteach, to supplement, to revise, to individualize–to be in control of learning in the classroom.

## ■ SUMMARY

Learning objectives describe the learning that is intended to take place as a result of instruction. In developing cognitive, affective, and psychomotor objectives, the teacher determines what should be included in the instructional design. Only when objectives are clearly defined can the teacher select appropriate instructional approaches. Evaluation procedures written at the time the objectives are developed enable the teacher to determine if what was intended has been achieved.

## ■ NOTES

1. Benjamin S. Bloom, ed., *Taxonomy of Educational Objectives: The Classification of Educational Goals, Handbook I: Cognitive Domain* (New York: David McKay, 1956).

2. Gilbert Ryle, *The Concept of Mind* (New York: Barnes & Noble, 1949), 25–61.

3. Ivor Davies, *Objectives in Curriculum Design* (Maidenhead, Berkshire, England: McGraw-Hill Book Company (U.K.), 1976), 125–126.

4. D. R. Krathwohl, B. S. Bloom, and B. B. Masis, *Taxonomy of Educational Objectives, Handbook II: Affective Domain* (New York: David McKay, 1964).

# Chapter 3

# Organizing Content

## *Course, Unit, and Lesson Design*

Mrs. Jones's classroom is always so much fun to visit. The children seem happy and are always busy working on interesting projects. Can one conclude that Mrs. Jones is a successful teacher? Perhaps. However, it is possible that the children are experiencing a series of interesting and entertaining episodes that have little relationship to each other. It is essential to determine if Tuesday's instruction relates to what was taught on Monday and what will be taught on Wednesday, and next week and next month. Is there a plan for how content is introduced to the learners, and are the connections between the lessons clear?

When children are taught without a careful plan for the presentation of content, they may have an experience akin to putting together a jigsaw puzzle with some of the pieces missing. The act of putting it together is fun, but when all the pieces have been assembled, it is impossible to tell what the picture was intended to be.

Subject areas of study in U.S. schools are generally organized into sequentially related courses, which are further subdivided into units and lessons. A good design depends on the teacher's ability to organize course, unit, and lesson content in a systematic and interesting manner. The main concepts to be considered in the course must be identified and then arranged into a hierarchy of importance. Obviously, an effective process is needed to plan a unit, organize a lesson, and prepare a lecture.

In a well-structured course design, the learner will be able to recognize the order behind the plan, determine how the parts fit into the whole, and how each part is related to other parts. Only when teachers consider the organization of content carefully and can explain the reason for the order in which material is presented, is it possible for students to have an overall understanding of what they are learning.

Frequently, the organization of material for a course is determined by the textbook or by a curriculum guide. Although both textbooks and guides can be important tools in the organization of content, the teacher needs to consider all of the factors related to the learner, the society, and the subject matter, which were discussed in Chapter 1. Each class presents a challenge to the teacher: how best to organize the content to fit the needs of *this* class and *these* individual students.

## Analyzing Content

We can divide most of the data that is processed in the classroom into three categories—facts, concepts, and generalizations. These broad categories will be discussed in more detail in Chapter 6, but dealt with briefly here.

### ■ Facts

Paul D. Eggen, a specialist in information processing models of instruction, has defined facts as the types of content "which are singular in occurrence, which have occurred in the past or exist in the present, which have no predictive value, and which are acquired solely through the process of observation."[1] Facts may be gathered through the direct observation of an event, such as an experiment in a laboratory, or through the retrieval of information from reliable sources, such as from dictionaries or encyclopedias.

### ■ Concepts

Concepts are the names given to the categories formed as a result of classifying factual data. Learners of all ages form concepts and give them names in order to make sense of all the various stimuli in the world. Imagine the cognitive overload if everything in the world were seen as a separate and unrelated entity. To form concepts, learners pay attention to likenesses, ignore differences, and place similar objects in the same category. A pussycat asleep by the fire and a tiger in the jungle have many differences, but by attending to similarities and ignoring differences, the concept of *cat* is formed.

### ■ Generalizations

Statements that link two or more concepts are generalizations. Unlike facts, generalizations contain more than one element and are predictive.
Consider the following:

> Ten of the fifteen students in Ms. Brown's fourth-grade class brought peanut butter sandwiches for lunch today. Nine students brought peanut butter sandwiches yesterday. Eleven students brought peanut butter sandwiches the day before.

These are factual statements formed on the basis of observation. They do not tell us if the sandwiches were eaten by the students or who made the sandwiches but are simply statements of what was observed.

*A majority of the students in Ms. Brown's class prefer peanut butter sandwiches for lunch.* This is a generalization based on the data from observation and from our understanding of concepts such as peanut butter and sandwich. We have inferred from observation that the students prefer peanut butter sandwiches, and we may predict that a majority of students will bring peanut butter sandwiches tomorrow.

None of these statements are necessarily true. The students may not prefer the sandwiches; they may simply have no choice in the matter. Peanut butter may have been on sale in the local market this week and next week cheese may be the main ingredient. However, from the observed fact of peanut butter sandwiches brought to school over a period of time, we formed a generalization that allowed us to draw inferences and to make predictions. Only data from additional observations would prove the accuracy of the generalization.

Since facts, concepts, and generalizations make up a large part of instructional content, the teacher must select the most important combinations of these in the design process. Which facts are most important, and which facts seem most accurate and relevant? Which concepts are familiar to the students, and which ones need to be explained before the students can understand the content? How do the students learn to infer and predict through forming generalizations, and how do they learn to test the reliability of data? Teachers must ask these questions as they select and organize the content of instruction.

## Ordering Content

A good system for ordering and presenting content is based on the work of David Ausubel,[2] to whom all educators owe a great debt as one of the founders of cognitive psychology. Ausubel's approach is rooted in principles of learning psychology: (1) the single most important factor influencing new learning is what the learner already knows, and (2) any concept is explainable at many different levels of generality, the highest or most general level being most easily understood, the lowest or most specialized level being the most difficult.

### ■ Principle One

*New learnings are built on prior learnings.* The very young child develops a concept of locomotion by observing the world in motion. He or she then tries to move, at first in a clumsy way, until the idea of full-fledged crawling is mastered. On that foundation walking begins, though for a while crawling is easier. From walking comes running, skipping, dancing, ballet—the repertoire is limitless. Notice, though, that each stage of locomotion is a specialized refinement of the one that preceded it.

Concepts develop in the same way. At first, to the very young child, people are faces. Later, the child distinguishes mother from not mother, then moves to the stage that all men are daddy, and so on. Anyone familiar with very young children knows that almost all their learning begins with the simplest idea and develops greater and greater specificity. The child's understanding of complex mathematical puzzles began many years before with the idea of combining parts into wholes; studying forms of government traces to the learner's first ideas of fair play and equity in human relations; arranging things into successively inclusive groups (species, genera, families, orders, classes, phyla, and kingdoms) follows, at least indirectly, from the child's earliest notion that like objects can be grouped on the basis of their likenesses.

### ■ Principle Two

*Any stage of learning and understanding builds on previous, more general levels.* Every concept imaginable subsumes other more complex concepts and is at the same time subsumed by more general concepts. Imagine an analogy here between concepts and the nested boxes young children play with, the kind that fit one into the other, each one exactly fitting the one next larger than itself. Think of the boxes as successively inclusive concepts. Each larger concept has the same structure as all the related concepts, whether more or less inclusive, so that if a person understands the structure underlying any one of the concepts, he or she can potentially understand any of the other concepts. Here is where the second principle of learning comes into play: The easiest concept to learn will always be the one at the next level of generality from a concept already understood. In deciding what to teach, find the "box" that contains the concept you wish to teach and ask yourself whether the learners already understand the next most inclusive concept.

## Unit Design

Courses and textbooks are often organized into manageable parts that span an instructional period of up to several weeks. These parts are called units of study. Units are usually centered around a broad concept or a cluster of related concepts. For example, a unit in earth science might be entitled "Seeds and Plants" or "Ecological Systems;" a unit in U.S. history might be entitled "The Colonial Period: Plymouth Rock to Revolution;" a unit in English literature might be entitled "The Short Story" or "Stories and Poems of the Black Experience." Units provide a structure or framework for the design of a course or an interdisciplinary program. The plan for a series of units helps to define a course of study.

There are three essential aspects to unit design: scope, focus, and sequence. *Scope* defines the breadth and range of content to be covered, *focus* determines what will be emphasized in the content, and *sequence* specifies the order in which the content will be arranged.

### ■ Scope

Every teacher is faced with the frustration of having too much to cover in too little time. There is an ever-present danger that in the hope of teaching much, the teacher may fail to take the time to teach well. Since all the conceivable content and information related to a course cannot be covered within the time frame of a course, choices have to be made as to the actual breadth and depth.

These choices will rest on two considerations: (1) the relative importance of facts, concepts, and generalizations that might be taught in terms of the continuum of the overall curriculum and (2) the relative importance of the content to be taught in respect to the needs of society and the age, interests, and abilities of the learners. Given the choice, one would always want to teach comparatively more important rather than less important content. Likewise, one would always want to choose content most appropriate to the learners, relative to their prior knowledge, abilities, and needs.

In general, learners will retain more of what they understand than of what they try merely to memorize; it is less important for students to remember all the facts of a topic than it is for them to understand the main ideas and concepts.

Teachers learn one lesson early on: if you try to teach everything possible, nothing may be learned well. However, if what is taught is taught well, it is nearly impossible to keep learners from learning everything they possibly can. Beginning teachers generally feel they have to pack in as much information as possible into every lesson. Such an approach overlooks how learners learn: by practicing new skills and having material presented in a variety of ways. There is no point in giving students more than they can learn and thereby miss the opportunity to have students learn the content well through a variety of instructional approaches.

## ■ Focus

A good way to start bringing focus to the planning process is to title the units within a course. Titling and organizing units around particular themes or ideas adds interest and helps learners understand the purpose of the study. For instance, the sixth-grade science teacher described in Chapter 1 titled her rationale "Our Window On the World." Next, she listed the major concepts that might be included in the course: Communities, Terrain, Resources, Habitat, Environment, Animals and Plants, Erosion, Water Sources, Climate, and Ecosystems. Each of these major concepts could potentially form the basis or serve as a major

part of a unit of study within the course. The teacher decided that "Environment" would serve as the basis of one unit. The next step was to put the components of the unit into a framework that accommodated the general and specific content. Thus, the unit on environment took the following form:

Organizing Idea: The *environment* consists of a number of carefully balanced ecosystems all of which are interrelated.

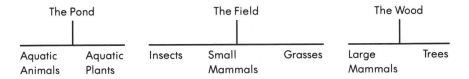

| The Pond | | | The Field | | | The Wood | |
|---|---|---|---|---|---|---|---|
| Aquatic Animals | Aquatic Plants | Insects | Small Mammals | Grasses | Large Mammals | | Trees |

The construction of a diagram like this one allows the teacher to clarify the focus of the work to be done in the unit. The focus of this unit will be on the pond, the field, and the wood. Furthermore, the focus for study of the pond will be aquatic animals and plants; the focus for study of the field will be insects, small mammals, and grasses; and the focus for study of the wood will be large mammals and trees.

The organization of the main concepts in the structure of a unit may take many forms, but organization is essential if the learners are to understand how the parts of the unit relate to each other and what the focus of their study is at any given time. The chart used to plan each unit can serve as an excellent organizer for the students. Putting the chart on the board at the beginning of the unit of study allows teacher and students to track their progress through the concepts and activities on which the unit is built. Decisions regarding the focus of a unit will lead directly to the formulation of unit objectives.

For the unit on the woods, the objectives might be as follows:

- Students will identify three mammals who live in the woods and list their distinguishing characteristics.
- Students will compare the habitats of woodland animals with those of meadow animals.
- Students will analyze the impact of environmental changes on the eating habits of woodland animals and evaluate the effectiveness of three different conservation plans.
- Students will develop a concern for limiting the use of pesticides.

Within any subject there are many interesting possibilities for study; however, it is impossible to include everything in a single course or unit. As Figure 3.1 illustrates, the first step is to survey the content in the field to be studied, considering all possible material for inclusion. As a result of this survey, the teacher draws together various strands of the material and determines a focus for the study. This focus enables the teacher to select related content and develop

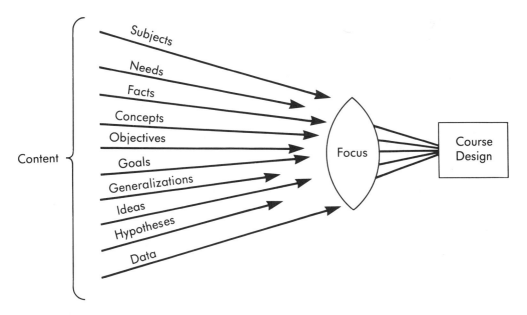

**FIGURE 3.1**    Focus on the Planning Process

the learning objectives to complete the design process. Without a focus, the selection of material may be random and disconnected.

### ■ Sequence

A third set of decisions to be made concerns the order in which to place subject matter. Subjects may be ordered chronologically or thematically. There is an obvious logic to ordering historical events chronologically, but they might also be ordered thematically, by bringing together topics such as civil unrest, wars, or migrations. The resulting comparisons and contrasts can enrich students' grasp of the material.

Basic skills, such as the fundamentals of reading or arithmetic, usually require that the sequence of skills proceed from the simpler to the more complex. However, even in such areas as math and reading, it is sometimes appropriate to sequence learning according to interest and variety. For instance, a unit on percent, in which winning percentages of the basketball team are studied, might be undertaken during basketball season, or a unit on consumer spending might be timed to coincide with the holiday season in December.

One important consideration in the sequencing of material is that new learning should be based on previous learning. Even when that is done, it is important to provide the connections that help the learner identify how the new learning fits into what is already known. In short, there should be a logical order for the sequence and the links between the parts to be learned should be made obvious.

## Exercise 3.1

Describe the scope, focus, and sequence of the following courses, as indicated by the unit titles.

1. Secondary Science – The Earth
   - Structure and History
   - Atmosphere and Weather
   - Continents and Oceans

2. Elementary Social Studies
   - Our Neighborhood
   - Our City
   - Our State
   - Our Nation

3. Secondary English
   - The Short Story
   - Poetry
   - The Novel
   - The Play

4. Consumer Math
   - Math in the Marketplace
   - Math in the Home
   - Math in the Factory

For each of these courses, develop another set of unit titles using a different organization.

Possible Answer to one course in Exercise 3.1

The focus for the secondary science class in this example is for earth science only. The scope includes the earth, the atmosphere, the oceans, and the continents. The sequence is from a general description of the earth to more specific descriptions of air, climate, oceans, and continents.

Another more general approach might be as follows:

The Earth and the Solar System
Life from the Sea to the Land
Man Settles the Continents

The first step in unit design is to decide how many units are needed in a course. The content must be examined to determine how much actually to undertake, what order to place it in, and what focus to utilize. In working through this process, the goals and objectives need to be reviewed and revised. Perhaps the time allowed is too short to cover all the goals, or perhaps the content mandated for the course by state or local requirements does not fit the rationale. In any case, the decision-making process is circular, with each decision necessitating a review of prior decisions.

## Activity 3.1

Diagram the content for the course you plan to teach. Title the main units and write unit objectives. In sharing your organization with the class, have you considered the scope, focus, and sequence of your design? Be prepared to explain your reasons for the way in which you organized the content, and then select one alternative approach. ■

## Developing Lesson Plans

Lesson plans are the component parts of the unit design. A lesson may span several days or it may take only one day. Just as a course is divided into units, units are divided into lessons. In deciding how many lessons are necessary to accomplish the unit objectives, it may be necessary to rethink and modify the unit objectives because they may prove too ambitious or too limited. The design process is always circular, in that prior decisions may be modified as the teaching progresses. Each lesson should be a logical part of the unit plan. If you have developed a clear chart of the main concepts to be studied, lesson planning will flow more easily.

We offer four guidelines to the development of effective lessons:

1. Limit the concepts and content to be covered in a lesson to allow time for the students to review, to practice, and to get feedback on what they have learned.
2. Be sure that new material is connected to what has been learned previously and that the connections are clear.
3. Check frequently to ensure that the students are acquiring the intended knowledge, attitudes, and skills, and be prepared to alter your plans or to reteach if the learning is not taking place or the students seem to be disengaged.
4. Never accept students' failure to learn as inevitable or unavoidable.

## ■ Deductive and Inductive Organization

In a deductive model of instruction, the lesson usually begins with the presentation of a generalization, a rule, or a concept definition. Students are then given specific examples, along with facts associated with the generalization, concept, or rule. In moving from the general to the specific, students are encouraged to draw inferences and make predictions based on the examples.

In inductive lesson designs, the students are first presented with the specific data and facts, and gradually, through the process of investigation and reasoning, the students form the generalization, rule, or concept definition. Most of the models presented in Part Two of this text are inductive, since induction is more conducive to stimulating students' thinking. However, deductive models, particularly the lecture, can be very effective when used judiciously and sparingly in delivering information.

## ■ Advance Organizers

An advance organizer is a term developed by David Ausubel for what he described as "anchoring foci for the reception of new material."[3] An advance organizer is presented at the beginning of the lesson and is usually a general statement or analogy that helps the learner place in context the material to be learned. About organizers, Ausubel wrote:

> First they provide advance ideational scaffolding. Second, they provide the learner with a generalized overview of all of the major similiarities and differences between the two bodies of ideas before he encounters the new concepts individually in more detailed and particularized form. Finally, they create an advance set in the learner to perceive similarities and differences, and by avoiding overly explicit specification, encourage him actively to make his own differentiations.[4]

In one of the earliest experiments on the use of advance organizers, Ausubel introduced learners to the topic of alloys before studying material relating to the Bessemer process of making steel. Knowing something about the more general idea, alloys, facilitated an understanding of the more specific idea, steel production, because knowledge of alloys provides a context for new information about steel, a specific alloy.

Organizing concepts may be presented in statements made by the teacher or through experiences such as viewing materials or reading assignments. An organizer might take only a few minutes to present or it might take an extensive amount of time, depending on the instructional design and the type of organizer. Organizers can be either *expository* or *comparative*.

### *Expository Organizers*
Expository organizers begin at a higher level of generality than the concept to be presented in the lesson. Alloys, for instance, are more general than the concept of steel and thus set a general context for more specific understandings.

The concept of *independence* could serve as an organizer for a lesson on the Revolutionary War, *nutrition* for a lesson on the basic food groups, *punctuation* for a lesson on the comma. For another example, the teacher might begin a lesson on insects using this expository organizer:

> Before we begin our study of insects, it is important for us to remember that both insects and man belong to larger families. The honey bee, the bear, the fish, and all human beings are part of the animal kingdom. Let us think of all the things that we share as animals and then we will talk specifically about what makes the insect special and different from other animals.

The discussion of the more general concept, animals—all require oxygen, reproduce their own kind, take in water and food, and so forth—sets the stage for learning about a particular instance of animals, the insects. The focus of the study can then be on how insects in particular perform the functions common to all animals.

### Comparative Organizers

Comparative organizers connect the new learning to previously learned material or to experiences that are familiar to the students through analogy and comparisons. For instance, a lesson on the Industrial Revolution could begin with a discussion of the word *revolution*.

> We may think of the word *revolution* as a turning around in a complete circle, like the revolution of a wheel or the revolution of the earth around the sun. Another way in which we use the word is to describe a complete change or turning around of a government, often by violent means, such as our own American Revolution.
>
> When we speak of the Industrial Revolution, we are also talking of a complete change or turn around from the way things had been. This change occurred, however, not as a result of war but as a result of technology—of machines.

In this example, the teacher is comparing a familiar meaning of the word *revolution* to a new meaning that she is introducing to the students. The students thus have a framework or a context within which to place the new learning.

Advance organizers are generally thought of as part of a deductive lesson plan. However, an organizer that sets the stage for learning to take place can be equally effective in an inductive lesson plan. For instance, following the organizer for the lesson on insects, the teacher could present the students with a series of examples from which they are asked to observe similarities and differences and draw conclusions.

Advance organizers, like the statement of objectives, help students comprehend more clearly the purpose of the lesson. The intent is to involve students in the process as participants; the more they understand what is to take place the better.

## Exercise 3.2

Determine which of the following examples is an expository organizer and which is comparative. Also, what is the topic of each organizer and what is the idea being compared to?

**1.** It would be hard for us to dance without the rhythm of music to follow. The music determines how fast we will move and what kind of dance we will do. The rhythm of the music makes us feel like dancing. There is also rhythm in the way in which words are used in poetry. This rhythm determines how fast the poem will move and how we feel about the poem.

**2.** Imagine a shepherd in the fields long, long ago. He was to take care that not a single sheep was lost, but there were so many. How could he possibly keep track of them all? He had an idea. What if he picked up many little twigs and tied them in a bundle each morning when the sheep were put out to pasture. Each stick would represent one of the sheep. At night, he could check to see if there was one sheep for each of the twigs in the bundle. His system worked well, except that he had so many sticks. He thought and thought and then he said, I will have a bigger stick and put one notch on it for each sheep. Now I will not have to carry so many sticks. For a long, long time, people have been trying to devise systems for keeping records of the number of things in the world. Today, we will learn about sets and how they help us to keep track of the numbers of things that we have.

Answer to Exercise 3.2

The first example is a comparative organizer in which the rhythm of music is being compared to the rhythm of poetry. The second is an expository organizer with the broader generality of counting introducing the idea of sets.

## Activity 3.2

Write lesson organizers for three of the following subjects. Have your classmates determine if you have written expository or comparative organizers.

The Gettysburg Address
Administering CPR
The multiplication tables
Pronouns
The basketball dribble
The metric system ■

### ■ Objectives for Lessons

When a lesson is not part of an instructional design for a unit, there often seems to be no logical reason for its delivery. The parts of a lesson are related to each other, and lessons are related to the integrity of the unit design. Each lesson should clearly be a part of a whole.

The objectives for each lesson should be related to the objectives of the unit and of the course. The students should be able to trace the purposes of their lessons as they move from step to step through an instructional design. The objectives for each lesson will determine the instructional strategies. There are always many instructional options; in order to choose one that is appropriate, the lesson objectives should be clearly defined. For example, here is a unit-level objective for a study of the Civil War: *The students will analyze the major events leading to the Civil War.* The objectives for one of the lessons in the unit could be as follows:

- Students will describe the operation of the Underground Railroad.
- Students will analyze the effect of the development of the cotton gin on the economy of the South.

From the diagram below, one can determine that the objective for the lesson on the Underground Railroad relates to the larger issue of the morality of slavery, which is one of the issues being studied in this unit, "Causes of the Civil War." The invention of the cotton gin is one factor related to an increase in the demand for cotton which, in turn, increased the demand for slaves.

**Three Causes of the Civil War**

| Morality/Economics | — | Expansion of the United States | — | Invention of the cotton gin |
| Slavery | | Tradition of state's rights | | Demand for cotton |
| Underground Railroad/ Abolitionists | | | | Increase in number of slaves |
| Slave trade in New England | | | | |

Diagramming the main ideas to be considered in the unit, from the most general to the most specific, and relating the information across categories helps the teacher organize the material and determine what is to be included. In addition, such a diagram can be presented to the students as part of the advance organizer for the unit or lesson to be studied.

**Activity 3.3**

Write lesson objectives for a unit in the course that you are planning. Check to determine if the lesson objectives fulfill the objectives for the course. You may find that either the unit objectives or the lesson objectives will need to be revised for them to be congruent. ■

The following outline exemplifies one type of lesson plan that could be followed, incorporating some of the ideas described in this chapter:

## Sample Outline for Lesson Planning

1. Title of lesson:
2. Date(s) to be taught:
3. Part of unit:
4. Lesson objectives:
5. Advance organizer:
6. Relevant textbook pages, supplementary reading materials, and demonstration materials needed:
7. Instructional design (This step would include the instructional models to be incorporated into the plan from Part Two of this text and the examples and illustrations that would accompany the lesson.)
8. Questions for classroom discussion:
9. Guided and independent practice:
10. Feedback and evaluation strategies:

At this point, you should be able to complete the first five steps of this lesson plan. You should also have some ideas about how to evaluate the objectives. Before you decide on the instructional design, however, you need to consider some of the instructional options that will be described in Part Two of this text.

## ■ SUMMARY

The design of a course consisting of units and lessons is one of the most rewarding professional experiences for an instructor. Since there is so much content in every subject that could be included, the instructor must decide what to put in and what to leave out, what to emphasize, the order in which to present the material, and whether to begin with the general and work to the specific or begin with specifics and work to the general. Effective examples must be selected and an organizing statement that will help the students fit the new learning into what they know already must be determined. Like the design of a building or an automobile, the design for instruction determines the quality of the finished product.

## ■ NOTES

**1.** Paul D. Eggen, Donald P. Kauchak, and Robert J. Harder, *Strategies for Teachers* (Englewood Cliffs, NJ: Prentice-Hall, 1979), 36–37.

**2.** David Ausubel, *The Psychology of Meaningful Verbal Learning* (New York: Grune & Stratton, 1963).

**3.** David Ausubel, "The Use of Advance Organizers in the Learning and Retention of Meaningful Verbal Material," *Journal of Educational Psychology* 51 (1960): 267–272.

**4.** Ausubel, *Psychology*, 90.

# Chapter 4

# Selecting Instructional Tools

## Criteria for Choosing Textbooks and Supplementary Materials

A child once remarked to a visiting consultant in the classroom, "Can you help me?"

"What seems to be the problem?"

"I'm having trouble reading this book," he said, pointing to his fifth-grade American history text. "I can't find the story."

Out of the mouths of babes! Textbooks and other informational sources often present a challenge to young readers, and for the wrong reasons. Wrong because the books in which they *learn to read* differ from the books in which they are asked to *read to learn*. How so? Under pressure to convey vast amounts of information, instructional texts leave out "the story" which would make information interesting and memorable. Unless instructional materials are chosen wisely and used discriminately, the result is boredom for learners.

Experts in evaluation speak of the relationship among three variables in instruction: input, process, and outcome. The latter two, outcome and process, are discussed elsewhere in this book. *Outcome* refers to instructional objectives, that is, intended learning outcomes. Outcome variables might be described as what the teacher expects as a result of instructional effort. The outcome variable is addressed in the first two chapters of this book. *Process*, on the other hand, refers to instructional approaches, techniques or models of instruction the teacher employs. It may also refer to the student's mental activity. Process is the focus of much of our discussion in the remainder of this book.

*Input,* the first of the instructional variables listed here, is the issue we raise in this chapter. Input refers to all the equipment and tools for instruction, the many instructional materials, textbooks, and technology that serve the teacher as tools of the trade. Thus, input includes the textbooks issued to students in most classes at every grade level of instruction. But more than textbooks are necessary to effective instruction, and all teachers must make choices in the use of instructional tools, particularly those chosen from school resource centers to supplement issued textbooks. The tools of instruction include workbooks, laboratory exercises, library books, pamphlets, computer software, and all the mimeographed exercises that pervade classroom instruction. We propose specific criteria that will help teachers choose instructional material (input) appropriate to the intended learning outcomes and instructional processes.

It is the wise teacher who is able to offer students many alternative sources of informational materials. But on what basis can one choose from among all the instructional material available, including textbook material?

## Activity 4.1

Examine a few of the textbooks and instructional materials that are appropriate for the grade levels and subjects you anticipate teaching. A cursory inspection will give you some notion of what might be the best and worst features of these books. Try to read as if you knew very little (and cared even less) about the subject. Would the text excite you or bore you, engage you or dissuade you from learning? Make a mental list of the good and the poor features of the several books you survey. ■

## Selection of Instructional Materials

If you were to buy a new car, you would be faced with judgments ranging from safety, economy, and general suitability to style, make, and color. To make those judgments, you would rely on a more or less subconscious preconception of what the ideal car might be for you. Likely, it would get very high gas mileage, or perhaps be fueled by something very cheap; it would probably be very safe to drive; and, ideally, would express and fit your personality and perfectly meet all your needs for efficient travel. But, of course, the perfect car does not yet exist, and may never exist, leaving you forever in the troublesome position of having to decide what compromises you are willing to make and what features you are willing to sacrifice in favor of others.

The process of selecting a new car is in some ways analogous to the process of selecting textbooks and instructional materials for use in your teaching.[1] Though the perfect teaching material does not and probably could not exist, there are certain qualities on which you will have to decide how far you are willing to compromise. The selection of instructional tools needs to be made on the basis of more than one or two criteria, taking into account a number of considerations beyond readability. The difference between selecting instructional materials and selecting a car is that you may be even less sure of your conception of the ideal instructional material than you are of the ideal car. Therefore, we suggest eight qualities that you might want to bear in mind when evaluating materials for possible selection and use. We present them as a series of questions, each accompanied by a brief explanation of why we think it a useful question to ask.

## Criteria for Selection of Instructional Materials

The criteria we choose as important in evaluating instructional materials are: (1) emphasis, (2) unity, (3) coherence, (4) repetition and elaboration, (5) appropriate vocabulary, (6) audience appropriateness, (7) format, and (8) caliber of questions. As you consider these criteria and the examples meant to illustrate each, think about what it means to become a judge of instructional materials. Have in hand a textbook or two, a workbook, a script for a filmstrip, or a manual that you can look at and analyze against each criterion. Our aim here is to help you become aware of elements of instructional materials that make them clear or unclear to readers.

## ■ Emphasis

*Are the main ideas of the material clearly stated for the learner and are ideas given appropriate emphasis relative to their importance to the intended meaning and purpose of the material?* If you look at the title and headings of a textbook chapter or a pamphlet or a newspaper or magazine article, you should get some idea of what the author wanted to stress. But look carefully at the paragraphs and sentences within and ask yourself, Is there information in the paragraphs that leaves no doubt in your mind what the author is talking about?

Ideally, important ideas should be stated in positive, not negative, terms and should be highlighted by position and repetition. Important principles are better retained if they are stated at the beginning or end of sections of text, rather than being buried in the middle, and if they are repeated in the discussion, both by restatement in different words and by an example or two. Furthermore, when several important ideas are being presented, they should be clearly enumerated or set off from the rest of the text.

Instructional material should cue the reader to think about the specifically intended learning outcome. When a writer inadvertently diverts the reader's attention, the emphasis is clouded and the reader's thinking becomes confused in regard to the writer's intent. Thus, instructional material should guide the learner to realize what is being emphasized.

## ■ Unity

*Are all the ideas in the material clearly related to specific main ideas and major points of the material?* Learners have a right to assume that the material they are given to study has a clear point and that the content of the material is logically related to that point. Unfortunately, instructional material is frequently subjected to a number of rewrites and editings by different people, thereby losing the single vision of its major points and purposes. As a result, you will often find irrelevancies in the material. Interesting as the occasional sidelight may be, unless the learner is already quite familiar with the topics treated in the material, every idea needs to be clearly and explicitly related to some overarching main idea. Every sentence and every paragraph in a text should contribute to an understanding of a clearly stated topic.

One good test for this quality is to ask yourself how easy the parts of the material would be to outline. To demonstrate to yourself just how unified the ideas in the following example are, try to outline it sentence by sentence. You'll see that every sentence has a place in this very nearly perfect paragraph, quoted directly from an elementary science textbook.

### Honeybees

#### Winter Organization

The honeybee colony, which usually has a population of 30,000 to 40,000 workers, differs from that of the bumblebee and many other social bees or wasps in that it survives the winter. This means that the bees must stay warm despite the cold. Like other bees, the isolated honeybee cannot fly if the temperature is below 7°C. Within the wintering hive, bees maintain their temperature by clustering together in a dense ball; the lower the temperature, the denser the cluster. The clustered bees produce heat by constant muscular movements of their wings, legs, and abdomens. In very cold weather, the bees on the outside of the cluster keep moving toward the center, while those in the core of the cluster move to the colder outside periphery. The entire cluster moves slowly about on the combs, eating the stored honey from the combs as it moves.

The first sentence of this paragraph is a transition from an earlier discussion (or presumed knowledge) of "other social bees or wasps." The sentences that follow the main idea statement in the second sentence are then all unified in their relationship to that idea; they tell how it is that honeybees stay warm despite the cold.

This paragraph was taken from a textbook in elementary life science, but it could as well be the script of a movie or a slide presentation or a paragraph in a reading exercise. The same criteria of unity applies to all kinds of text.

You may have the impression that we are describing a minimum quality of instructional material. After all, aren't we merely saying that authors should stick to the point? Yes, but we invite you to take a close look at some instructional material you might use in teaching; you may find that not all the paragraphs have the clear unity one might wish.

### ■ Coherence

*Are the ideas in the text clearly linked together in an easy-to-follow, logical way?* Coherence and unity are related to one another, but the question of coherence refers to whether ideas are tied together; unity refers to whether all the ideas in a text relate to the same topic. For example, take a look at the following paragraph from a middle-school social studies text as an example of good unity but poor coherence.

> The region called the Far East is a region of great extremes. It contains the highest mountains in the world, the Himalayas, as well as fertile lowland plains. It has one of the world's driest deserts, the Takla-Makan in western China, as well as many areas covered with lush tropical rain forest. It is also the home of some of the most ancient civilizations on earth. The Indus River Valley civilization on the Indian subcontinent developed at almost the same time as the Nile River civilization of Egypt, and the Chinese can claim a civilized culture as far back as 1500 B.C. Yet, there are people living on islands in Indonesia who have remained in the Stone Age right up to the present. The Far East is a region of economic extremes, too, from terrible poverty in parts of India to high prosperity in Japan.

The main idea of this paragraph is clearly stated, setting up a pattern for the discussion that follows in the next two sentences: highest mountains in contrast to lowland plains and driest desert in contrast to rain forest. But then problems arise. The contrast between ancient civilizations and Stone Age is not at all clear; also, the reader is left with the inadvertent implication that Egypt is part of the Far East, which of course it is not. The reader needs to see more clearly that the Far East is home to civilizations that have flourished for centuries as well as cultures that have never progressed beyond the Stone Age. But somehow the author loses the thread of the argument in the text's midsection. The thread is there, but it has no beads or knots that the reader can use to pick his or her way through the discussion. When examining instructional materials for their potential clarity, ask yourself whether you find the knots and beads on which clarity depends.

### ■ Repetition and Elaboration

*Does the material present new concepts in relation to other concepts previously introduced?* Teachers know that, at times, the major function of teaching is to remind students of what they already know; they also know that information must be given to students repeatedly in different forms. Repetition helps remind readers of what they know and helps them relate new concepts to known ones. Text should hang together in such a way that things said are interrelated, concepts are interconnected, and ideas build on one another. To assess this quality, ask yourself whether the main ideas of the text are explicitly referenced to ideas previously introduced. Look for repetitions of ideas from previous sections or chapters, for use of technical vocabulary previously defined, and for statements such as "Recall that we said before . . . ." Look also for cues to elaborations, phrases and expressions such as "to elaborate on this idea," "to extend this analogy," or "what this is taken to mean . . . ."

Often, textbooks are accompanied by workbooks, laboratory activities, and supplementary material meant to elaborate, enhance, and provide practice with the information in the textbook. To be most effective, these materials should be designed with the same specific instructional objectives. Learners should be able to see a direct link among all related materials—media material, ditto sheets, exploratories, workbooks, and so forth. All too often, unfortunately, these different pieces seem to have been prepared by different people with different purposes in mind. And, in fact, that is often the case. A publisher may contract independently for the preparation of textbook and workbook material, even in a basic reading program organized around a common set of skills objectives.

Helpful instructional materials refer the reader to previous sections that explain a concept the author is now assuming the reader understands. The student is thereby encouraged, and given the necessary guidance, to review the work as it becomes progressively more complex. Look carefully at any instructional material for *explicit* ties between information in the present context and information presented earlier.

Instructional materials should also provide opportunities to see important information in several elaborated forms, *unpacked* as much as possible from its technical context. You will see this in the form of graphs, tables, charts, and illustrations as well as in verbal elaborations and expansions of information.

### ■ Appropriate Vocabulary

*Is the vocabulary in which ideas are expressed appropriate to the academic level of the students who will be asked to read the book?* Here the question is whether new ideas are put in familiar as well as technical terms. If key ideas are expressed in very technical vocabulary, then those ideas will escape the unfamiliar reader. Authors are often put in a bind, though, since the introduction of precise terminology is part of what they are seeking to accomplish. Take note of how the author of the material in the next example gets around this paradox.

All new technical terms should be defined in familiar language, set off in boldface or other highlighting, and introduced gradually to the naive reader. The net effect, happily, is to raise the academic level of the students rather than to ignore it. In this first paragraph, notice how tightly packed the concepts are and how this high school textbook author's approach is anything but gradual.

> The basic nerve cell is called a neuron. Neurons are composed of a cell body, containing the nucleus, with the addition of threadlike projections of the cytoplasm known as nerve fibers. The nerve fibers are of two kinds: dendrites, which conduct impulses *to* the cell body; and axons, which conduct impulses *away from* the cell body. The dendrites of sensory neurons are very different from those of other neurons. They are usually single and they may be very long (as much as 3 feet) or they may be short; but in any case, they do not have the treelike appearance so typical of other dendrites. Each sen-

sory nerve fiber (dendrite) has a special structure called a receptor, or end organ, where the stimulus is received and the sensory impulse begins.

By contrast, here's a paragraph on a related topic, which does a fine job of carefully introducing some technical concepts in familiar terms.

The organs of the nervous system are the brain, the spinal cord, and the numerous nerves of the body. Often the brain and spinal cord together are referred to as the *central nervous system* (CNS)—an appropriate name for them in view of their central location in the body and their central role in the functioning of the nervous system. In contrast, all the nerves of the body together are referred to as the *peripheral nervous system* (PNS). Peripheral means outlying. So nerves, reaching out as they do from brain and cord to all parts of the body, seem well named as the peripheral nervous system.

## ■ Audience Appropriateness

*Has the author made reasonable assumptions about the prior experiences of the students for whom the material is intended?* Instructional materials are usually written for a very specific audience, identifiable by subject area and grade level. Authors, then, should rarely produce materials that miss their target. But, at times, they miss by a surprisingly wide margin, as in the following example from an elementary science textbook:

### How Seeds Are Made

A bee flies from flower to flower. It is getting food. But the hairs on its body pick up pollen from a flower. Some of that pollen sticks to the pistil of the next flower. That flower is pollinated.

When a flower is pollinated, here's what happens. A tiny bit of pollen sticks to the pistil of the flower.

A tube grows from the bit of pollen. The tube goes down into the pistil. It goes into an ovule, one of the tiny round things like beads. The ovule grows into a seed.

The pistil gets bigger and bigger. It becomes a fruit. Inside the fruit are the plant's seeds.

Can you explain how seeds are made? If so, you knew before you read this selection, *included in a third-grade textbook*. Actually, there is so much wrong with this text that it misses its target completely. The text is little better than a series of statements about bees and flowers and pollination—all of which are related to the main idea of the text but not strung together in any coherent or helpful way. We can't imagine any audience for whom this text is appropriate, much less the third-graders for whom it was intended. Part of the problem is vocabulary—technical vocabulary that goes unexplained. The text is accompanied by a draw-

ing of a flower with some of the internal parts labeled to ease the vocabulary load. Unfortunately, the pistil was not labeled.

Instructional materials may be inappropriate because they contain vocabulary, analogies, metaphors, figurative language, and examples that are unfamiliar to learners. At times, these problems can be dealt with in the preparatory phase of instruction. Sometimes, however, instructional materials are inappropriate because the author explains ideas in ways that confuse rather than clarify for the reader. As you examine instructional materials, look not just at the information given but at *how* it is presented to learners.

## ■ Format

*Does the format of the text facilitate readers' comprehension?* Comprehension is often aided by italicized type, bold-faced headings, spacing (e.g., partitioning of key ideas and examples), and inclusion of clearly related, supportive illustrations, definitions, and references to other instructional materials and books. Learners should respond favorably to the format, not feel overwhelmed by print size or pages of continuous, unbroken print. Consider the next example, from a fifth-grade history textbook, noting especially the embedded question.

### Special Taxes

One of the laws passed by Parliament was called the Stamp Act. The Stamp Act was to force the colonists to buy stamps and put them on newspapers, wills, almanacs, playing cards, and many other things. Pictures of some of the taxes are on this page. Which two stamps have the same value?

Students are then asked to examine seven pictures to select the stamps of an identical amount. Such a format distracts and confuses learning. You will notice in some textbooks that the illustrations have little to do with the main points stressed in the text, almost as if they were put in the text for decoration.

Consider the supplements attached to most textbooks—for example, glossaries and workbook exercises or problem sets. Does the glossary provide adequate definitions of previously explained concepts? Are workbook exercises and problem sets printed in an attractive, uncluttered format that invites study? We think of format in a rather theatrical analogy: Does the supporting cast (spacing, figures, charts, illustrations) clarify and amplify the stars (main ideas) in the show? Or do they detract from an otherwise good performance?

### ■ Caliber of Questions

*Do questions accompany the instructional material and, if so, are they written to elicit varied levels of thinking?* In Chapter 2, there is a reference to Bloom's taxonomy and to the importance of writing cognitive objectives that require more than mere recall of information, for example, analysis, synthesis, and evaluation of content. One effective way to achieve these objectives is to use questions in the classroom that call for thinking in these areas.

One quick way to judge a text is to look at the kinds of questions that follow the chapters. Do they require thinking that is of a higher order than recall? A certain number of questions will demand recall, certainly. But the simplicity of recall questions can be deceiving and may depend on different kinds of thinking that make recalled information memorable in the first place. Thus, readers may recall only those portions of text they have been able to interpret or evaluate successfully. Therefore, a substantial proportion of the questions should require students to interpret, apply, analyze, synthesize, or evaluate the content. Here are examples of questions in each area:

1. *Knowledge* (recall):

   a. What do the Eskimos call their homes?
   b. Where does the play *Macbeth* take place?

2. *Comprehension* (requires students to state new understanding in their own words):

   a. Explain how the word *interloper* is used in the short story "The Interlopers" by Saki.
   b. State in one or two sentences the main point of the previous page.

3. *Application* (requires students to apply previously learned principles to new material):

   a. Compare the character of Montresor in "The Cask of Amontillado" with the character of General Zaroff in "The Most Dangerous Game."
   b. Contrast the treatment of property in Russia (studied previously) and in the United States.

4. *Analysis* (requires students to break subject matter into parts and study those parts or their relationships):

   **a.** Analyze the story *Cinderella* by identifying the introduction, rising action, climax, denouement, and conclusion.
   **b.** How does setting affect plot in Chapter 1 of *Great Expectations?*

5. *Synthesis* (requires students to put parts together in new ways, to look for patterns, to create new ideas):

   **a.** Find three reasons to attack or support the theory that the institution of slavery was not the central issue of the Civil War.
   **b.** Design a utopia that expresses your sense of justice.

6. *Evaluation* (requires students to evaluate material in reference to a particular value system):

   **a.** What do you think of the King's system of justice in "The Lady or the Tiger"? Is it just? Why or why not?
   **b.** What are some of the disadvantages of abstract art as a form of communication?

There are many gray areas in analyzing types of questions in this way. For example, if the disadvantages of abstract art have been discussed already, you are simply asking for recall. If not, you are requiring students to exercise judgment and to call upon their own value systems. Accurately classifying questions as to type or level is confusing because there is so much overlap in the thought processes. Usually, it is necessary to recall, to comprehend, and to apply meaning when analyzing material, and to do all of those when synthesizing. It is not necessary to think of these processes hierarchically. For example, sometimes it requires more complex thinking to comprehend very sophisticated content than to analyze simpler material. What is important is that you begin to analyze questions, and especially the kinds of thinking processes that those questions demand. As you do, you will find it increasingly easier to nurture students' learning with your questioning. Soon it will become second nature to nudge students into more complex thinking. Try the following exercise, and don't be discouraged if your answers differ from the answers we offer. Your reasons for putting the questions into a particular category may be as sound as our own.

## Exercise 4.1

Decide which category the following questions fall into by analyzing the thought processes the students must perform to answer them.

1. Write a brief dialogue that might have taken place between Abraham Lincoln and Robert E. Lee had they met on the eve of the Civil War.
2. Contrast our national anthem and the British national anthem with regard to the meaning of the words and the emotions evoked by the music.
3. Where was the Gettsyburg Address written?
4. Was the colonies' cause in the American Revolution a just one?
5. Why did Jack go up the beanstalk for the third time?

Possible Answers to Exercise 4.1

1. Synthesis—students must draw on the relevant parts of their knowledge of these two leaders to create a new product.
2. Application—students must draw on principles learned in music, poetry, and psychology.
3. Knowledge—this requires recall.
4. Evaluation—students must articulate and evaluate this cause in light of their personal value system.
5. Analysis—students must distinguish among Jack's motives at different times.

---

### Activity 4.2

Make up two questions that fall into each of the categories, questions that you could use in your first unit. If you feel unsure about which category a particular question falls into, don't worry. It is probably because it calls for thinking that falls into more than one category, in which case it would be given the more complex label. The important thing is to diversify the required thinking processes, which is necessary if your students are going to master the material. ■

### Activity 4.3

Label the end-of-chapter questions in the text you are evaluating. In your best judgment, are there questions from each category? If not, look in another chapter. If the questions seem to be drawn from only the first two or three categories, you should consider this a serious drawback. ■

With all we've said about the criteria for excellent instructional materials, we hope you're ready to practice your own evaluation skills. To make the task easier, we've condensed the criteria for judging materials into a series of questions, although reluctantly as there is danger here of reductionistic thinking. It would be a great mistake to try to translate qualitative judgment to a quantitative checklist, something you could use as a rating sheet to derive a numerical score.

The criteria we're presenting now in question form is meant as a guide to your thinking about text, not as a test of text quality. Keep in mind this question as you evaluate teaching materials: How appropriate is this material for the students who will use it? Answer that question in a paragraph or two using the seven criteria for ideal material as a framework for evaluation. Be specific and cite evidence for each criterion.

### Criteria for Evaluating Instructional Materials

1. *Emphasis*

   a. Are the main ideas clearly stated for the learner?
   b. Are the main ideas critical to study of the discipline? That is, are the ideas the author has chosen to emphasize the ones *you* think important to the topic of study?
   c. Do subheadings accurately predict the content that follows them?
   d. Are main ideas for the chapters and parts stated clearly at the beginning of the section and repeated at the end?
   e. Are important ideas stated in positive, not negative, terms?
   f. Does the author maintain the focus on discussion of important ideas?
   g. Are subtopics directly defined or explained apart from examples?

2. *Unity*

   a. Are all the ideas in the material clearly related to the main ideas and major points?
   b. Does the material avoid irrelevancies; does it stick to the point?
   c. Do the paragraphs of the text lend themselves to easy outline such that each sentence has a place in relation to all the others?
   d. Do you find it easy to pick up the thread of the argument and follow it through the material?

3. *Coherence*

   a. Do the paragraphs that comprise the written portion of the instructional material and/or text lend themselves to easy outline with the effect that each idea in each paragraph has a place in relation to all other ideas in the text?
   b. Do the pronouns the author uses all have very clear reference?
   c. Are important conceptual relations explicit in the text? Look for clearly stated cause-effect, conditional, comparison, and contrast relationships.

4. *Repetition and elaboration*

   a. Are new concepts clarified in relation to related concepts previously discussed in the material?
   b. Are newly introduced concepts restated to reinforce readers' understanding?
   c. Do the different components of the material reinforce each other so that each part elaborates on the same ideas as other parts?
   d. Are there references to other parts of the text where ideas have been previously mentioned?
   e. Are there aids in the material to help students locate previously discussed concepts?
   f. Are important ideas highlighted by repetition?
   g. Do specific ideas build on more general concepts familiar to the students?
   h. Are examples clearly related to the points they are intended to illustrate?

5. *Appropriate vocabulary*

   a. Are new ideas put in familiar rather than technical terms?
   b. Are technical terms defined in familiar language, set off in boldface or other highlighting, and introduced gradually?
   c. Are concepts developed with terms that are well understood?
   d. Does the material avoid conceptual explanations that are vague, imprecise, or too abstract?

6. *Audience appropriateness*

   a. Has the author made reasonable assumptions about the prior experiences of the students for whom the material is intended?
   b. Does the material *relate* new information to previously learned information that students might reasonably be assumed to bring from sources external to the text?
   c. Are the vocabulary, analogies, metaphors, figurative language, and examples appropriate to the intended readers?
   d. Are the concepts presented and discussed in the material placed in a context appropriate to the body of knowledge of which they are a part, and is that context likely to be familiar to the intended learners?

7. *Format*

   a. Is the layout of the material appealing?
   b. Are graphic aids in the material pertinent to the ideas discussed, illustrative of concepts already introduced in the text?
   c. Is appropriate use made of italicized type, boldface headings, and spacing (e.g., partitioning of key ideas and examples)?

    **d.** Does the material provide adequate aids to reading and study, such as a good index, glossary, chapter summaries, and the like?

**8.** *Caliber of questions*

    **a.** Do the questions require thinking in all six of Bloom's levels?

    **b.** Do the initial questions require recall, comprehension, and application, thus laying the groundwork for the other levels?

    **c.** Are the questions stated clearly? Are they appropriate for *your* students? (Remember, texts are written for a very broad audience. You are the best judge of what is appropriate for your students.

    **d.** Do the questions challenge or excite you? Do they require students to draw from other materials or experiences, thereby promoting connections from new material to known content?

    **e.** Do the questions included in the text help readers' thinking?

    **f.** Do the questions and exercises attached to the material require of students the level and kind of thinking you consider most important and appropriate to your instruction?

Perhaps the most important thing one could say about judging the appropriateness of instructional materials is this: *Judge the material from the perspective of the student learner.* We have seen many instances where teachers perceive instructional material to be appropriate from their own point of view and are genuinely puzzled when their students have difficulty comprehending it. To avoid this situation try to forget all that you know about the topic and view the material from the perspective of one of your students, a naive, uninformed learner. Go through the reading and exercises in the material from the students' perspective. If you keep your students in mind when examining each criterion, your overall rating will be close to the mark even while you are becoming an expert.

## ■ SUMMARY

Many of the learning problems that students face in schools can be traced to the difficulty of the textbooks and resource materials they are asked to use. No matter how appropriate the rationale for your course or the objectives of a lesson you want to teach, if the textbook materials are inappropriate, learning will be impeded. Furthermore, given the range of interests and abilities of students in a typical classroom, no single information source can possibly serve every student.

This chapter has focused on criteria for the selection of a variety of instructional materials. We hope that where choices exist, we have enabled you to make wise choices. Keep in mind that students, like all learners, have a right to the "story." If care is taken in the selection process for instructional materials, we think fewer children will say they can't find it. Good writing always makes it apparent.

■ **NOTE**

**1.** Portions of the discussion that follows previously appeared in Joseph L. Vaughan and Thomas H. Estes, *Reading and Reasoning Beyond the Primary Grades* (Boston: Allyn and Bacon, 1986). Used by permission.

# *Planning for Instruction*

In Part One of the text we have discussed the planning phase of instruction. Goals, needs, and objectives have been defined and a technique for writing rationales described. In addition, we pointed out different types of evaluation strategies for different types of objectives. An organizational strategy for unit and lesson planning was included together with a description of the processes necessary for textbook selection.

In the following sections we will describe a series of instructional models that can be incorporated into the design process. A repertoire of instructional models allows the teacher to select the appropriate teaching strategies for each instructional design. From the hundreds of possible models, we have selected six that we feel form the basis for a variety of teaching approaches.

# Part Two

# Matching Objectives to Instruction: A Models Approach

Remember what it was like to make something from a pattern for the first time – a dress, a model airplane, a birdhouse, a cake? The task seemed very difficult in the beginning, if not impossible. You made many mistakes and needed advice and coaching from more experienced hands. Gradually, the skills and techniques were acquired, and when many dresses or birdhouses or loaves of bread had been made, you could work without following a pattern and even design patterns of your own that others could follow.

Instructional models, like patterns or blueprints or recipes, present the steps necessary to bring about a desired outcome. The selection of a particular model to use in an instructional design depends on the desired outcome or objective of the instruction. The methods selected for teaching a lesson should depend on what the students are expected to learn as a result of the instruction.

When planning to build a birdhouse, it is necessary to select a pattern for a birdhouse, not a pattern for a garage or a picket fence. A recipe for a meatloaf will not produce a loaf of bread; a pattern for an evening gown will not result in a pair of blue jeans. Likewise, a model of teaching designed to bring about the recall of facts will not produce creative thinking or problem-solving skills. A model for teaching generalizations is not effective in teaching the skills necessary for learning to swim. *An instructional model is a step-by-step procedure that leads to specific learning outcomes*. The best models have been used extensively and found to be effective in bringing about specific objectives of instruction. Effective instructional models

- Allow students to become active participants in the learning process;
- Take students through specific sequential steps; and
- Reflect research about thinking, learning, and behavior.

67

Bruce Joyce and Marsha Weil selected 22 models to describe in their classic work on instruction titled *Models of Teaching*.[1] In their research, they identified hundreds of instructional models that could be used by classroom teachers in developing a range of instructional approaches in the classroom.

Instructional models can be found in a variety of sources. Joyce and Weil gathered their models from classrooms, psychology labs, and training institutions, as well as from the techniques and ideas of teachers, therapists, military personnel, educators, and philosophers. The models-of-teaching approach emphasizes the need for variety in the classroom by developing a teacher's repertoire of instructional approaches to meet a range of objectives.

Earlier in the text we spoke of the varied needs of learners in the classroom. Some students learn better in a highly structured environment, some in a more open and student-centered atmosphere. Some students want to solve problems for themselves, others feel more comfortable if solutions are presented to them. Some learners think deductively, some are more comfortable with inductive thinking. Some students learn better by themselves, some work better in groups.

If a teacher creates a single environment in the classroom or utilizes the same instructional approach over and over, only those students who learn well in that environment or with that approach will succeed. The teacher who utilizes a variety of instructional approaches is more likely to reach all students in the classroom; moreover, students are encouraged to learn in a variety of ways.

Ironically, professional educators have frequently divided into camps, asserting that one approach is infinitely more desirable than another. Those who believe in behavioral psychology scoff at those who insist on problem solving and inquiry. The renewed emphasis on the teaching of thinking skills has rekindled the controversy between those who insist that thinking is a product of behavioral conditioning and those who believe that thinking is related to perception and psychodynamic forces.

It is our belief that such controversy is wasteful, since there is no one correct manner in which to instruct all of the students all of the time. Even special populations, such as the mentally or physically handicapped, can benefit from a variety of instructional approaches. No group or stratum of society needs to be relegated to one type of approach even though it may be reasonable to use certain approaches more often than others.

In Part One, we discussed instructional planning and identified the range of objectives that teachers can design into an instructional plan. Some objectives focus on cognitive learning, some on attitudes, some on the acquisition of skills. It's only logical that instruction to bring about this variety of learning in the classroom needs to be varied.

In addition, we have stressed designing instruction so that a variety of approaches are used in each unit. A careful instructional design takes into account the age and interests of the learners, the knowledge that they bring with them to instruction, and the conditions under which instruction will occur.

In Part Two of this text, we present eight models, selected from a variety of sources, that provide a solid repertoire for the beginning teacher. Some of these models, such as concept attainment and concept development, are familiar to many teachers. Others, like the discussion model based on the Great Books program, are presented in model form for the first time. To provide our readers with a good foundation for understanding and utilizing these models, we have devoted a chapter to each model.

The *direct instruction model* is most effective with information recall and skill acquisition. The *concept attainment model* is effective in defining, comprehending, applying, and using concepts. The *concept development model* is designed for categorizing, generalizing, and synthesizing information. *Synectics* is a model that encourages creative thinking through the use of analogy and metaphor. The *Suchman inquiry model* is designed for problem solving and inquiry. The *classroom discussion model* is particularly effective in meeting objectives related to formulating questions, developing insights, and fostering critical-thinking skills. In the *cooperative learning models*—Teams Games Tournaments, STAD, and Jigsaw— students develop cooperative attitudes through learning to work together, and cognitive and psychomotor objectives are achieved. Finally, the *explorations of feelings and resolution of conflict model* is valuable in helping students relate learning to their feelings and attitudes and in resolving conflict situations in the classroom.

For each model, we describe the steps in order to provide a theoretical base for the approach and instructional situations in which the model might occur. It is important to practice these models under conditions where coaching from an expert can take place and where there is an opportunity for periodic peer review. Our experience in promoting models of instruction warns us that teachers may have difficulty relating instructional models to appropriate objectives, emphasizing the learning of concepts rather than activities, and in finding the time to properly learn to use these models in the classroom. "Most teachers use a very narrow range of instructional practices [and] will expand that repertoire only when they are provided substantial and carefully designed training."[2]

Joyce and Weil recommend that beginning teachers master a repertoire of four or five models; however, they point out that creative and experienced teachers should "use these models not as recipes, but as stimulators to their own activities."[3] Following the steps in the instructional models is essential in the beginning, but as the teacher gains experience and confidence, the possibilities for designing new approaches and for personalizing the models are endless.

When teachers have multiple instructional procedures available, they no longer have to rely on one technique to gain the interest of the class and to teach the material. When one process is ineffective they can switch to others. The teacher becomes a professional problem solver and decision maker.

The models presented in Part Two meet a wide range of instructional objectives. Each can be used to teach individual objectives and, combined in an instructional design, they can meet a variety of student needs and interests. Most of the models are directed toward the acquisition of cognitive objectives, as these are the ones that are most emphasized in our schools. And they are designed to include all learners—no student, even the nonreader, is excluded from the process. Thus, many affective objectives related to participation and feelings of achievement are met through the use of these models.

**1.** *Direct Instruction:* A highly structured model that is used most effectively in teaching basic skills such as reading and mathematics when the tasks to be learned can be broken into small discrete segments. This model is also effective in teaching cognitive objectives related to recall and recognition of facts and data. Psychomotor skills, such as holding a pencil, playing the violin, and throwing a baseball, are also effectively taught through this model.

**2.** *Concept Attainment:* By teaching the thinking skill of categorizing, students comprehend and analyze the meaning of a particular concept. Through a series of positive and negative examples, students define the concept and determine its essential attributes. This model is particularly effective in meeting objectives related to comprehension, comparison, discrimination, and recall.

**3.** *Concept Development:* Originated by Hilda Taba, this model teaches students to group data on the basis of perceived similarities and then form categories and labels for that data, effectively producing a conceptual system. In the process, students learn to think about their own thinking and to understand how concepts originate. This model is effective with objectives related to contrasting, applying, categorizing, and analyzing data.

**4.** *Synectics:* This model uses group interaction to stimulate creative thought through metaphorical analogies. Far from being a lonely, isolated process, creative thinking and expression becomes a group activity in which each individual can participate. The synectics model is particularly effective for those objectives related to exploration, comparison, identification, and insight.

**5.** *Inquiry:* From a puzzling situation, learners follow a scientific process that leads to a hypothesis. The emphasis of this model is on the need for careful, logical procedures in problem solving, on the tentative nature of knowledge, and on the need for group endeavor in solving problems. Learners are encouraged to seek more than one answer for a question. The inquiry model is effective in meeting objectives related to problem solving, analysis, hypothesizing, and evaluation. Group process, cooperation, and communication are also emphasized in this model.

**6.** *Classroom Discussion:* Based on the Great Books approach, the discussion model guides the planning and selection of questions to be used in classroom discussions. Both students and teachers learn to identify different levels and types of questions. This model also helps the teacher direct the process of classroom interactions for effective classroom discussions. This model is effective with cognitive objectives ranging from knowledge acquisition to synthesis and evaluation and with affective objectives related to receiving and responding to learning.

**7.** *Cooperative Learning:* These models, Teams-Games-Tournaments (TGT), Student Teams-Academic Division (STAD), and Jigsaw, describe ways in which the teacher can encourage students to work with and help other students in the classroom. The use of these models helps to create a positive environment in the classroom and to meet affective objectives related to cooperation and understanding. In addition, these models are effective in reaching cognitive and psychomotor objectives.

**8.** *Exploration of Feelings and Conflict Resolution:* This model is also based on the work of Hilda Taba. It helps students understand their own feelings as they learn to explore the feelings of others in real-life situations as well as in literature. This model is particularly effective in meeting affective objectives related to feelings and attitudes and in resolving conflicts in the classroom.

We have chosen to present the steps for each model before discussing the theoretical base, because many teachers become mired in the theory of an approach before seeing how it works in the classroom. Each model is presented with a brief introduction, a description of the steps in the model, a theoretical explanation of the model, and finally a scenario in which the model is used.

These models are appropriate for any age, with all abilities, and with any subject matter. It is up to the teacher to apply the appropriate subject matter for the age and interests of the learners. We have used these models with learners from kindergarten to postgraduate, with special education students, with classes for the gifted, and with teachers and school administrators. The more we use these models for instruction, the more convinced we become of their effectiveness.

## ■ NOTES

**1.** Bruce Joyce and Marsha Weil, *Models of Teaching*, 3rd ed. (Englewood Cliffs, NJ: Prentice-Hall, 1986), 1–23.

**2.** Bruce Joyce, Beverly Showers, and Carol Rolheiser-Bennett, "Staff Development and Student Learning: A Synthesis of Research on Models of Teaching," *Educational Leadership*, 45 (October 1987): 11–23.

**3.** Joyce and Weil, *Models*, 1.

# Chapter 5

# The Direct Instruction Model
## *Teaching Basic Skills, Facts, and Knowledge*

Every teacher should periodically learn a new skill to understand how students feel in the classroom as they are introduced to the new and the unfamiliar. If tomorrow you had to learn to ski, make buttonholes, read Hebrew, arrange flowers, or program a computer, the experience would be humbling. Yet, children in school encounter such experiences constantly as they confront new tasks and strange material that must be mastered. Those experiences are made easier by carefully planned *direct instruction*. In fact, we present direct instruction first because so many aspects of this model apply to all well-planned instructional designs.

Surely there is much in the curriculum of schools that cannot be taught *directly*–literary appreciation, and inferencing skills, for example. Most attempts at direct instruction of composition and rhetoric fail to have any affect on language use. Models other than direct instruction are appropriate here. By contrast, consider how very many objectives do lend themselves to direct instruction: mathematical procedures, grammatical rules, the states of New England, alphabetizing, carburetor overhaul, scientific equations, and the periodic table of the elements, to name a few. Every teacher, in every subject, at every level of schooling has some learning objectives related to basic skills that must be mastered before the learner can move to other levels of thinking and learning.

The direct instruction model is presented first in this series of models because the steps of this model are essential in planning for any instructional design. It should be noted that all of the other models in this text could be incorporated into this model at Step 3–presentation of new material; however, direct instruction is treated as a separate model because certain types of objectives require that practice and feedback receive particular emphasis. Objectives in the psychomotor domain, in particular, necessitate drill and practice, as do those learnings that must be committed to memory, such as the multiplication tables.

The model is based on behavioral research on how effective training occurs. It is most useful in teaching those skills that can be broken into small, discrete segments, with each segment building upon the prior one. Direct instruction is characterized by relatively short instructional periods followed by practice until mastery learning is achieved.

Teachers are frequently criticized for the predominance of rote learning in the classroom. We would emphasize that the direct instruction model is a necessary but not a sufficient instructional tool because it depends, in part, on rote learning. Many of the steps in this model are useful in all the other models and to be without this effective tool is a handcap; however, to use this model exclusively is deadening. Direct instruction should be used whenever the objectives of instruction indicate such an approach will be effective. Used with other models in an instructional design, direct instruction provides a base for instructional practice.

## Steps in the Direct Instruction Model

There are a number of excellent studies of effective teaching that relate to the direct instruction model, including the research of Anderson, Evertson, and Brophy,[1] Rosenshine,[2] and Good and Grouws.[3] Many classroom teachers have been introduced to direct instruction through the work of Madeline Hunter, who describes seven steps in the process: (1) an *anticipatory set,* which causes the learners to focus on what they are about to learn, (2) a description of *objectives and purpose,* in which the teacher makes clear what is to be learned, (3) an *input* stage, in which a new knowledge, process, or skill is presented to the students, (4) *modeling,* in which the new learning is demonstrated, (5) *checking for understanding* to determine if students have grasped the new material, (6) *guided practice* under the careful supervision of the teacher, and (7) *independent practice* that encourages learners to perform or utilize the new learning on their own.[4]

Closely related to these steps, Barak Rosenshine has identified six steps in direct instruction, which will be described in detail in this chapter.

1. Review of previously learned material
2. Statement of objectives for the lesson
3. Presentation of new material
4. Guided practice with corrective feedback
5. Independent practice with corrective feedback
6. Periodic review with corrective feedback if necessary

### ■ Step 1—Review of Previously Learned Material

In direct instruction the students must understand clearly what they are expected to learn, the steps they will follow in that learning, and how the new learning connects to what has been learned previously.

1. Mrs. Jones is preparing to teach a lesson on alphabetizing. She begins by reviewing with the class what they learned the day before: "Yesterday we

grouped words according to the first letter. On the table are the word stacks we made, each beginning with the same letter. Today, we are going to order these stacks by the first letter's place in the alphabet, starting with the *A* stack. First, let us review the names of the first letters in each of the stacks we made yesterday."

II. In the gym, Mr. Terry instructs his swimming class: "Last week you learned how to float. First, get in the water and practice floating for about 5 minutes, so I can see if everyone remembers that skill. Then, you will learn how to move your hands in order to propel yourself in the water."

III. In math class Miss Tomlin says, "Yesterday, we learned about using *X* to represent an unknown. Sara, will you please put the first homework problem on the board, Tom will you put up the second, and Frank will you please put up the third? When we are sure that we understand how to use the unknown *X*, which you practiced for homework, we will learn how to use the *X* in an equation."

Each of these teachers is practicing an essential technique of the direct instruction model as described by Rosenshine:[5] *Begin with a short review of the previous learning, which is necessary for the new learning, and state clearly the objectives for the new learning.* Homework assigned for the previous lesson should be checked before proceeding. Putting problems on the board or examining the material learned the day before through questioning or testing is important before proceeding to a new skill level. If necessary, reteach the previous lesson before going on, particularly when the new skill is dependent on mastery of the preceding one.

Pretesting of the class to determine skill levels is essential before teaching a new skill. Analyzing students' abilities to learn the skill helps the teacher determine the pace at which to proceed and allows the teacher to prepare for individual differences in the class.

## ■ Step 2—State the Objectives

Lesson objectives should be stated clearly and written on the board in language the students can understand. We visited one second-grade classroom during a writing lesson and saw this objective written on the board: *The students will practice holding the pencil in the proper position in order to form the letters for cursive writing.*

Do you see the problem here? The language is not appropriate for the age of the students or even for the instructional objective—that is, practice in forming cursive letters. The purpose of stating objectives is to clearly and simply tell the learners what the purpose of the instruction is and what outcomes they should expect. Lesson objectives should be connected to previous learning and within the reach of all the students.

## ■ Step 3—Presentation of New Material

Whether it is a new skill to be learned or information to be presented, the teacher's analysis and preparation of content is essential in this step. It is not sufficient to know the content or the procedure; many experts in a subject are unable to convey their expertise to others. Preparation for this step is to ensure that what is known by the teacher can be learned by the student. The effective teacher spends preparation time analyzing the steps needed to learn a new skill and the order in which the steps will be presented. One does not introduce multiplication before addition, semicolons before commas, or the swan dive before floating.

Instructions and explanations must be given in a clear and detailed manner in each step of the presentation. Frequent and varied examples, punctuated with ample questions and corrective feedback, serve to focus learners on the material and avoid digressions. At every point, it is important to be sure that instructions and explanations are understood by the class.

The classroom teacher should combine effective verbal presentation with audiovisuals, questions, demonstration, and student participation. Information should be interesting, highly structured, well organized, and limited in scope.

Content should be analyzed in the same manner. If the learners do not know the meaning of basic concepts in a definition, they will not comprehend the definition. For instance, a lesson on building a table will have little meaning to learners if they cannot identify certain basic tools, such as the level, the plane, and the square. One must know the parts of speech before diagramming sentences and the parts of a right triangle before learning the Pythagorean theory.

### *Organizing Content*

The process involved in organizing new material for presentation is similar to the process for organizing content for a unit of study, as described in Chapter 3. The content to be learned must be selected and then analyzed according to the needs of the learners. Material that is too difficult or too much material presented at one time hinders learning and defeats the purpose of the presentation. Presenting a few significant points accompanied by many illustrations and questions is generally more effective than covering many points. When introducing a new skill, the procedures should be broken into small segments that can be introduced in a sequence.

Organizing the content from the most general concepts to the most specific is helpful. For instance, content for baking a cake might be organized and diagrammed as follows:

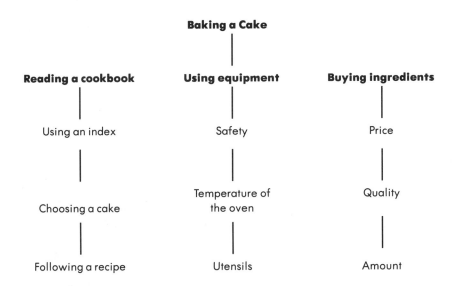

The most general, inclusive concepts in this process appear in the first line of the diagram followed by the details under each part. These parts are related to each other and to previously learned information at each step in the process. For instance, using an index in a cookbook can be related to the use of indexes in textbooks and other familiar material. Choosing a recipe is related to the equipment one has to use and the ingredients that are available, so that each part of the design is related to other parts. Illustrations and examples should be selected to illustrate each point as it is presented. These should be drawn from experiences already familiar to the learners so that the new learning can be hooked to that which is already familiar.

The teacher must determine how much content can be offered in one presentation, based on the age of the learners and their abilities. The less experienced the learners are, the more they need to have each step carefully explained and the more the teacher needs to limit the content in each presentation. Again, content should be organized so that the most general information is presented first followed by more detailed and specific data, and new material should be related to material previously learned at each step in the process.

### Advance Organizers

After the content of the lesson is diagrammed, the advance organizer, described in Chapter 3, can be selected. Keep in mind the importance of selecting an idea that is more general than the new material and that can provide the learner with a context within which to relate the new learning. For instance, a lesson on baking a cake might begin with an advance organizer on the theme of baking in general or a description of the development of cakes from simple patties prepared by native tribes to the complex confections available in bakeries. A teacher might begin by showing pictures of a simple pancake and an elaborate wedding cake and discussing what these two cakes have in common and what makes them so different. An advance organizer for a lesson sets the stage and serves as a point of reference throughout the lesson.

### Demonstrations

If the lesson is to include a demonstration, the teacher prepares the material to be learned in small segments and checks for understanding at the end of each segment. One of the most difficult tasks of the expert is to anticipate the learning steps of the beginner, particularly for the beginner who may not have the same aptitude or enthusiasm for the skill the teacher has.

Visual examples work particularly well in the presentation stage of this model. Too often, teachers depend on *telling* when *showing,* either through pictures or live demonstration, can be more effective and can provide learners with a memory hook for new information. Imagine a lesson on baking a cake without a demonstration phase; yet, many teachers forget that one picture (activity, experiment, or demonstration) can be worth a thousand words. In summary, the steps of the process of presenting information are as follows:

1. Analyze the content to be presented according to the needs of the learners.
2. Chart the content from the most general to the most specific material to be presented.
3. Break all skills into small segments to be presented in a logical order.
4. Develop an advance organizer for the lesson that will provide a reference point for the new material.
5. Select the main points or steps to be presented and limit these to a reasonable number depending on the learners.
6. Select examples to illustrate each of the main points and connect each of the points or steps presented to the one preceding and to the advance organizer.
7. Ask questions to check for understanding and watch for signals from the class that indicate lack of attention.
8. Summarize the main points and connect them to the next phase of the lesson.

## ■ Step 4—Guided Practice

Practice, both guided and independent, is an essential part of direct instruction. New material is presented in small steps, with ample opportunity for practice following each step of the process. In guided practice, the teacher controls the process and monitors the practice of the group and of individuals within the group.

I. To tie our shoes we start with holding a lace in each hand. Now take the lace on the model shoe in front of you and hold a lace in each hand.

Good. The next step is to cross the lace in the right hand over the one in the left hand (be sure to plan for left-handed children). Let's all practice putting the right lace over the left lace like this. Tommy, hold up your right hand. Good. Now cross the lace in that hand over the one in your left hand, like this. Very good.

II. To operate a computer we must first turn it on. Please locate the switch in the left-hand corner and switch it to the on position.

III. We have just seen a filmstrip on the four chambers of the heart. Let us review each of these four chambers as we fill in this diagram on the board together.

### Questioning

The most common form of guided practice is questioning by the teacher to check for understanding. A number of questions should be prepared ahead of time and there should be more than enough for the lesson. Teachers frequently err in feeling that the class will become bored if too many questions are asked during instruction; however, in learning new material, repetition and review are essential. There is a greater risk that too few questions will be asked to only a small number of students than that there will be too many questions.

Since few students want to announce their ignorance to the world, the request "Raise your hand if you don't understand" is usually an ineffective diagnostic. Questions like, "Are there any questions?" are hardly better. Nor should the teacher call on those students who always raise their hands in response to a question. A better technique is to say: "In a minute I will ask someone to do this problem on the board, so be prepared," or "After we view the filmstrip, I will ask the following questions."

A checklist of students responding to questions can be maintained in order to monitor participation. If the same students are answering most of the questions, evaluate the questions being asked and determine if the rest of the class is comprehending the material.

If there are a few students who never raise their hands, plan a conference to discuss their class participation. For some students, speaking out in class is frightening even when they know the answer. One technique is to ask students to write a short answer to each question on a sheet of paper and pass it to the front of the row. If the answers given by the students who never speak out in class are correct, ask them to read their answers aloud. Gradually, this may help them to gain the confidence needed for class participation.

There is a story about a teacher whose principal praised her at her retirement dinner by saying how impressed he had always been in observing her classroom, that whenever she asked questions all hands went up, and whoever was called on knew the answer. The teacher confessed that she had told her students to raise their hands when a guest was present—"Raise your right hand if you know the answer, your left hand if you don't know the answer." Actually, that's not bad technique—it would at least give the teacher a way to know how many students claim to understand the material and, thus, some way to adjust the pace of instruction to accommodate the needs of the learners.

Effective teachers set up a situation in which those who need further explanation or help can get it. They ask students to repeat the directions or the information. They ask students to summarize for each other and share those summaries. They call on students for additional examples and applications of information.

Rosenshine identifies four types of student responses to questions:[6]

1. **Correct, quick and firm**—The teacher response to this type of answer is to ask a new question to keep the pace of the lesson moving, avoiding overemphasis on success.
2. **Correct but hesitant**—This type of response usually occurs during the initial stages of learning and the teacher should provide some encouragement (That's good. Keep up the good work.).
3. **Incorrect but careless**—Simply correct and move on. The student knows the process but made a careless mistake.
4. **Incorrect and lacking knowledge of facts or process**—The teacher may provide hints, ask a simpler question, or reteach.

### Correcting Error

Rosenshine emphasizes that *"Errors should not go uncorrected . . .* students learn better with feedback—as immediate as possible; and errors should be corrected before they become habitual."[7]

*Don't blame students for not learning the material, and don't go on if what you have done has not worked.* The swimming coach does not allow students to drown if they are in the deep end of the pool and cannot tread water. He or she goes back to a more basic step. The same approach is needed in learning any skill or new content. If students do not meet the instructional objectives, evaluate and analyze the original presentation, determine the problem, and then find a way to reach the entire class. The success rate for the learning of directly taught skills should be as close to 100 percent as possible. Students who understand the first presentation will benefit from any reteaching, particularly if the presentation is

different from the first. Better yet, early learners can help others by putting their understandings into their own words for others to follow.

It is important to realize that there are as many potential teachers in a classroom as there are people who understand what is to be taught. In addition, individualized materials, programmed learning materials, and computer-assisted instruction are potential resources for those students who need additional learning time.

Watch for signals from the class. Learners who are confused will usually act out in some manner. They will turn to a neighbor, put their heads on the desk, tap their pencils, grimace, yawn. If the class has not understood, don't get angry, try again. It is possible that the skill level at which you began the instruction was too high for most of the class and you need to start at a lower level. Expect a success rate of 85 percent or higher by the students before proceeding to the next level. In some cases 100 percent is the only acceptable success rate. (For the math teacher, a 100 percent mastery of the multiplication tables through the 12-times table at high speed may be the goal.)

Jere Brophy's report on the behavior of effective teachers in inner-city schools pertains to instruction at all levels. Brophy writes, "If the curricula, instructional methods, or evaluation devices that (effective teachers) intended to use do not work, they find others that will work. If something is not learned the first time through, they teach it again. In general, these teachers treat student failure as a challenge."[8]

## ■ Step 5—Independent Practice

Independent practice requires careful monitoring of students working on their own or in small groups to practice a new skill. Before assigning students to work independently, however, sufficient time must be spent in guided practice to insure that they are prepared to work on their own.

The teacher should circulate during independent practice, checking to insure that no student is repeating the mistake, or actually *practicing error*. In addition, there should be some way for students to check their results as they proceed independently. Sometimes, the answers in the back of the textbook are an excellent resource. And some teachers provide checkpoints, or stations, in the classroom where students can go periodically to check their work.

### *Worksheets*
If worksheets are used for independent practice, they should be introduced in a setting of guided practice. The class completes the first problem together as the teacher demonstrates the process. After the next problem is done individually, the entire class examines the problem and its solution together as the process is explained for all to see. If necessary, have the class complete several of the problems as a group or have small groups or pairs of students work on the problems before individuals attempt to work on their own.

The problem with many worksheet assignments given for independent practice is that students may repeatedly make the same error, and that error then becomes fixed in their learning. Often, the purple dittoes come to dominate instruction in inappropriate ways, as time fillers and busywork. A consultant hired to evaluate a reading program was visiting a classroom, just walking around to get a feel for the place, when a child looked up from his hunched-over position to ask, "Can you tell me what I'm supposed to be doing?" On the dimly printed sheet before the lad was the following: "Each of the following words has a blank space where a letter has been left out. Place a vowel that says its name in each blank space to make a word."

c__me     m__ne     r__in

With prompting, the child tried "a" in the first blank and successfully made "came." Then he announced, "I get it. The next one is 'mone.' "

This child was *required* to practice a behavior he had not been taught and that, furthermore, was abstracted from any context in which it could have meaning. The task is an abstract exercise, all too typical of worksheets.

### Unitization and Automaticity

These terms have been used to describe the two stages through which students pass in independent practice.[9] In the unitization phase, students are attending carefully to each component or unit of the skill. They are working with few errors, but slowly and with considerable effort. As they reach automaticity, they are able to work more quickly and to respond automatically without having to think through each step in the process. In order to reach automaticity, students need to overlearn the skill through practice and repetition at the unitization stage.

Homework is most effective when students have reached unitization of learning but have not yet reached automaticity. As the most frequently used form of independent practice, homework is often abused by sending children home to practice material before they understand it clearly and before there has been ample guided practice in the classroom. Much of the frustration with homework assignments comes from the fact that students are asked to work independently with material before they are ready.

### ■ Step 6—Periodic Review with Corrective Feedback

Periodic review of the material should be built into every instructional plan. Overlearning is essential to acquiring a new skill, particularly when each skill is necessary to learning the next. While students are in the process of learning a new skill, review of skills learned before is essential for automaticity. (How many English teachers say that they never learned so much grammar as when they taught it five times a day!)

Homework should be checked as a part of the review before proceeding. If homework is worth assigning, it is worth checking, yet research indicates that many teachers neglect this important part of the review process.[10] If the students have not understood the assignment, then do not go on to the next step. Reteach the material and analyze the reasons for failure to learn.

If a weekly review indicates that a skill has not been retained, then reteaching is necessary. Students often forget skills and information during the summer, so it is particularly important to test for retention at the beginning of a new school year or semester.

Teachers should demand a high success rate for their students. If they are not learning there must be a reason. Some questions to be asked are:

- Did the students have the required background to learn the new set of skills or material?
- Were the steps in the learning process broken into sufficiently small steps?
- Was each step learned before a new step was introduced?
- Were the learning objectives and the directions stated clearly?
- Was the content organized logically and were the examples and demonstrations effective?
- Were there a sufficient number of questions asked to determine if the class understood what was being taught?
- Was there enough guided practice? Were all of the students involved in the practice, and were errors corrected quickly?
- Was there independent practice of the skill or learning? Was this independent practice checked carefully to determine if the students were performing without error?
- Was there periodic review and opportunities for practice of the new learning?

## Summary of Steps in the Direct Instruction Model

**1.** *Review previously learned material:* Make certain that students have mastered the material taught previously and that they understand the connections to the new learning.

**2.** *State the objectives of the lesson:* The objectives should be presented to the students at the beginning of the lesson in language they can comprehend.

**3.** *Present new material:* New material should be well organized and presented in an interesting manner. Frequent checks should be used to determine if the students are comprehending the information.

**4.** *Conduct guided practice:* The teacher guides the students through practice sessions, making certain that they are performing correctly.

**5.** *Assign independent practice:* The teacher continues to supervise the students as they work independently, checking for error. Homework should be assigned for independent practice only when the teacher feels certain that the students can practice correctly.

**6.** *Periodic review with corrective feedback:* Homework is checked before new instruction is given, and reteaching is conducted if necessary. The teacher conducts periodic checks to make certain that the new learning has been retained.

## Exercise 5.1

Evaluate the following remarks according to the steps in the direct instruction model.

1. Who wants to put the homework problems on the board?
2. Because you all failed the quiz this morning, there will be no recess today.
3. Today we will learn about mytosis. Listen carefully because you don't know anything about this and there will be a quiz tomorrow.
4. As you watch the filmstrip, pay attention to the names of the oceans and rivers. I will ask you questions about these later.
5. Because you were not paying attention during the lesson, I am assigning three pages of problems for homework tonight.
6. While the class is reading quietly, I will ask some individuals to come to my desk and review the reading skills that we learned last week.

Possible Answers to Exercise 5.1

**1.** In the first example, the teacher would gain better information in the review process by designating specific students to go to the board: Mary, Joe, and Tom, please put the first steps of the problem on the board. Watch carefully, class, because I will ask three other people to complete the problem.

**2.** The failure of the class to learn should be countered by a different instructional approach, not punishment. Teachers who blame students consistently for a failure to learn do not grow professionally. Blaming students repeatedly prevents teachers from analyzing what needs to be done differently.

**3.** Students are more likely to learn new material if it is presented in an interesting manner and connected to something with which they are familiar than if they are threatened by an exam.

**4.** The teacher is preparing the students for guided practice by instructing them to focus on the important material to be learned. A study guide for students to fill in as they view the filmstrip, with periodic pauses during the presentation to make certain that everyone is keeping up, is an even more effective procedure.

**5.** The students are probably going to practice error. The independent practice of homework should be based on successful guided practice in the classroom. If the class was inattentive and did not learn the material, it would be futile to assign homework that requires applying that material. At this point, the teacher needs to determine what prevented learning from taking place and then plan to reteach the material.

**6.** This is a good technique for evaluating individual students to determine if retention has occurred. It is also an excellent way to establish independent contact with children in the classroom.

---

## Basis for the Direct Instruction Model

We describe here some of the background and basis for this model in order to help readers determine its appropriateness for use in their classrooms. It is not the intention of the authors to endorse one approach over another but rather to describe as fairly as possible the background of each model presented.

The direct instruction model is based on behavioral psychology, which originated with the work of Pavlov in 1927.[11] However, it is more directly linked to the work of B.F. Skinner[12] and to training psychology and cybernetics techniques developed primarily for the military. In the behavioral approach, the emphasis is on controlling those behaviors of the learner that can be measured and observed rather than focusing on inner psychodynamic forces like thinking and feeling.

Skinner was able to train a rat to push a lever only when a light was turned on by providing food each time the rat exhibited the desired behavior. Conversely, the rat was given no food if it pushed the lever when the light was not on. The rat was conditioned to perform the desired behavior through selective reinforcement, a process termed *operant conditioning*. Operants are behaviors that are voluntarily performed by the learner. Because the reinforcement was contingent on the performance of the desired behavior, the process of conditioning is called *contingency management*. To be effective, the reinforcement following the desired behavior must be immediate, consistent, and regular.

Many educators are repelled by the idea of teaching people by methods related, even remotely, to the way in which rats are trained to push a lever. But for certain types of learning, training through contingency management has proven to be highly effective. By breaking the learning task into small steps and by reinforcing the learning at each step in the process, the teacher conditions the desired behavior and increases the probability that it will occur again. Each step in the process is followed by feedback, and the learner is rewarded for correct performance. Behaviorists point out that the instructor, by carefully determining the steps necessary to learn the desired skill and conditioning the correct response, provides the conditions for learners to gain control of their environment. Critics of this approach point out that conditioned behavior may not be of long-term duration. Once again, the reader is cautioned that this model should be used with others in a total design.

### ■ Concepts of Training Behavior

Some of the important concepts of training behavior are *shaping, modeling, practice, providing feedback,* and *reinforcement.*

### Shaping

Once the teacher determines the desired outcome of student learning, the learning task is broken into the steps, or *successive approximations*, necessary to acquire the new learning or skill. The students' behavior is gradually shaped through reinforcement as they progress through the steps necessary for mastery of the desired skill.

### Modeling

Learners acquire knowledge and skills by witnessing and imitating the teacher, who acts as a model. In some situations, a student can learn segments of information or steps in a skill much more efficiently by copying the behavior of another than by working independently.

Models can also be procedures that have been developed for the learner to follow (such as the models of teaching in this text) or carefully designed self-teaching materials that carry a learner through each step in the process. For instance, drawing in China is taught by having very young students copy the works of masters over and over. Originality is not valued until years later. These young students become proficient at reproducing very sophisticated work through this process.

### Practice

In the early stages of practice, the teacher leads learners through each step in a regimented and structured manner. It is essential in this phase that errors be corrected and that correct behaviors be reinforced. After students are able to perform a skill with 85 to 90 percent accuracy, they then practice independently with periodic supervision until they can perform the task accurately and independently.

Beginning practice should occur in frequent, intense, highly structured segments. Depending on the age of the learners, these segments may vary in length of time, but the students should always be motivated and involved during these sessions. Monitoring by the teacher to assure accuracy in performance is essential.

Practice sessions should gradually be spaced farther apart as learning is mastered; new learning can be introduced while mastery of the previous learning is still being practiced. For instance, a student learning scales on the piano may begin to practice the G scale, but should return to the C scale periodically to reinforce the learning.

### Feedback

Feedback should be as specific as possible and is most effective when the reinforcement given through feedback is positive and frequent. Negative statements (e.g., "That was a stupid thing to do." or "Why can't you keep up with the rest of the class?") generally discourage performance. Corrective feedback should describe the behavior and specify the way to correct it.

As practice proceeds, students need to receive feedback, either verbally or through grades or alternative evaluation devices (smiley faces) regarding their performances. In the beginning, the teacher provides continuous feedback through reinforcement of correct behavior or through correction and reteaching. As the learning progresses, feedback can become less frequent.

### *Reinforcement*

Reinforcement can be continuous or intermittent—that is, the teacher reinforces behavior each time it occurs or follows a periodic schedule of reinforcement. In the early stages of learning, behavior should be reinforced after every correct response and after those responses that are moving in the right direction. Few learners can do everything right the very first time, but they need encouragement as they proceed.

As learning progresses, reinforcement should be provided at intervals determined by the teacher. These intervals may be based on a certain number of correct responses, for instance after four correct responses, or after a certain amount of time, by checking for retention on a schedule and reinforcing the correct response.

### ■ Basic Principles of Conditioning Behavior

The following are some basic principles related to conditioning behavior:

**1.** Identify the specific goals or target behaviors that you want the learner to achieve. Be specific in describing these behaviors and the success rate you will accept. For example:

- Students will be able to list the 12 major battles of the Civil War with 85 percent accuracy.
- Given 10 problems in long division, the students will solve the problems with at least 85 percent accuracy.
- Students will be able to recite the multiplication tables from the 2 times to the 12 times table with 100 percent accuracy in 2.5 minutes, or less.

**2.** Pretest to determine how much of the target behavior the learner already possesses. Keep accurate data on the skill development of learners in order to provide accurate feedback to students regarding both their current level of performance or knowledge and their progress toward mastery.

**3.** Set realistic goals for learners. Consider the age of the learners, their interest in the learning, and their present level of knowledge. Here, transfer of learning is an important consideration because skills related to interest and prior knowledge are more easily acquired. For instance, if a person can tune the motor of a lawn mower, he or she can more readily learn to tune the engine of an automobile.

**4.** Break the task to be learned into small interrelated segments and introduce a single step at a time.

**5.** Use positive reinforcement to change behavior whenever possible and reinforce a behavior immediately after it occurs.

**6.** Reinforce continually when first introducing a new learning, but then gradually schedule reinforcement at periodic intervals.

**7.** Keep careful records of the progress of learners and encourage them to monitor their own progress in achieving their learning goals.

## Exercise 5.2

Indicate which of the following objectives could be effectively taught using the direct instruction model. Explain the reasons for your decisions.

1. Students will be able to diagram sentences indicating subject, verb, and direct object.
2. Students will be able to utilize metaphorical language in describing situations.
3. Students will perform the swan dive.
4. Students will be able to follow directions in cutting out a skirt.
5. Students will be able to utilize effective group problem-solving skills.

Answer to Exercise 5.2

Objectives 1, 3, and 4 are appropriate because a very specific sequence of behaviors can be identified and practiced. In 2 and 5, some aspects of these objectives can be learned through direct instruction but other models would be more appropriate.

## Scenario

A science class is studying a unit on chemical changes that necessitates the use of the Bunsen burner, which has not yet been used in the class. Mr. Brown begins by determining how many people have used the burners before. Two students raise their hands, and he asks them to come to his table and serve as assistants.

Mr. Brown begins by reviewing briefly the preceding lesson: "Yesterday we discussed safety in the laboratory and established some basic safety rules. Let's go over those together. Sue, please state the first rule."

Then Mr. Brown describes the objectives of the lesson for the day: "Today, we will learn to use the Bunsen burner, an important piece of laboratory equipment. By the end of this lesson you will be able to identify the parts of the burner, and you will be able to use it with a group to perform a simple activity."

As an organizer, Mr. Brown uses an analogy familiar to the students. He asks the students if they have ever watched a welder using a blow torch.

> Tommy: Sure, it turned the pipe red hot when they were fixing our sink.
>
> Mr. Brown: What was the plumber able to do with the pipe when it was hot?
>
> Tommy: I think that he bent it.
>
> Mr. Brown: Right. Heat can change the way a substance behaves, especially when the heat is intense and can be directed to a particular area; therefore we frequently need such heat in the laboratory. A safe and convenient source of such heat is the Bunsen burner.

For the next 10 minutes the teacher presented information on the Bunsen burner, using pictures to illustrate the parts and their function. He frequently asked questions to determine if the students were understanding the material.

After the presentation, an overhead projector was used to show the class the steps for using the burner. Mr. Brown demonstrated each of the steps and then asked the assistants to demonstrate them as well. After each step the class discussed the procedure. For the guided practice step, the teacher assigned teams of students to work together to use the burners as he moved about the classroom checking on the progress of each pair. When there was an error, he corrected it immediately.

At the end of the period, Mr. Brown distributed a worksheet for a homework assignment on which the steps were out of order, directing the students to place the steps in the proper order and then to label the parts of the burner. He told the class that they would review the steps the following day and then each student would use the burner to complete a simple experiment.

If Mr. Brown discovers the following day that one or two students are still having difficulty with the lesson, he may decide to assign them some additional practice, work with them individually, or ask them to work with one of the students who has mastered the procedures. If a period of time elapses in which the burners are not utilized, he will review the use carefully to make certain that the students have retained the necessary information.

### Activity 5.1

Considering the lessons you plan to teach, develop a lesson plan that uses the direct instruction model to present new material or to teach a new skill. ■

### ■ SUMMARY

It's important to repeat a statement we made in the beginning of this chapter: the direct instruction model is a necessary but not a sufficient instructional tool. To be without this effective tool is a handicap, as the steps in this model provide a framework for instructional design; but to use this model exclusively is deadening.

In a general sense, the other models presented in this text can be incorporated into the *presentation of material* phase of the direct instruction model. More specifically, this model can also be used to reach many knowledge-level objectives and skills.

## ■ NOTES

1. L. M. Anderson, C. M. Evertson, and J. E. Brophy, "An Experimental Study of Effective Teaching in First Grade Reading Groups," *The Elementary School Journal* 79 (1979): 193–223; and J. E. Brophy, "Successful Teaching Strategies for the Inner-City Child," *Phi Delta Kappan* 63 (April 1982): 527–532; and J. E. Brophy and T. L. Good, "Teacher Behavior and Student Achievement," *Handbook of Research on Teaching*, 3rd ed., ed. Merlin C. Wittrock (New York: Macmillan, 1986), 328–375.

2. B. Rosenshine, "Teaching Functions in Instructional Programs," *The Elementary School Journal* 83 (March 1983): 335–350.

3. T. L. Good and D. A. Grouws, "The Missouri Mathematics Effectiveness Project: An Experimental Study in Fourth-Grade Classrooms," *Journal of Educational Psychology* 71 (1979): 355–362.

4. Madeline Hunter, "Knowing, Teaching and Supervising," in *Using What We Know About Teaching*," ed. Philip L. Hosford (Alexandria, VA: Association of Supervision and Curriculum Development, 1984), 175–176.

5. Rosenshine, "Teaching Functions," 338.

6. Rosenshine, "Teaching Functions," 344–345.

7. Rosenshine, "Teaching Functions," 345.

8. Brophy, "Successful Teaching Strategies," 527.

9. S. J. Samuels, "Some Essentials of Decoding," *Exceptional Education Quarterly* 2 (1981): 11–25.

10. Good and Grouws, "Missouri Mathematics Effectiveness Project," 355–362.

11. I. Pavlov, *Conditioned Reflexes: An Investigation of Physiological Activity of the Cerebral Cortex*, trans. G. V. Anrep (London: Oxford University Press, 1927).

12. B. F. Skinner, *Science and Human Behavior* (New York: Macmillan, 1963).

# Chapter 6

# The Concept Attainment Model
## *Defining Concepts Inductively*

One of the great paradoxes of language is that though the world is full of a practically infinite number of objects and ideas, humans manage somehow to talk about them all with a few thousand words. What makes this possible, in part, are the dual processes of concept development and concept attainment. *Concept development,* the topic of Chapter 7, is the process of creating categories by grouping similar objects and ideas, which greatly eases the burden of having so many different things to recall or understand. *Concept attainment* is the process of defining concepts by attending to those attributes that are absolutely essential to the meaning and disregarding those that are not; it also involves learning to discriminate between what is and is not an example of the concept.

The natural tendency toward concept attainment is illustrated by every child. If the child spends her first year in the presence of a cat for a house pet, she will certainly make the generalization that small furry animals with four legs are cats. It is this tendency to overgeneralize a concept, for example, by calling the neighbor's dog a cat, that frequently strikes adults. How does that happen? In the companion process of attaining the concept of cat, the child encounters multiple examples of cat (short-hair and long-hair, adult and kitten, etc.) and examples of animals that are not cats—the canary in a cage, the neighbor's German shepherd, grasshoppers in the yard. All of these examples of cats and not-cats allow the child (1) to intuit a set of attributes for cat, characteristics that define and distinguish a cat as a cat, and (2) to test her hypothesis of what a cat is and is not by trying the label "cat" on animals that might fill the bill for what a cat is. The role of the adult in the child's concept attainment process is to provide an enriched object- and idea-filled environment so that many examples of many concepts are encountered, as well as information and feedback to the child regarding the accuracy of the concept definition.

Teaching concept attainment is, in many ways, a formal enactment of the natural process of concept attainment that we just described. It is all too easy to take for granted that children possess certain concepts, which in truth they do not, and thus to base instruction on false and instructionally harmful assumptions. Adults find much humor in the misconceptions children often develop for what they are taught in school. For instance, Art Linkletter once used a directional microphone to pick up the individual voices of children in a group saying the Pledge of Allegiance. He later heard renditions like the following:

I pledge ul-ee-junce to the flag of the public . . . 4 witches stand. One nation under God invisible with lemon trees and jello for all!

Cute as this story is, one has to wonder how many of the concepts that are taught to children in school are misunderstood or misinterpreted, just as these children do not really understand the very complicated single sentence that forms the Pledge they say every day. Too often, we who teach delude ourselves and our students into thinking that memorization is the same as understanding, while ignoring our responsibility for helping children acquire a strong conceptual foundation on which to base their learning.

There are many children who say the Pledge every morning just as Art Linkletter heard it, and so we're left with all sorts of questions: What's the use of teaching if what we teach has no meaning for the learners? Isn't conceptualization more important than memorization? Why is it so easy to take for granted that learners understand the meaning of the concepts used in the classroom?

Using the concept attainment process in the classroom is aimed at helping learners attain the meaning of concepts through the inductive process of comparing examples and non-examples of the concept until the learner derives a definition. In taking ownership of concepts which they have a part in developing, students can become "authorities" in what they are taught.

## Steps in the Concept Attainment Model

Steps 1–3 are done by the teacher prior to instruction.

1. Select a concept and write a definition.
2. Select the attributes.
3. Develop positive and negative examples.
4. Introduce the process to the students.
5. Present the examples so that students can identify the essential attributes.
6. Have the students write their own concept definition.
7. Give additional examples.
8. Discuss the process with the class.

### ■ Step 1—Select and Define a Concept

Concept attainment is most appropriate for teaching concepts that have clear criterial attributes. For example, the parts of speech are teachable as concepts with clear attributes. The classification system in biology is a natural, as are the North and the South in the Civil War, concepts of *freedom* and *slavery* in the Civil War, triangles and other shapes in geometry, different artistic styles in fine arts, and so on. Distinctions between facts and opinions are likewise teachable as an attributional concept, as are each of the types of sentences (simple, compound, etc.). Select concepts for teaching with this model that are definable by features that clearly distinguish them from other similar concepts.

In addition, it is important that students be able to recognize the relationships among various concepts. For instance, in teaching the concept of *apple,* the teacher must consider those concepts that are coordinate to apple, those that are subordinate to apple, and those that are superordinate to apple. Apples, pears, and oranges (coordinate) are all fruits (superordinate). Mackintosh, Stayman, and Winesap (subordinate) are all types of apples. Although all apples are fruits, not all fruits are apples, and a Winesap is both a type of apple and a fruit.

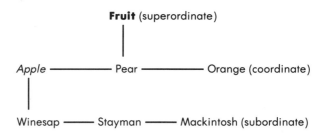

Once you have identified a concept that is teachable by concept formation, write a definition that is satisfactory to you and that the learners can comprehend. Concept definitions in many textbooks are incomprehensible, so don't rely solely on the text or on the dictionary. It may take a while to find a definition that will serve as an adequate base for the lesson; there are usually multiple meanings for a concept, and thus it is necessary to limit the definition to the one most appropriate for the lesson. At the close of the concept attainment process, you may discuss with the students other meanings of the concept.

The point is not merely to find a definition that will, in turn, be *given* to the students but for the teacher to formulate a definition that will be used in the design of the concept attainment lesson. The major purpose of the lesson is to allow students the chance to author their own definition; for many reasons, student-generated definitions are often superior to the initial definition created by the teacher. In any event, the outstanding function of the concept attainment model is to provide an alternative to telling learners what to understand, allowing them, literally, to participate in their understandings.

### ■ Step 2—Select the Attributes

Once you have completed the first step of selecting and defining a concept, the next step is to select those attributes that are essential to a definition of the concept—attributes or characteristics of *examples* of the concept that determine their placement into the conceptual category. For example, the concept *rectangle* is a four-sided geometric figure containing all right angles in which the opposite sides are both parallel and equal. The essential, defining attributes are

> geometric figure
> four-sided
> containing all right angles
> opposite sides parallel and equal

### ■ Step 3—Develop Positive and Negative Examples

Create as many examples of the concept as possible. Each positive example must contain all of the essential attributes. For instance, in the case of the rectangle, some examples can be drawn on the chalkboard, some can be made of cardboard, some can be projected with an overhead projector, and others can be cut out of construction paper; but each example must contain all of the essential attributes—four sides that meet at four right angles, each pair of sides parallel and of equal length (see Figure 6.1).

Prepare some negative examples that do not contain all of the attributes. For instance, a triangle is a geometric figure, but it does not contain all the attributes of a rectangle. These negative examples will help students focus on the essential attributes.

### ■ Step 4—Introduce the Process to the Students

Explain carefully to the students that the goal of the activity is to define the concept by identifying what is essential to the meaning. You may talk of this as a game, and you may keep the concept a secret until the end of the activity. The purpose is for the students to gradually arrive at an understanding and for them to define the concept in their own words.

Place two column headings on the chalkboard, one for positive features, one for negative features. Tell the students that you will show them positive and negative examples of the concept you want them to learn. Their job is to formulate a list of features that distinguish the positive examples, which will then lead to a clear definition of the concept.

### ■ Step 5—Present the Examples

Start with a positive example. Allow students to mention any attributes that they note. There are no wrong answers. If a student says that the figure is made

Positive Exemplars                     Negative Exemplars

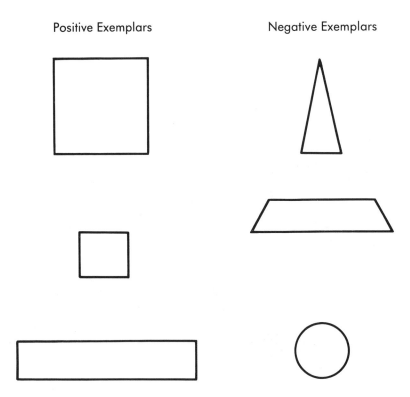

**FIGURE 6.1**   **Positive and Negative Examples for a Concept Attainment Lesson**

of paper write *made of paper* on the chalkboard under the heading "Positive." ("Paper" will be eliminated when there is another positive example of a rectangle that is made of another substance.) *Stress that every positive example needs to contain all the features, attributes, and qualities of the concept.* Nonessential, or "noisy," attributes, like color or texture, can be pointed out in the discussion. For instance, a teacher has fashioned the first positive example of a rectangle from green construction paper. When they see it, the students volunteer the following list of attributes:

> green
> four sides
> made of paper
> a shape
> opposite sides are alike

The second example is a solid block of wood painted white on one side. The teacher reminds the class that every positive example must contain all of the attributes of the concept. This time the class eliminates two of the attributes from the original list. (The teacher marks out the words eliminated but does not erase; the students need to see how they arrived at their definition.) Now the list looks like this:

~~green~~
four sides
~~made of paper~~
a shape
opposite sides are alike

As a result of looking at the new example and comparing it to the first they also add to the list "contains all right angles." Now the teacher gives them a negative example:

The teacher reminds the class that the negative example may contain some but not all of the attributes and that it will help them focus on the differences. The students note that this figure also has four sides, but that the opposite sides are not equal and the angles are not right angles. Then one student notices that in the positive examples, the opposite sides are parallel to each other. This fact is now added to the positive list of attributes. The negative example helped the students to note a positive attribute that they had missed. The list now looks like this:

~~green~~
four sides
~~made of paper~~
a shape
opposite sides are alike
contains all right angles
opposite sides are parallel

At this stage, the teacher asks the students to clarify some of their terms: What is another name for alike? (Equal.) Is there another word that we could use with *shape* to make it more descriptive? (Geometric shape.)

Negative examples serve to emphasize the positive attributes, as the trapezoid did in the previous example. Attributes of the negative examples listed on the board can be used for emphasis and comparison. Some negative examples will have some, but not all, of the qualities of the concept. Make it clear to the students that negative examples do not eliminate any attributes from the positive list; only positive examples that do not contain an attribute on the list allow elimination of an attribute.

This process teaches learners to attend to likenesses and differences and to understand the essential attributes of a concept. It is not enough to give examples that illustrate the attributes. For instance, if the concept is *fruit,* just having different fruit listed on the board will not bring about a definition. Students must first identify the essential attributes in order to form a definition, and the examples must give learners a clear indication of the *attributes*. In this case, the examples could be pictures showing different fruit cut open or actual fruit in different stages of development.

Attributes can be demonstrated in many ways. For instance, if the teacher is introducing the concept *romanticism* to a literature class, pictures from the Romantic period in art provide excellent positive examples; negative examples could be drawn from art that represents other styles.

Different forms of this model can be used. The form described above begins with a positive example and then adds either negative or positive examples one at a time. Another version is to give all of the examples, positive and negative, to the students at once and allow them to draw their own conclusions. Still another is to put all the examples before the students and let the students try to determine which are the positive and which are the negative examples.

Select appropriate media; pictures, vignettes, three-dimensional objects, and verbal examples are all effective. Guard against reading long passages aloud to the students, as they will not be able to remember the information. Instead, give textual examples to students on a sheet of paper that they can read. Most importantly, examples should always be clear and interesting.

### ■ Step 6—Students Develop a Concept Definition

With a reasonably complete list of significant attributes on the board, the teacher then asks the students to try to develop a definition for their new concept. Often, definitions in students' own words will be surprisingly more comprehensible than the textbook definition.

Be patient with this part of the process; students are not accustomed to stating definitions in their own words. Encourage one student to make the initial effort so that others can add to or change the definition. With experience, the class will gradually become more adept at this part of the process.

Keep in mind that the objective of a concept attainment lesson is not that the students derive *the* definition or anything like a perfect definition. The major objective is for students to *engage in* the process of defining and of forming concepts.

### ■ Step 7—Give More Examples

Once students have developed an initial definition of the concept they are learning, show them a few more positive and negative examples to test whether they can identify examples of the concept. Ask the students to provide their own examples and then to explain why their examples fit the concept definition.

### ■ Step 8—Discuss the Process

This step is essential in making sure that students understand how they reached the definition and are able to link this process to the natural process of their own thinking. "As students learn how to categorize more effectively and as they learn how they arrived at their categories, their ability to attain concepts increases."[1] Attention to likenesses and differences is essential in any type of research or analysis, in both formal and informal thinking; the more conscious a learner is of the process of his or her own thinking, the sharper that thinking will be. Thus, as you use concept attainment in teaching, have students identify the point at which they understood the essential attributes and which examples were the most helpful.

## Summary of Steps in the Concept Attainment Model

Steps 1–3 are done prior to instruction.

**1.** *Select and define a concept:* Determine if the concept is appropriate and teachable according to this model. The definition should be clear and the attributes should be identifiable.

**2.** *Select the attributes:* Determine those qualities that are essential to the concept.

**3.** *Develop positive and negative examples:* This is the key step because the positive examples must contain all of the essential attributes, though they may contain some nonessential attributes that are gradually eliminated. Negative examples may have some but not all of the essential attributes.

**4.** *Introduce the process to the students:* It is important to take the time to explain clearly what you will be doing and what each step will entail. You may find it helpful to remind students of how often in their daily lives they engage in the concept attainment process—in their interactions with and reactions to one another, to objects in their surroundings, and to ideas they encounter in all their classes in school.

**5.** *Present the examples and list the attributes:* List positive and negative attributes in separate lists. Items are crossed out when a new example does not contain the attribute. Remember, only positive examples can delete attributes from the positive list. Items on the negative list are there to emphasize qualities.

**6.** *Have students write their own concept definition:* Using the positive attributes, students will write a concept definition. Be patient. It takes a while to work through the ideas.

**7.** *Give additional examples:* Determine if the class understands the concept. (One advantage of this model is that all the students can participate even though some get the meaning more quickly than others. There may be some students that do not comprehend the concept until this step; meanwhile, the other students are gaining reinforcement of the concept.)

**8.** *Discuss the process with the class:* Be sure the students understand how they arrived at the definition. This is important because it helps them to see how concepts are formed.

## Basis for the Concept Attainment Model

The concept attainment model is based on the research of Jerome Bruner, Jacqueline Goodnow, and George Austin, which was reported in the landmark work, *A Study of Thinking.*[2] Bruce Joyce and Marsha Weil, in *Models of Teaching,*[3] first described this research in the form of a teaching model, and a number of educators since have built on and refined this material.[4]

Bruner and his associates were concerned primarily with the process through which individuals categorize data and attain concepts. Educators have been particularly interested in the use of this research in teaching concepts to learners. Bruner wrote, "To categorize is to render discriminably different things equivalent, to group the objects and events and people around us into classes, and to respond to them in terms of their class membership rather than their uniqueness."[5] It is this process of categorizing that allows learners to simplify their complex environment through the development and attainment of concepts.

The particular aspect of the Bruner research used in the concept attainment model in this text is based on what Bruner called reception strategies in concept attainment, and he described three basic rules for this approach:

1. Take the first positive instance and make it in toto one's initial hypothesis,
2. Consider what is common to your hypothesis and any positive-infirming instance you may encounter, and
3. Ignore everything else.[6]

In school, students are constantly bombarded with propositions (statements of which truth or falsehood can be asserted), both in what they are told and in what they are asked to read. Always these propositions are composed of discrete concepts; often, the truth or falsity of a concept embedded in a proposition will determine how the proposition is understood. For example, every schoolchild knows the proposition "Columbus discovered America." The truth of that assertion depends, however, on how one defines the concept "discover." There were, it is estimated, ten million people living on the North American continent when Columbus stumbled onto the islands he misnamed the West Indies, in his mistaken assumption that he must be somewhere near India. That error was further compounded, and remains so today, in the reference to Native Americans as "Indians." Critical thinkers, schoolchildren and adults, who understand the process of thinking in terms of concept attainment will be wary of such simplistic propositions.

To summarize, *concepts* are the ideas or abstractions that are formed as a result of categorizing data from a number of observations. Learners of all ages form concepts and give them names in order to make sense of all the various stimuli in the world. Imagine the cognitive overload if everything in the world were seen as a separate and unrelated entity. To form concepts, learners pay attention to likenesses rather than their differences, and place similiar objects in the same category. Apples come in many sizes, shapes, and colors, but by attending to their similiarities and ignoring their differences, we form the concept of *apple*.

Many concepts used in the classroom are abstract and have many interpretations; however, they frequently are used as though every student shared the same definition. Consider the concept *democracy*. If you asked a class of university students to write their own definition of the term, you would get many different answers. Yet, we often expect that learners in elementary school have a shared definition of concepts just like this one in their vocabulary.

Teaching students to understand the meaning of the concepts taught in the classroom is one of the most important challenges of teaching. Concepts have names and they have definitions that contain essential attributes, which place them in a particular category. For instance, take the concept *table*. The concept definition is "a piece of furniture consisting of a smooth, flat slab fixed on legs." The essential attributes of *table* are (1) piece of furniture, (2) smooth, flat slab, and (3) fixed on legs. The students are more apt to understand the meaning of the concept and be able to recognize the essential attributes if they arrive at a definition through numerous examples rather than memorizing the concept name and definition.

In the concept attainment model, the emphasis is on the learner attaining the meaning of the concept that has been preselected by the teacher. The final step of this model encourages learners to explore how concepts are formed through a process of attending to similarities and ignoring differences. The model serves both to teach a meaning of a particular concept and to teach students how the thinking process occurs.

In preparing to use the concept attainment model, one must determine ahead of time the following basic elements of the concept to be learned:

1. Name of the concept,
2. Concept definition or rule,
3. Conceptual attributes,
4. Examples of the concept, and
5. Relationship of the concept to other concepts.

## Activity 6.1

In using this model, the teacher often learns as much as the students regarding the definition of concepts. Test yourself and see if you can write a definition of such concepts as *freedom, law, family, line, area,* or *liquid* without looking in a text. Now look up the concept in a dictionary and decide which of the definitions are attainable in a lesson. ■

## Scenario

Mrs. Jones is teaching the concept of *metaphor* to her eighth-grade class. She explains that they are going to learn the meaning of a new concept and that the word will be a secret until they have all the essential parts of the definition on the board and the class is able to derive the meaning. "We will find the meaning of the concept by searching for the essential qualities that define it. I will give you positive examples that illustrate this word and some negative examples that may contain some but not all of the essential qualities of this concept."

The first example was "The moon is a silver ship sailing in the night sky." The students came up with the following possibilities, which the teacher wrote on the board:

ships
night
comparison
poetry
sentence
quotation

The next example was also positive: Superman – The Man of Steel. The students were able to eliminate all but the word *comparison* with this example. Now the list looked like this:

~~ships~~
~~night~~
comparison of different things
~~poetry~~
~~sentence~~
~~quotation~~

Next the students were given a negative example: "He had a heart like a lion."

Teacher: What about this example is different from the ones you have seen before?
Student: It is still a comparison, but this time there is *like* in there.

Under the negative examples column the teacher wrote: *uses like*. Another negative example, "Frightened as a mouse," was given, and the word *as* was added to the negative list.

Student: If the negative examples contain *like* or *as* then *not* containing *like* or *as* should be on the positive side.
Teacher: Here is an example. Tell me if you think that it should be a negative or a positive example: "The father was a tower of strength."

Student: That is positive because it is a comparison without using *like* or *as*.

Teacher: Is there anything you can add about the things that are compared?

Student: Well, they are very different. Ships and moons, people and towers, people and steel.

Teacher: How about this example, which is also positive: "The ship plows the sea."

Student: The ship is being compared to a plow that is used in the earth.

Student: The ship has really become the plow in this example.

Teacher: Are you ready to state the definition of this concept?

Student: A comparison of things that are very different.

Student: Don't forget that you don't use *like* or *as*.

Student: One object actually becomes another, like the moon plowing the ocean of the night.

Student: How about a joining of things that are very different to make a new image without using the words *like* or *as*.

Teacher: That is an excellent definition and better than the one that I had written. We call this concept of using language *metaphor.*

Teacher: Notice how you arrived at this definition. How did you determine the main attributes?

Student: By picking out what was similar in the different examples and what was different.

Teacher: Here is a selection of quotations. See if you can identify the metaphors.

The teacher need not use this teaching strategy every day, but it makes for an interesting and effective variation. By forming the rule after the examples have been given, students who learn best through inductive reasoning have had their needs met. In addition, the students are more likely to remember the meaning of *metaphor* as a result of attaching it to the examples than if the meaning were learned in isolation.

A final step in the concept attainment model is to discuss with the students the process they just went through. Ask the students questions such as, "When did you realize that a particular characteristic was essential to the meaning of this concept?" or "How did we eliminate a particular characteristic?" Help the students to understand how concepts are formed and to think about their thoughts.

**Activity 6.2**

Select a concept from a lesson you plan to teach. Determine if it can be taught effectively by using this model and then design a concept attainment lesson. ■

## ■ SUMMARY

The concept attainment model describes the steps in teaching the meaning of a concept by presenting positive and negative examples of the concept to the class until the students can identify the essential attributes and state a concept definition. In addition, this model helps students understand the process through which concepts are defined. The teacher may present a new concept to the class or focus on one particular aspect of the definition of a concept. Because the understanding of concepts is so essential to learning in the classroom, the time taken to identify and clarify these concepts is time well spent. In addition, teachers find that in preparing to teach this model, they clarify their own understanding of essential concepts.

## ■ NOTES

1. A. M. Kilgore, "Models of Teaching and Teacher Education," in *Using Research to Improve Teacher Education: Teacher Education Monograph No. 1,* ed. R. L. Egbert, and M. M. Kluender (Lincoln, NE: The Nebraska Consortium, 1984), 108–126. Available also in ERIC, No. ED246029.

2. J. S. Bruner, J. J. Goodnow, and G. A. Austin, *A Study of Thinking,* (New York: John Wiley & Sons, 1959; Huntington, NY: Robert E. Krieger Publishing, 1977).

3. Bruce Joyce and Marsha Weil, *Models of Teaching,* 3rd ed. (Englewood Cliffs, NJ: Prentice-Hall, 1986).

4. One outstanding example of a work building on the models approach is *Strategies for Teachers* by Paul D. Eggen, Donald P. Kauchak, and Robert J. Harder (Englewood Cliffs, NJ: Prentice-Hall, 1979).

5. Bruner, Goodnow, and Austin, *Study of Thinking,* 1.

6. Bruner, Goodnow, and Austin, *Study of Thinking,* 131.

# Chapter 7

# The Concept Development Model

## *Analyzing the Relationship between Parts of a Concept*

In one passage of James Michener's *Centennial* he describes Potato Brumbaugh's acquisition of two words important to him:

> He was only a peasant, but like all men with seminal ideas, he found the words he needed to express himself. He had heard a professor use the words *imprison* and *replenishment* and he understood immediately what the man had meant, for he, Brumbaugh, had discovered the concept before he heard the word, but when he did hear it, the word was automatically his, for he had already absorbed the idea *which entitled him to the symbol* (closing italics are ours).[1]

## Understanding Concepts

Michener is making the point that individuals acquire vocabulary in direct relation to the acquisition of concepts. When a concept is understood, a new word takes on meaning because it is useful in communicating that concept. The concept and its label become a permanent part of the individual's mental framework. On the other hand, when a new tag is given and then a definition follows before conceptualization has occurred, the tag seldom becomes a part of the individual's mental framework for more than a few days.

*The American Heritage Dictionary of the English Language* defines a concept as:

1. A general idea or understanding, esp. one derived from specific instances or occurrences.

2. A thought or notion . . . [Late Latin *conceptus*, a thing conceived, thought, from past participle of *concipere*, to take to oneself, CONCEIVE.][2]

There is a tendency to think of a concept as something highly abstract, out there, like beauty or truth, but remember the words of the dictionary, "to take to oneself." Anything that has attributes, even a concrete object, projects an idea of itself, an idea in our heads that we take to ourselves. It is this idea or concept of the thing that we build in our heads that we are emphasizing in this chapter.

Plato spent a great deal of time and energy exploring what attributes make up our concept of objects like trees–"treeness," he called it. A table is often defined as a a flat surface supported by legs on which we place objects. Is a board supported by two unattached cinder blocks on which we place our lunch a table? Is a board lying on the ground on which we place our lunch a table? The attributes of table that you have "taken to yourself"–the attributes you have put in your conceptual basket marked "table"–will determine your answer to these questions.

Two attributes most often associated with the concept apple are "red" and "round." If, however, a youngster grew up where Granny Smith apples are grown, he might consider the most common attributes to be "green" and "round." Actually, the conceptual basket into which we place our apple attributes should contain information on size, taste, texture, skin, seeds, stem, curved surfaces, color, pulp, and so on.

The word concept, therefore, refers not only to the object-in-itself, which many think is unknowable since one can never step out of one's understanding, but also to those attributes that make up one's notion of the object. Jerome Bruner asserts that when "we see an object that is red, shiny, and roundish and infer that it is an apple, we are then enabled to infer further that 'if it is an apple, it is also edible, juicy, will rot if left unrefrigerated, etc.' The working definition of a concept is the network of inferences that are or may be set into play by an act of categorization."[3] Bruner further asserts "that virtually all cognitive activity involves and is dependent on the process of categorizing."[4] This statement points out the importance of the mental processes introduced in this chapter.

Hilda Taba, the educator who developed this model, emphasizes that the mental processes a person employs to select attributes and arrive at his or her idea of what an object is are identical to the processes involved in arriving at more abstract ideas.[5] In other words, whether we study an object such as a table, or an idea such as democracy, we are using the same processes. These processes are mirrored in the steps of this model.

Further, she asserts that the more practice students have in extending, developing, and refining their concepts of simpler objects, the more efficient they will be at refining, developing, and extending their concepts of more abstract ideas.

One of the popular features of the HBO comedy series "Not Necessarily the News" is the segment on sniglets, defined as "words that don't appear in the dictionary, but should." These are usually nouns that refer to objects everyone knows but no one has a name for. These sniglets illustrate how names can be given to an object already familiar to us; thus the concept name follows the concept definition.

- per'-cu-burp–The final gasp a coffee percolator makes to alert you it is ready.
- may'-pahp–A bald automobile or bicycle tire.
- spork–The combination spoon/fork popular in fast food restaurants.[6]

In the previous chapter on the topic of concept attainment, our instructional focus was directed at how concepts are learned; in this chapter, the emphasis is on how concepts are refined. Instruction is built on baseline concepts established from the learners' prior understanding. In the exploration of these prior understandings, and as conceptual interrelationships emerge, a framework for new understandings is established. Thus, instruction builds on what is known, with the effect of adding to and modifying the information and understandings learners bring to that instruction. The important principle underlying this model is that *understandings are built, not acquired*. For example, our concept of what a table is will change and grow more sophisticated as we become interested in our own furniture and learn that there are bedside tables, coffee tables, formal card tables, and lowboys. The foundation and framework for understanding is the prior knowledge and experience of the learner.

One further difference between the concept attainment model and the concept development model is that the teacher has more control over the students' concepts of an object or an idea in the concept attainment model. Because the teacher chooses the examples, he or she can direct the students' thinking. In the concept development model, however, the items in the data base come from the students, as well as the categories and the reasons for the categories.

The concept development model has several other advantages. In addition to refining and extending students' understanding of the topic to be studied, practice in performing these processes in a group situation increases the students' abilities to perform them alone. Reacting to and building on the ideas and connections made by others helps students become more flexible and creative in their own responses. Furthermore, by calling attention to a process that is often performed subconsciously, students become more reflective. Once aware of the steps, students may use them to generate original ideas. More details of this use will be mentioned later in the chapter in the section "Optional Writing Assignment."

## Steps in the Concept Development Model

1. Listing–naming or enumerating the items
2. Grouping–categorizing the items
3. Labeling–defining the relationships between the items
4. Regrouping–reanalyzing or subsuming the individual items or whole groups
5. Synthesizing–relabeling and summarizing the data and forming generalizations[7]

When done consecutively, these five steps mirror a process humans employ individually as they marshal their thoughts on a particular subject, as they organize and reorganize these thoughts, as they seek out new relationships and new meanings, and as they make their way through the uncharted terrains of cognition. For example, by investigating the idea of *enmity* developing between two characters in a short story (termed *grudge* for the students and presented later in this chapter) a group of middle school students became aware of how something relatively small and unimportant can feed on itself and grow into something large and formidable. By enumerating many specifics associated with the word grudge and by examining the relationships between these specifics, students expanded their understanding of this concept and, thereby, their understanding of the short story in which a grudge played a central role. By using this model to explore a central idea from an upcoming work of literature or era in history, you can broaden and enrich the students' comprehension of that work or era. Students enjoy the process, because the ingredients are *their* contributions and the product is *their* product.

The steps in this model will probably seem long and perhaps intimidating. When you first teach the model, try it in parts. Do one or two steps. Each step, while an integral part of a whole, has merit on its own. One option is to have the categories serve as the basis of study and research over a period of time before the generalizations are drawn. In a unit on dinosaurs, for instance, kindergarten children formed the following categories: Shapes of Heads, Types of Food, Where They Lived, and What Happened to Them. After the teacher read stories about dinosaurs and the children viewed films, the class finished categorizing the data on large picture charts and then formed generalizations.

### ■ Step 1—Listing—Naming the Items

In the first step, students are asked to enumerate items related to a subject. This data may be drawn from their own experience or from material that has been studied in the classroom. A teacher might say, "Tell me everything you know about astronauts" before the class begins a study of space. Or, after viewing a movie on witchcraft, the teacher might say, "Let's name everything that comes to mind when you hear the word 'superstition.' "

Taba was very precise in the way she worded the questions in the steps. Table 7.1 provides an overview of the question-response-follow-through sequence that Taba established in this model. Although she changed the wording slightly, her variations had similar meanings. The wording of our questions are precise replications; therefore, we have used quotation marks.

Items should be written on a chalkboard, or somewhere where they are visibly accessible to all participants. Items listed must be specific or the next step, grouping, will be confusing. If you are asking the class to enumerate items about Halloween, for example, and a student says, "scary things," ask the student to be more specific. If he has trouble you might ask, "What sort of things are scary?" You hope he will name some scary things, like "a beckoning finger" or "a rattling skeleton." The problem with writing down "scary things" is that it doesn't name, it groups, and that gets you one step ahead in the process.

**TABLE 7.1**  Developing Concepts

| Teacher | Student | Teacher follow through |
|---|---|---|
| What do you see (notice, find) here? | Gives items. | Makes sure items are accessible to each student. For example: Chalkboard Transparency Individual list Pictures Item card |
| Do any of these items seem to belong together? | Finds some similarity as a basis for grouping items. | Communicates grouping. For example: Underlines in colored chalk. Marks with sumbols. Arranges pictures or cards. |
| Why would you group them together? [a] | Identifies and verbalizes the common characteristics of items in a group. | Seeks clarification of responses when necessary. |
| What would you call these groups you have formed? | Verbalizes a label (perhaps more than one word) that appropriately encompasses all items. | Records. |
| Could some of these belong in more than one group? | States different relationships. | Records. |
| Can we put these same items in different groups? [b] Why would you group them that way? | States additional different relationships. | Communicates grouping. |
| Can someone say in one sentence something about all these groups? | Offers a suitable summary sentence. | Reminds them, if necessary, to take into consideration *all* the groups before them. |

*Source:* Hilda Taba, Mary C. Durkin, Jack R. Fraenkel, and Anthony H. McNaughton, *A Teacher's Handbook to Elementary Social Studies* (Reading, MA: Addison-Wesley, 1971). Reprinted with permission by Addison-Wesley Publishing Company.

[a] Sometimes you ask the same child "why" when he offers the grouping, and other times you may wish to get many groups before considering "why" things are grouped together.

[b] Although this step is important because it encourages flexibility, it will not be appropriate on all occasions.

It is important to have a comprehensive list from which student generalizations can emerge, because generalizations have far more validity when they are based on a variety of data. Encourage students to continue listing, even after they appear to have run out of information. Some items that follow the first pause are the less obvious ones, which frequently derive from greater insight and more thought.

We emphasize the importance of participation by all students. To encourage the fullest possible participation, call on the more reticent students during this first step; they will find it easier to respond at this stage. Also, wait until many hands have gone up before calling on someone to give a response. This implies that you value thoughtful answers.

## ■ Step 2—Grouping—Categorizing the Items

When the teacher feels sufficient items have been listed, it is time to move to the other half of the blackboard and ask, "Which of the items we have listed go together because they are alike in some way?" In this step students begin to examine the relationships between items. For example, one student might say beckoning fingers, rattling skeletons, unfamiliar noises, and complete darkness go together.

It is important in this step to ask students to explain the reasons for their choices. (Their explanations are often surprising!) Even if the reasons for grouping seem obvious, ask students to articulate their reasons. Having to explain the label they gave a particular group of items forces students to articulate and defend their reasoning processes. Frequently, they express connections they sense but have not precisely verbalized. Student thinking must be understood by everyone at this stage, as Taba's amusing story illustrates.

> Dr. Karplus at the University of California . . . tells about some seven-year-olds who were grouping and labeling some rocks on their desks. Dr. Karplus was interested in how the children were doing and so as he walked around the room he asked one little boy, "How are you grouping your rocks?" and the reply was, "By age."
> This was really impressive. So Dr. Karplus said, "Tell me more about that."
> And the little boy replied, "You know, big rocks and little rocks."[8]

## ■ Step 3—Labeling—Defining Relationships between Items

In this step, students give labels to the newly formed groups. The student who put beckoning fingers and rattling skeletons together might label the group "scary things." The sophistication of the labels depends on the age and background of the group. Older students, for instance, might use a label like "habitat" whereas younger students might label the group "places where animals live."

The teacher must remain passive so students feel their judgments are valued by the teacher and the rest of the class. If the teacher steps in, students will expect help the next time they are puzzled, and they will not find answers for themselves. The purpose of labeling is not to teach particular inferences or generalizations but to develop the students' skills in drawing inferences and in making generalizations as they decide how to label the items they have grouped together.

### ■ Step 4—Regrouping—Reanalyzing or Subsuming Items

Step 4 centers on the questions "Are there items now in one group that you could put in another group?" and, later, "Are there whole groups that could be placed under one of the other labels?" Again, ask for the learner's reasoning here: "Why do you think _____ belongs under _____?"

For example, a student might want to add "witches on broomsticks," which had been under "decorations," to the group of scary things. If you feel the groupings were done for rather shallow or superficial reasons and that the students can go further, try erasing the second half of the board, leaving the initial items clearly visible. Ask the class to reexamine the items from a slightly different point of view, and to regroup the items. Remind them that the list of items is not final; if they create a new group, they may add other items.

Just as during the naming step the more obvious items come first, so with grouping, the more obvious relationships are pointed out first. Also, the connections seen when the model is first used are much less complex than those recognized after practice. As time goes on, students will find out for themselves that every person, object, or idea has many characteristics and may be grouped in many different ways. For example, when a ninth-grader observed that the item "leering pumpkin" could be labeled decorations or food or scary things depending on how you thought about it, he showed his understanding that the same object may be viewed from different perspectives. We all tend to put constraints on our thinking. If A is B it cannot be C. In this model, students discover that one item can be viewed from several vantage points and can, therefore, appear in several groups. Also, whole groups may be included in other groups.

### Exercise 7.1

Group the following items and then label each of the groups. Then regroup the items and relabel. Remember, be flexible. You may use an item more than once, or you may omit an item.

| rocks | tigers | kittens |
| stars | cars | the sea |
| ponies | cakes | roses |
| cookies | sausage | grass |
| motorcycles | rollerskates | flowers |

Possible Answers to Exercise 7.1

## Group A

| Parts of Nature | Means of Transportation | Foods |
|---|---|---|
| rocks | cars | cookies |
| stars | motorcycles | sausage |
| flowers | rollerskates | cakes |
| roses | ponies | |
| grass | | |
| the sea | | |
| tigers | | |
| kittens | | |
| ponies | | |

## Group B

| Nonliving Parts of Nature | Cats | Plants | Foods High in Cholesterol |
|---|---|---|---|
| | tigers | flowers | |
| rocks | kittens | roses | cakes |
| stars | | grass | cookies |
| the sea | | | sausage |

### ■ Step 5—Synthesizing—Summarizing Data and Forming Generalizations

In step 5, the teacher asks the class to look over the entire chalkboard, consider all the labels, and try to summarize all the information in one sentence. Students must differentiate various items, decide what the larger categories are to be, and what information is subordinate and what is superordinate. This step offers an opportunity for students to begin to appreciate the richness and complexity of ideas. Students tend to think in terms of either/or. Either Halloween is a "good" holiday or a "bad" one. They do not see that Halloween can have two faces. Scary situations need not be dangerous if controlled, and can even be fun. A private party can offer some thrillingly terrifying moments that pose no danger. If not supervised, however, trick-or-treaters can be in danger from traffic, over-zealous pranksters, or the occasional sick mind. By looking at all the conflicting data on the chalkboard at once, students begin to realize that the idea of Halloween is complex, fraught with pleasures and dangers.

## Summary of Steps in the Concept Development Model

1. *Listing or enumerating:* Involves itemizing or listing ideas, associations, memories, and concepts related to a target idea or concept of which learners

have some prior knowledge and understanding. Thus, what the learners already know is *identified*. The information may be based on general knowledge that students have of a subject or on what they know or think they know already. Or it may come from an experience they have had, such as a field trip, a preparatory reading, or a film.

**2.** *Grouping or categorizing:* Involves grouping items by finding ways in which they are similar or related. Thus, what learners know is *qualified*. Similar ideas, or ideas related to a common concept, bear similar qualities. An important part of learning consists in the identification of these qualities.

**3.** *Labeling or defining relationships:* Involves labeling groups according to the reasons for grouping them together. Thus, what learners know is *defined*. Qualities that are borne in common by ideas form the basis of the categories into which those ideas will fit.

**4.** *Regrouping—reanalyzing and subsuming:* Involves analyzing through regrouping and subsuming additional items under already established labels or subsuming labels under other labels according to relative inclusiveness. For example, under the heading democracy, the category "campaign," containing items like shaking hands and making speeches, might be subsumed under another category, "elections." It is in this step that the most creative connections occur.

**5.** *Synthesizing and summarizing:* Involves summarizing the information in the briefest terms possible. Thus, what learners know is *synthesized*. To synthesize is to put the parts of an object or idea together.

## Comments on Taba's Questioning Techniques

Let us return to The American Heritage definition of a concept: "a concept (is) a general idea or understanding, esp. one derived from specific instances or occurrences." The important point is made here that an understanding is more accurate when it derives from a data base of specific information. This is why the model begins by establishing a data base in Step 1 from which our understandings emerge.[9] This is also the reason why inductive questioning processes are recommended over deductive questioning processes when refining and extending our understanding of a concept.

What does this mean? Suppose you had just finished teaching a unit on the American Revolution. You want to know what kind of man your students think George Washington was. Remember, Washington was an individual man, but your students' understanding of that man constitutes their individual concepts of him. No one shares precisely the same idea. Even his contemporaries, who saw him, talked to him, worked with him, and fought with him, saw very different sides of him and had very different impressions.

Instead of beginning by simply asking your students what kind of man Washington was and having them list characteristics such as brave, honest, energetic, and so on, go back a step. Establish a data base by asking students to list all the things they remember that Washington did. Here is a sample list:

- At the age of 21 he led British and colonial troops against the French at Fort Duquesne.
- He was defeated at Fort Duquesne in 1754 and again in 1755.
- He attended the First Continental Congress, which produced a declaration of grievances against England.
- He crossed the Delaware River with his troops at night.
- He tried to change farmers who were crack shots into European-type fighting machines instead of capitalizing on their strengths.
- He repeatedly risked his life for the colonies; yet, he wrote that he was sick of their squabbling and dissension.

Next ask, "What sort of man would cross the Delaware at night?" and other similar questions. The adjectives that emerge will be based on specific information rather than vague impressions. By using this inductive questioning process, a picture will emerge of a man who was rich with complexities and contradictions, a picture grounded in supporting evidence. The class will see a man who was doggedly persistent, even in the face of defeat, painfully torn, even in the face of victory.

As you question students, proceed slowly. Pause after asking a question to give students time to think, and do not call on the first student who raises his hand. Continue to give the others time to ponder. You are asking for more than simple recall, and students will learn that you value thoughtful responses.

## Basis for the Concept Development Model

Listing, grouping, labeling, regrouping, and synthesizing—these are descriptions of the essential components of higher order thinking, the thinking that makes the concept development model so powerful for teachers and students alike. From the early weeks of life to old age, all humans learn in something like the way we've described as concept development.

The philosopher of language Ludwig Wittgenstein said that to know a language is to participate in a form of life.[10] Likewise, to know a subject, a discipline, is to participate in a way of thinking, to become disciplined in thought with other thinkers, human beings whose thought is no different in *process* from your own. And what, exactly, is the process of disciplined knowing? Every field of inquiry, whether biology, algebra, literature, physics, geometry, history, geography, or any other of an almost limitless list, represents a way of thinking. Each field of human inquiry centers on a different kind of phenomena, names those phenomena, examines their various qualities, establishes categories for them, analyzes them, and synthesizes them. Ruth Benedict, in discussing scientific study in *Patterns of Culture,* says,

> In all the less controversial fields like the study of cacti or termites or the nature of nebulae, the necessary method of study is to group the relevant

material and to take note of all possible variant forms and conditions. In this way we have learned all that we know of the laws of astronomy, or of the habits of social insects, let us say.[11]

In their study, the expert and the novice, the teacher and the pupil are different in *what* they can think but similar in *how* they can think. To teach, especially to teach conceptually, is to invite learners to exercise their thinking processes on new phenomena in familiar ways. The essential purpose of teaching on the model of concept development is that such teaching builds on a manner of thinking and a store of knowledge already familiar to the learner. Listing, grouping, labeling, regrouping, and synthesizing are *built upon* so that learning becomes actual *growth in understanding* and *participation in a way of thinking*.

### ■ Conceptual Thinking Is Learned

A child will not approach his or her intellectual potential without guidance and practice in the *process* of thinking. And much possible critical thinking will never take place if curriculum is so strongly content oriented that processes of learning and thinking are left to chance. To awaken, to encourage, to stretch children's abilities to think for themselves is the highest goal of education. To develop thinking skills is to develop an increasingly complex mental organization with which to view the world and to solve problems. Cognitive skills are seen as products of a dynamic interaction between the individual and the stimulation he or she receives.

Learning is not merely the passive absorption of information, but is rooted in perceived experience. Understandings are based on the interpretation of data available through the senses, and there is an immediate and subconscious attempt to reconcile new information with previously observed information. To illustrate the process, we recount a story about a college professor who, while walking across campus, encountered a student wearing a lampshade on her head. He nodded, trying to behave naturally, while searching for a conceptual basket, a mental file in which to put this bizarre behavior. Was the student unbalanced? Her past behavior had not been unusual. Was this a new craze in women's fashion? That seemed unlikely. Not until he saw a second student with similar headgear did the correct "file" present itself; they were both freshmen. This was hazing day for freshmen.

Our senses are constantly transmitting signals to our brains, which our brains are constantly screening. Even at a sensory level, individual perception does not record literal descriptions of the environment. Each perception is a result of the incoming stimuli combined with overlays of past experience with similar stimuli and with the object situated in the environment. Humans see, qualify, and categorize in order to understand. What they see may be completely new, but the basis of qualification and the criteria for classification are what learners bring to any experience and what they use to learn from it. Concerning the subject matter of education, John Dewey concluded "that education must be conceived as a continuing reconstruction of experience; that the process and goal of education are one and the same thing."[12]

### ■ Concepts Are Creative Ways of Structuring Reality

Concepts function like files in a storage cabinet—they provide a way of classifying and thus simplifying incoming information so that it may be stored in meaningful ways and retrieved later. Concepts make it possible for us to mentally process data. Take for instance the concept *color;* in fact, there may be over a million discernible colors. No one, however, can manage that many colors in a concept of color. As a result, the National Bureau of Standards has developed a means of describing and naming 28 hues arranged into 267 colors. (This is an example of an institutionalized conceptualization.)

Since our senses are being constantly bombarded by myriad stimuli, our ability to simplify, as much as our ability to absorb complexity, allows us to act upon our environment. Driving is an activity that would be impossible if we were attuned to every sign, tree, house, vehicle, or person that we passed. Safety and the dictates of driving demand that we screen data and assimilate only certain relevant noises, landmarks, and conditions. Unconsciously, as we drive along, we put incoming data into categories marked relevant or irrelevant.

As young children we learn to pick and choose, to assimilate only stimuli that we determine has meaning, or, more accurately, to which we can assign meaning. When children come to school, the process doesn't change; what they can learn is what they can accommodate. Teaching is, literally, helping children in their natural process of learning new information and assigning meaning to that information. Hilda Taba makes the point that facts are important, but only as they relate to a theory. She felt that the teacher who said her students needed to learn facts first, before they could do any thinking in the area, may not have understood the nature of thought.[13] Facts—disparate items of information—have meaning only in relation to something more inclusive, in relation to a conceptual framework.

We give meaning only to those stimuli that get past our initial screening, so we can begin to bring order out of what would otherwise remain chaos. We group these stimuli because they are alike in some way, and we call these groups concepts. To repeat, concepts are creative ways of structuring our perception of reality.

### ■ Concepts Are Building Blocks of Patterns

This process is quite natural and forms the basis of our understanding of the world. Touching a hot stove leads to an understanding of heat. "Hot" becomes a category into which we place many things (see Figure 7.1), including the idea of caution. Experiments with falling objects (including oneself) lead to an understanding of gravity. We impose order in our world by observing and creating

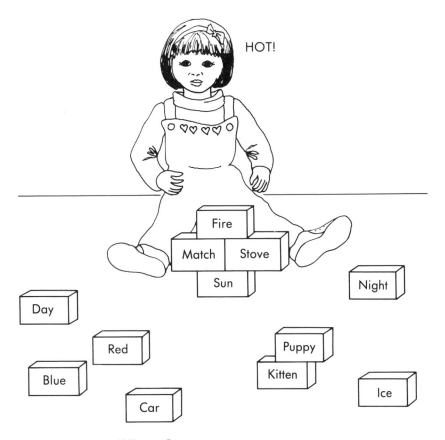

**FIGURE 7.1**    **Building a Concept**

patterns. We divide time into hours, minutes, seconds. We divide space into miles, feet, inches—manageable, bite-size pieces. We attempt to predict the future by observing patterns.

Taba points out that "generalizations are . . . taken as representing a higher level of thinking than concepts in that they are a statement of relationships among two or more of these concepts."[14] Concepts are, therefore, the building blocks of theories from which hypotheses spring. By refining and extending our understanding of concepts, we refine and extend the precision of our hypotheses about life. In the concept development model, a ministructure that mirrors how the human mind works is created. The focusing question produces data, not miscellaneous, indiscriminate data but data relevant to an idea contained in the focusing question. From the data come comparisons, contrasts, and finally a theory that makes sense of the myriad data.

The concept development model parallels the stages of our mental development—from observing concrete data to making comparisons and contrasts to abstracting a theory. Concept development mirrors the actual processes humans use as we move through life attempting to reconcile new, and sometimes startling, data with our present world view.

## Scenario

The following is a description of the concept development process as a seventh-grade class explored the concept of *grudge*. The class was about to read a story in which a grudge was a cause for the conflict.

### ■ Step 1

Listing should result in a large number of items on the chalkboard following the question "What sort of things does the word *grudge* bring to mind?"

| | | |
|---|---|---|
| hurt | binge | friends |
| mean | evil eye | enemies |
| fight | stare | stiff |
| cruel | hold | hard |
| fudge | hate | cold |
| Cindy | yell | deep |
| whisper | stomach | dark |
| secrets | empty | wrinkled |
| not talking | argue | nose |
| silent | talking behind back | brown |
| faces | silly | trench |
| eyes | children | ground |
| cloud | childish | school |
| mist | people | heavy |
| fog | feelings | cut off |
| embarrassed | fat | burden |

### ■ Steps 2 and 3

Grouping and labeling followed the questions: "Which of these items are alike in some way? Which of these items do you think belong together?" and "Why do you think _____ and _____ go together?" Here are two examples:

#### *Feelings caused by grudge*

| | | | |
|---|---|---|---|
| hurt | hate | hard | brown |
| mean | empty | cold | heavy |
| cruel | silly | cut off | burden |

*Things done while holding a grudge*

| | | | |
|---|---|---|---|
| whisper | not talking | embarrassed | nose in air |
| secrets | fight | hold | cut off |
| evil eye | yell | hate | hurt |
| stare | argue | childish | mean |
| talking | talk behind back | cold | binge |

### ■ Step 4

Regrouping by subsuming produces additional groups when the students are told to look at the list again and are asked, "Are there other groups that could be made?"

| *Things associated with food* | *Things that cause a grudge* |
|---|---|
| binge | anger |
| people | friends |
| fudge | gossip |
| stomach | enemies |
| heavy | fights |
| silly | misunderstandings |

### ■ Step 5

Synthesizing culminates the activity when students try to summarize all of their information into one sentence, forming a generalization about the concept. Here are some examples of the students' statements about grudges:

"Holding a grudge is not good for you."

"Holding a grudge can make you do things you will be sorry for later."

"A grudge can grow from something little to something very destructive."

"Fighting is just another way of acting when you feel bad because someone has hurt you. I eat; some other people fight; neither way is really solving the problem."

## Optional Writing Assignment

The authors have found that the concept development model is a superb tool for teaching paragraph unity. Grammar texts tell us that a paragraph is a series of sentences developing one topic. In spite of the fact that this definition seems reasonably straightforward, students frequently have trouble with this conceptual division. Many simply indent half way down the page, if at all.

When students have finished listing, grouping, and labeling a concept or a topic, ask them how they would write about the topic if they had to write a paper. Could the items on the board be useful? If so, which categories would they use? Try to let them see the connection between categories and paragraphs, between labels and topic sentences. Let them pick a category and write a paragraph. The label becomes the topic sentence and the items in the category are ways of developing the idea in the label. Tell the students that they may add more items to the list in the category, and that they do not have to use all of the items.

After students have performed the model several times in class, they can follow the steps independently. It is an effective technique for generating original ideas about a concept or a topic. When they have practiced writing coherent paragraphs, structured around one thought – the thought contained in the label – they can use this technique to write whole papers on a main topic. They can develop a central theme or idea and support that idea with three or four paragraphs derived from related categories.

Here is a paragraph written by a ninth-grade student who had just finished exploring the concept "grudge." She had picked the group "things done while holding a grudge." She wrote the following:

> Have you ever held a grudge? A grudge is a cold, mean, nasty little animal that bites and causes you to do strange things. After you touch the grudge, it might make you start to be mean to a friend because of something that friend did to you, even though it might not have been that big a deal. Soon, you and that friend have become enemies, all because of the mean little grudge. Oh, the grudge loves it, too! It will get you talking about the person behind her back, whispering about her to her friends, and causing everyone else to choose sides between you and her. The grudge is a mean, nasty little animal. Don't ever hold one!

Building on ideas contributed by everyone, both the students and the teacher came away with an expanded idea of the concept "grudge" and of the consequences of holding one.

The teacher had been puzzled by the item "fudge" and assumed it was a rhyming response. When she asked for clarification the student said, "Because grudges make me unhappy, and when I'm unhappy I eat junk, like fudge." Frequently a student's reason for suggesting an item or for grouping items is quite different from what the teacher or other students may assume, so clarification is important. This model also led two students to use personification and analogy. As the ideas were student generated, introducing these new terms was done in a meaningful context.

## Activity 7.1

Teaching is, by its nature, related to concept development. Think of a unit of study you might one day teach in your intended subject area. Try to name one of the crucial concepts that might occur in this unit. (You may wish to check through a curriculum guide or typical textbook for help in identifying a concept.) Next, think of at least one question you might ask or activity you might assign at each of the five steps of the concept formation process: listing, qualifying, labeling, analyzing, and synthesizing.

If you have a copy (preferably a teacher's edition) of a textbook appropriate to your subject area specialty, compare your questions and activities to those suggested in the text. How do the authors assist students in the concept formation process? ■

## ■ SUMMARY

There are several benefits to performing the concept development model on a regular basis (once a month or more frequently). First, students learn much from each other about the concept, object, event, or person studied. They absorb a great deal of the accumulated knowledge and ideas of the whole group. They expand and refine their own concepts of the topic being studied; concomitantly, they expand and refine their ability to perform these mental processes.

Knowledge is not static. Knowledge of even a simple object can grow and take on new dimensions, or it can recede and grow hazy with lack of exposure. It might be helpful to think of growth in knowledge as a series of overlays on an overhead projector. We add to and change an already existing impression, much as one adds an overlay on a basic drawing. The model is helpful to teachers, because it not only allows them to enrich the original impression but it also affords a glimpse of that original impression on which to build.

## ■ NOTES

1. J. A. Michener, *Centennial* (New York: Random House, 1974), 678.

2. William Morris, ed., *The American Heritage Dictionary of the English Lanaguage* (New York: Houghton Mifflin, 1969).

3. Jerome S. Bruner, Jacqueline J. Goodnow, and George A. Austin, *A Study of Thinking* (New Brunswick, USA: Transaction Books, 1986), 244.

4. Bruner, Goodnow, and Austin, *Study of Thinking*, 246.

5. Hilda Taba, *Hilda Taba Teaching Strategies Program* (Miami, FL: Institute for Staff Development, 1971).

6. Rich Hall and Friends, *Sniglets* (New York: Collier Books, 1984).

7. Taba, *Teaching Strategies*, xv.

8. Taba, *Teaching Strategies*, 165.

9. Hilda Taba, Mary C. Durkin, Jack R. Fraenkel, and Anthony H. McNaughton, *A Teacher's Handbook to Elementary Social Studies* (Reading, MA: Addison-Wesley, 1971), 37.

10. L. Wittgenstein, *Philosophical Investigations* (New York: Macmillan, 1953).

11. Ruth Benedict, *Patterns of Culture* (Boston: Houghton Mifflin, 1934), 3.

12. John Dewey, *How We Think*, rev. ed. (Boston: D.C. Heath, 1933), 27.

13. Taba, Durkin, Fraenkel, and McNaughton, *Teacher's Handbook*, 10.

14. Taba, Durkin, Fraenkel, and McNaughton, *Teacher's Handbook*, 72–73.

# Chapter 8

# The Synectics Model

## Developing Creative Thinking and Problem Solving

*Fog*

The fog comes
on little cat feet.
It sits looking
over the harbor and city
on silent haunches
and then moves on.

–Carl Sandburg

Cat feet and fog are very different realities, but when the poet Carl Sandburg put the two together he created an image that delights and surprises the reader with its accuracy. Likewise, the child who says "Oh, look, Mommy, my ice has porcupines in it" is creating language to express meaning. Poet and child alike constantly exercise the ultimate creative power of language – the power of metaphor.

By bringing together two literally different ideas, metaphor creates a psychological tension that can only be resolved by seeing an otherwise hidden relationship. The best metaphors are those that lead to the most interesting insights, those that extend the resources of language to allow new meaning to emerge. In the words of the French linguist Paul Ricoeur, it is the purpose of metaphor "to shatter and to increase our sense of reality by shattering and increasing our language."[2] In exactly the same way, the synectics model is a structured approach to creating understandings that are not merely novel but unique to the learners who participate in them.

William Gordon is credited with the development of the process called *synectics,* which comes from the Greek term meaning "understanding together that which is apparently different." Synectics is a process that utilizes group creative processes to create new insights through this "understanding together" process. "It is an operational theory," writes Gordon, "for the conscious use of the preconscious psychological mechanisms present in man's creative activity."[3]

The synectics approach was originally developed for groups of individuals in industry who were responsible for developing new products. Synectics materials have also been developed by Gordon for use by classroom teachers; these are particularly effective in teaching creative thinking and writing.[4]

In synectics, metaphor is broadly defined to include all figures of speech (e.g., simile, personification, oxymoron), which join together different and apparently irrelevant elements through the use of analogy. Three forms of analogy stressed in the synectics model are (1) direct analogy, (2) personal analogy, and (3) symbolic analogy.

A *direct analogy* is a direct comparison between two objects, ideas, or concepts. For instance, how is a classroom like an anthill, or a teenage crush like a roller coaster? How is math like a crowded bus, or a summer day like watermelon slices? In each of these questions there is an implied metaphor, or an analogy by metaphor. With practice in analogy by metaphor, students become more able to extend their thought. In the beginning, they will usually see fairly obvious comparisons, such as the sun as a ball of fire. But then the sun may become a chariot, a dragon, lemon custard, or a burning seed. With practice, students are able to increase the tension or strangeness of their analogies.

A *personal analogy* invites students to become a part of the problem to be solved or the image that is being explored. How does it feel to be a zipper? How would you feel if you were a tree that had been attacked by acid rain? When does a sewing machine feel anxious? What is it like to be a rose? What if you could defy gravity? The goal here is empathy. Use of the personal analogy in synectics is to provoke the learner into projecting his or her consciousness into the object or idea under consideration in an effort to experience an emotional understanding that goes beyond the merely cognitive.

The *symbolic analogy,* or compressed conflict, involves descriptions that appear to be contradictory but are actually creatively insightful. This type of analogy extends the common understanding of metaphor to the realm of the oxymoron, which derives from the Greek "oxys," meaning sharp or keen, and "moros," meaning foolish. In ancient Greek, the word was "oxymoros," pointedly foolish. There are many examples in common language, not mere contradictions but carefully thought through creations, such as the play title *Alone Together* or the book title *Intimate Strangers*. In discussing this special trope, William Safire cites "cruel kindness," "thunderous silence," "deliberate speed," and "open secret," among others.[5] How can love be both kind and cruel? When is silence deafening? How can love nurture and smother? When is duty both ennobling and unkind? Even young children can participate in this compressed conflict when it is explained in terms of words that fight each other. The "fight" is the tension of the metaphor in compression.

By removing themselves from their realm of immediate personal experience, learners can gain a fresh view of whatever they are exploring. In addition, as learners participate in the creative experience of this group activity, their shared ideas and creations establish among them a shared pride of authorship.

## Steps in the Synectics Model

1. Describing the topic, idea, or word to be explored
2. Creating direct analogies

3. Describing personal analogies
4. Identifying compressed conflicts
5. Creating a new direct analogy
6. Reexamining the original topic

### ■ Step 1—Describing the Topic

The teacher begins by asking students to describe a topic with which they are familiar (e.g., a character of fiction, a concept, or an object), either in small-group discussions or by individually writing a paragraph. In the case of young children or handicapped youngsters who cannot write, discuss the subject with them and write down their descriptive words and phrases. Another possibility is to have them draw a picture or act out their interpretation of the subject. The purpose of this phase is to frame an initial description of the topic.

When the students have completed their writing or discussion, ask them to share the words they have used to describe the topic so you may write them on the chalkboard. (If there is no board space, use sheets of paper that can be torn from a chart and attached to the wall.) List the words or phrases without evaluating them—all student contributions are welcome.

### ■ Step 2—Creating Direct Analogies

In the second phase of the model, the students form a direct analogy between the descriptive words on the board from Step 1 and words from an apparently unrelated category. For instance, the teacher may ask them to examine the list and name a machine that reminds them of the words they have listed. Plants, foods, flowers, and colors are other possible categories.

Each student's contribution is listed on the board and each person is encouraged to explain why he or she chose a particular analogy. When the teacher feels that everyone has had an opportunity to participate and the class is ready, the students vote on one particular analogy that they would like to pursue in the next step of the synectics model.

In one class, students produced the following initial list of descriptive words while exploring the word *math*:

| | |
|---|---|
| difficult | obscure |
| sometimes hard, sometimes easy | necessary |
| frightening | a key |
| rewarding | a mystery |

When asked to name a machine that these words reminded them of, they listed the following:

computers—because they hold the key but they are hard to learn
pianos—because they have keys but they can be obscure and difficult
a dentist's drill—because it is frightening but necessary

### ■ Step 3—Describing Personal Analogies

In the third phase of the synectics model, learners are asked to view reality from the perspective of the metaphorical object that they have just selected. After they have had a short time to think, ask students to tell you how it feels to be this object, and then list their reactions on the board. Encourage each person to explain why he or she had a particular feeling. It takes older learners more time to accept this step in the model, but once they do the response can be exhilarating.

A group of teachers was participating in a synectics lesson and the subject was student behavior in the lunchroom. The teachers were comparing the children to a swarm of bees and when asked to consider what it would feel like to be a bee inside a swarm, they came up with the following perceptions:

- Helpless—I have to do what the others are doing.
- Powerful—I am the queen and I can make the others follow me.
- Frightened—I don't know what will happen next.
- Secure—I don't have to make decisions for myself.
- Dangerous—I can harm people with my stinger.
- Carefree—I can fly and I don't have to make decisions.
- Armed—I have my stinger.
- Imprisoned—I have to follow the swarm, and I am inside, and I can't escape.
- Vulnerable—I can be swatted if I get away from the group.
- Independent—I can fly away from trouble.

A group of third-graders was describing how it felt to be a rose blooming on a fence:

It feels like I'm safe because I have thorns all around me.
I feel fragile because I can't bloom very long and the heat makes me wilted.
Beautiful and admired—people come by and see how nice I look.

### ■ Step 4—Identifying Compressed Conflicts

This is the most exciting and important step in the synectics model. Ask the students to examine the list of descriptive feelings they created in the last step and to put together pairs of words that seem to fight each other. For instance, in our example of the teachers comparing the children to a swarm of bees, some words that fight each other are:

frightened and secure
helpless and powerful
armed and vulnerable

carefree and frightened
independent and imprisoned
armed and carefree

These are all combinations of words that seem to be in conflict, yet each pair is in metaphoric tension.

Take all suggestions and encourage the students to explain why they think the words fight each other. Then have the students vote once again on which combination of words contains the best compressed conflict.

### ■ Step 5—Creating a New Direct Analogy

Using the compressed conflict chosen by the class, ask them to create another direct analogy. For instance, if the combination chosen was *independent-imprisoned,* you might ask the students to describe an animal that is both independent and imprisoned. Some possible analogies would be:

a tiger in a cage
a human being in society
a powerful dog on a leash
an astronaut in a space shuttle

Once again, the students vote to select one of the direct analogies.

Another category to apply the compressed conflict to would be that of food—hot sauce in a bottle or seeds inside an orange are examples of foods that are both independent and imprisoned. The more experience teachers and students have with the model, the more categories they will be able to use with confidence.

### ■ Step 6—Reexamining the Original Topic

The final stage is to take the last direct analogy chosen by the class and compare it to the original topic. For instance, if the last analogy chosen was "a dog on a leash" and you had begun the process with "a character in a novel," you would ask the learners to describe the characteristics of the leashed animal and then to consider the character in terms of those descriptors.

*No mention is made of the original subject until this last step.* The purpose is to get away from the original topic, step by step, and then to return with all the rich imagery that has been developed during the process.

If you ask the students to describe the original topic in writing again, you may want to give them the opportunity to use any of the images that were generated during the exercise, not restricting them to only the last analogy. This works particularly well with older learners or with students who are experienced in working with this model. The chalkboard or paper listing the analogies provides a rich resource of words and images from which the students may draw.

## Summary of Steps in the Synectics Model

**1.** *Describe the topic:* Select a subject to explore with the class. This may be from any discipline. It may be a character from a novel that has been read or a concept such as freedom or justice. It may be a problem, such as behavior on the school bus, or a technique, like diving. Students are asked to describe the topic either in writing or verbally and the descriptive words or phrases are written on the board.

**2.** *Create direct analogies:* Select a category, such as machine, plant, or food, and ask the students to examine the list of words generated in Step 1 and describe how those words are like an item in the chosen category. Ask the students to explain the reasons for their choices.

**3.** *Describe personal analogies:* Have the students select one of the direct analogies and create personal analogies. Ask the students to become the object and describe how it feels and works. Write down the words used by the students to describe their feelings.

**4.** *Identify compressed conflicts:* Direct the students in creating a series of compressed conflicts using the words that described feeling from the personal analogy stage. Ask the class to pair words that seem to conflict or fight with each other and that seem to be charged with tension.

**5.** *Create a new direct analogy:* By using one of the pairs of words in the compressed conflict step, ask the students to create another direct analogy by selecting an object (animal, machine, fruit, etc.) that is described by the paired words.

**6.** *Reexamine the original topic:* Return to the original idea or task so the students may produce a product or description that utilizes the ideas generated in the process. They may concentrate on the final analogy or use ideas from the total experience.

### Exercise 8.1

The following words were used by the class to describe the character of Tom Sawyer. What vehicle do the words in this list make you think of?

| | |
|---|---|
| clever | young |
| naughty | old-fashioned |
| headstrong | original |
| brave | funny |
| smart | |

Possible answers to Exercise 8.1 (some responses given by seventh-grade students)

- model A Ford—because it is old-fashioned and an original
- red convertible—because it is naughty and headstrong and makes a person feel young and naughty
- bicycle built for two—because it is an original and fun
- roller skates—they are young and funny and they get you into trouble a lot of times.

---

### Activity 8.1

Select a topic and follow through the steps of the synectics model on your own. Then, repeat the experience with several friends. Compare the richness of the images created in both the individual and the group processes. ■

## Basis for the Synectics Model

Faraday, the chemist, Einstein, the physicist and philosopher, and Keats, the man of letters, all report a feeling of becoming the very thing they were trying to create, a knowing what it feels like to be a molecule, an atom, the sea itself. Gordon observes, "In both science and art, detached observation and analysis are abandoned in favor of Personal Analogy." [6]

Detached observation and analysis are essential to solving problems but the ability to utilize empathy, imagination, and feelings is equally essential. The flashes of insight and creativity that come from the nonrational part of our thinking create images and solutions that are unique and extraordinary. It is this irrational part of our thinking that synectics is designed to enhance.

The synectics process works, regardless of age and subject matter, most effectively when the objective is for students to look at reality in a different way and experiment with possibilities. Objectives calling for inductive thinking and seeing wholes in relation to parts require that students juxtapose seemingly disparate facts or occurrences. Since students seldom know how to do this, instruction that helps them to recognize analogous relationships is very important. Synectics is the ideal means to this end.

Originally, synectics was used in the development of new products for industry by having groups of individuals play with metaphor in solving problems. Gordon points out that in problem solving "the challenge is to view the problem in a new way. This new viewpoint in turn embodies the potential for a new basic solution." [7] In making the familiar strange, the mind is unlocked from the narrow confines that prevent creative insights and solutions.

In the following passage from a transcription in Gordon's book *Synectics: The Development of Creative Capacity,* the participants are working on the development of a new can opener for a client:

> B: We aren't going to get anywhere if we limit our thinking to improvements. My understanding is that the client wants a radically new can opener . . . not a slightly better one.
>
> A: I think you're right. Let's back way off from the problem . . . What does "open" mean?
>
> E: In nature there are things that are completely closed, then open up . . . a clam for instance.
>
> B: But with a clam the process is reversible. We don't need that for our problem. We don't need to close the can up again.
>
> D: I thought it would be great if we could.
>
> B: I guess not . . . How about a pea pod? That really opens up along a line . . . it's got a built-in weakness and splits along the weak line.[8]

By playing with the idea of "open" and identifying analogies in nature, the group developed the idea of a can that could be opened along a seam and then reclosed—a revolutionary new design concept.

Contrary to the common belief that creativity is an isolated activity that cannot really be understood or taught, Gordon maintains that it can be taught and that learners can understand how to use the process in solving problems or in developing more insight into descriptions and analyses. Using synectics in a group can actually enhance the creative process for many individuals by providing an important kind of interaction—the sparking of ideas from one person to another. "A synectics group can compress into a few hours the kind of semiconscious mental activity that might take months of incubation for a single person."[9]

Another advantage of synectics is that it encourages interdisciplinary relationships. The act of combining seemingly unlike entities causes both students and teachers to search for relationships across the artificial boundaries of knowledge that can be so restrictive. How are volcanic eruptions and civil wars alike? Frost's poetry and Euclid's geometry? Paragraphs and biological classification? Grammar and diplomatic protocol? Maps and story plots?

This ability to hold two very different concepts together in the mind has been described as Janusian thinking, after the Roman god with two faces, Janus.

> Janusian thinking consists of actively conceiving two or more opposite or antithetical concepts, ideas, or images simultaneously, both as existing side by side and/or as equally operative or equally true. In apparent defiance of logic or matters of physical impossibility, the creative person formulates two or more opposites or antitheses coexisting and simultaneously operating, a formulation that leads to integrated concepts, images, and creations.[10]

The ultimate goal of synectics is finding practical and realistic solutions to problems and more effective and powerful ways of communicating ideas. It is the means used to achieve these goals that is unique to the process. By insisting on the involvement of the irrational and emotional part of the brain before engaging the rational and the analytical, synectics seeks to open new dimensions of thought and new possibilities for problem solving.

## Scenario

Mrs. Jones's seventh-grade class has been studying the early colonists in New England and they are about to begin a unit on the Salem witch trials. Mrs. Jones asks the class to write a paragraph describing witches.

### ■ Step 1—Describing the Topic

Under the topic *witches* on the board she writes the ideas they share about the topic based on their writing:

Teacher: What words or phrases did you use to describe witches?

Student A: They are spooky.

Teacher: Why do you think they are spooky?

Student A: Well, you never know what they are going to do, and people are afraid of them.

Teacher: Would you say that they are unpredictable?

Student A: Yes, that is a good word.

Student B: I think they are powerful because they can make magic happen and they can cast a spell on people if they want to.

Student C: I think that witches are evil; some people think that they do the work of the devil.

Student D: There are good witches too. Remember in *The Wizard of Oz*, it was a good witch that saved Dorothy. I said that witches are like people—some good, some bad.

Student E: I said that they don't really exist. They are just based on superstition and ignorance.

Student F: When I was little I used to love to dress up like a witch at Halloween in a long black cloak and a pointed hat.

Student G: Me too. I put a big wart on my nose with clay and used an old mop to make stringy hair.

Teacher: I will add "looks strange" and "wears weird clothes" to the list.

Student H: Don't forget that they fly around on brooms.

### ■ Step 2—Creating Direct Analogies

>    Teacher: This is quite a list of descriptors. Look at it closely for a few minutes and then tell me what *plant* comes into your mind when you look at some of these words.
>
>    Student B: I think of a Venus's-flytrap because they can be beautiful but they trap insects.
>
>    Student A: How about an old oak tree in a swamp with moss hanging from the branches? I saw one like that on a trip and it made me feel really spooky.
>
>    Student D: How about a dead tree standing all alone in a field?
>
>    Student C: I think of those trees in the swamps with the big roots that grow down into the water.
>
>    Teacher: Are you thinking of a cypress tree?
>
>    Student C: Yes, that's the one. They seem to be powerful but they are frightening, too. They aren't really evil, but they can make you feel uncomfortable not knowing what is down below those roots.
>
>    Student G: It seems strange but it makes me think of a weeping willow blowing in the wind. They always seem to be flying and they make me feel sorry for them.
>
>    Student H: Well, I think about a potato. They usually have warts on them and they have rough, ugly skins.
>
>    Teacher: This is a good list. Let's vote on these and see which of the images you would like to pursue. (A vote is taken)

### ■ Step 3—Describing Personal Analogies

>    Teacher: It looks like the oak tree hanging with moss has been selected. Close your eyes and imagine what it would be like to be a tree like this.
>
>    Student B: It feels lonely. There aren't any other trees around that are like me. I am old and different.
>
>    Student A: It feels like I am being used, with all this moss hanging on me. I can't get away and this moss is taking advantage of me.
>
>    Student D: I feel strong and powerful. I am bigger than everyone else and this moss needs me.
>
>    Student G: I feel peaceful. It is very quiet here and the wind is stirring in my branches.
>
>    Student H: I feel trapped because I can't get away. I just have to stay here in this one spot forever.
>
>    Student I: I feel independent. There is no one around, and I am free.

### ■ Step 4—Identifying Compressed Conflicts

> Teacher: Look at this list and pick out pairs of words that seem to fight with each other and have very different meanings.
>
> Student A: How about "powerful" and "trapped"?
>
> Teacher: Why do those two words seem to fight with each other?
>
> Student A: Because if you are powerful you should be able to get away and not be trapped.
>
> Student C: I think that "lonely" and "peaceful" fight with each other. If you are peaceful you don't usually feel lonely.
>
> Student G: "Powerful" and "taken advantage of," because if you are powerful you should be able to keep people from taking advantage of you.
>
> Student B: "Lonely" and "powerful," because if you are powerful you shouldn't be lonely.
>
> Student A: How about "needed" and "taken advantage of"? Usually when people feel needed they don't feel that they are being taken advantage of.
>
> Student E: How about "trapped" and "independent"? Those two words really don't seem to belong together.
>
> Teacher: Let's vote again and see which of these compressed conflicts we want to work with in the next step. (A vote is taken) It looks like *trapped/independent* will be our compressed conflict.

### ■ Step 5—Creating a New Direct Analogy

> Teacher: Let's try an animal for our direct analogy in this step today. What animal seems to be both trapped and independent?
>
> Student A: A horse in a corral. It is trapped but it is still very independent in the way it moves about.
>
> Student E: It reminds me of an animal—a leopard—that is in one of those zoos where the animals seem to be free but they really can't get away.
>
> Student G: I know what you mean. You just walk around and there aren't any cages or bars. The animals seem to be free but you hope they really can't get away. There is always something that is stopping them. There was this beautiful big parrot that couldn't get away because its wings had been clipped.
>
> Student H: I saw a film about trapping otters. The animals caught in the trap always seemed to be independent and fierce even when they were bleeding and in pain.
>
> Student G: My grandmother has a parrot and that bird is so independent. She won't talk or do anything unless she wants to, but she is still in that cage.

Student D: My cat is like that. Even though she has to stay in the apartment and she can only sit in the window and look out, she is still so independent.

Teacher: Let us select one of these that seems to be the best example of something that is both independent and trapped. (A vote is taken) It will be the otter caught in the trap that we will examine further.

### ■ Step 6—Reexamining the Original Topic

Teacher: Now, here is the question. Suppose you lived back in the days when witches were condemned and put to death. How is a person who has been condemned as a witch like an otter caught in a trap?

Student C: They would probably be fighting for their life and would try anything to escape.

Student D: Trapping animals is illegal in most states now because it is so cruel to the animals. We don't believe that people should be called witches anymore either.

Student A: The animals are often hunted and trapped because they are beautiful. Sometimes people were jealous of the witches because they were different and people wanted to destroy them.

Student E: People used to trap animals because they didn't know any better and that was the way it was with witches. They just didn't know how wrong it was. There are still people today that think that it is OK to trap animals just like there are still people who believe in witchcraft.

Teacher: Using any of the images that we have on the board today, write another description of witches. (Figure 8.1 presents the information written on the board by the teacher.)

The following example of a before and after writing exercise on witches gives a flavor of the effect the synectics exercise had on the students' thinking. Here are two examples written before the exercise:

I. Witches are really spooky. They fly around on brooms and they snatch little children who are not inside their houses. I think that witches have long hair and snaggly teeth with warts on their noses.

II. Witches used to be taken seriously and people hung them and put them to death. I don't really believe in witches, but I think that it is fun to pretend that they really exist.

And two examples from after the exercise:

1. *List of Descriptors*—Question: What words would you use to describe witches?

> spooky
> unpredictable
> powerful
> casts spells
> some good/some bad
> imaginary
> based on superstition and ignorance
> looks strange
> wears funny clothes
> fly on brooms

2. *Direct Analogy*—Question: What plant does the list of words in Step 1 bring to mind?

> Venus's-flytrap
> *old oak tree in a swamp with moss* (chosen by the class)
> weeping willow
> cypress tree
> potato

3. *Personal Analogy*—Question: How does it feel to be an old tree in a swamp?

> | | |
> |---|---|
> | lonely | needed |
> | old | trapped |
> | powerful | independent |
> | different | used |
> | taken advantage of | strong |
> | peaceful | free |

4. *Compressed Conflict*—Question: What words from the list in Step 3 seem to be in conflict or to fight with each other?

> powerful/trapped
> lonely/peaceful
> trapped/free
> powerful/taken advantage of
> needed/taken advantage of
> *trapped/independent* (chosen by the class)

5. *New Direct Analogy*—Question: What animal could be described as being both trapped and independent?

> a horse in a corral
> leopard in a zoo
> parrot with clipped wings
> *otter in a trap* (chosen by the class)
> cat in a window

6. *Reexamine Original Topic*—Question: How is a person who has been condemned as a witch like an otter in a trap?

**FIGURE 8.1**    Synectics Model on Topic "Witches"

I.   People who were called witches must have felt like animals caught in a trap. The trap is really superstition and ignorance, because people want to blame someone for things that are wrong with the world.

II.  People who were called witches must have felt very lonely, like a tree standing all alone in the field when a lightning storm comes.

In the second writing, the students have gained insight into the problem and their language has deepened in power and imagery. Now the teacher can go on with the lesson on the Salem witch trials knowing the students have a heightened awareness of the subject. What seemed liked a common and familiar concept has taken on new meanings.

The value of this activity is that the students were doing most of the talking and drawing most of the conclusions. The teacher is in control of the process and can intervene at any time, but the ideas are coming from the students. When students think about values during this process, they are doing it on their own rather than being lectured to by the teacher.

### Activity 8.2

Design a lesson in which synectics is used as an advanced organizer for a unit. For instance, a unit on the study of amphibians could begin with a synectics lesson on *toads,* or a unit on the seasons could begin with a synectics lesson on summer. ■

## ■ SUMMARY

Synectics is a process that uses the power of metaphor to expand imagination and creative thinking. Students are encouraged to look at problems in new and more dynamic ways and to express their ideas more forcefully. The key to its success lies in getting learners to see relationships among ideas they might otherwise have never associated. The result is an altering of the way the learner sees information and ideas to be learned.

Synectics can be used with learners of all ages. Students and teachers enjoy the process and are often astounded at the interesting and imaginative products that result. Although synectics is particularly effective in teaching writing, it is also effective in any type of learning in which the objective is to develop new and creative insights into a problem. Participants, including both teachers and students, are amazed at the power of metaphor to capture the imagination of learners.

## ■ NOTES

1. Epigraph: Carl Sandburg, "Fog," from *Chicago Poems* by Carl Sandburg, copyright 1916 by Holt, Rinehart and Winston, Inc. Renewed 1944 by Carl Sandburg, reprinted by permission of Harcourt Brace Jovanovich, Inc.

2. Paul Ricoeur, "Creativity in Language: Word, Polysemy, Metaphor," *Philosophy Today* 17, no. 2 (1973): 111.

3. William J. J. Gordon, *Synectics: The Development of Creative Capacity* (New York: Harper and Row, 1961), 3.

4. Materials may be obtained from SES Associates, 121 Brattle St., Cambridge, MA 02138.

5. Willam Safire, "Whose Oxymoron is Gored?" *The New York Times*, 2 June 1985, Section 6, 16–18.

6. Gordon, *Synectics*, 38.

7. Gordon, *Synectics*, 34.

8. Gordon, *Synectics*, 125–126.

9. Gordon, *Synectics*, 10.

10. Albert Rothenberg, "Einstein's Creative Thinking and the General Theory of Relativity: A Documented Report," *American Journal of Psychiatry* 136 (January 1979): 39–40.

# Chapter 9

# The Suchman Inquiry Model

## *Teaching Problem Solving through Discovery and Questioning*

Why are caterpillars fuzzy? What causes snakes to slither and bears to growl? Why do cats always land right side up? What happens to the lightning bug's light during the day? Is a baby fish afraid of the water? Did something take a bite out of the moon? Who ever thought up the name "Brussels sprouts," and why does ketchup stick in the bottle? Was the red color in the leaves hiding under the green? Is my skin brown because I was toasted? Will the rain melt the flowers?

Remember when the world was full of questions to ask rather than answers to learn? Somewhere along the way to adulthood, children inevitably get the idea that becoming a grown-up means leaving the world of questioning for the world of knowing. Schools institutionalize the departure from questions to answers as success becomes putting the right answer into the blank or circling the correct response, knowing positively what is true and what is false. Almost all questions in school have one right answer, and questions for which there are no answers don't often arise.

True wisdom, however, might better be defined as the realization of how *little* one knows in contrast to how *much* one knows. The real excitement of learning is daring to challenge the vastness of ignorance with unbridled curiosity. Homo sapiens, meaning quite literally "humankind who *taste* of knowledge," have aptly named themselves. If, as we believe, knowing how to learn is more important than knowing all the answers, then the greatest realization of a person's intellectual life must be that *good questions are more important than right answers*. Thus, the road to wisdom is marked by the quality of the questions one can ask rather than the correctness of the answers one can give. Scientist and philosopher Lewis Thomas has described this intellectual journey.

Science, especially twentieth-century science, has provided us with a glimpse of something we never really knew before, the revelation of human ignorance. We have been accustomed to the belief, from one century to another, that except for one or two mysteries, we more or less comprehend everything on earth. Every age, not just the eighteenth century, regarded itself as the Age of Reason, and we have never lacked for explanations of the world and its ways. Now, we are being brought up short. We do not understand

135

much of anything, from the episode we rather dismissively (and, I think, defensively) choose to call the "big bang," all the way down to the particles in the atoms of a bacterial cell. We have a wilderness of mystery to make our way through in the centuries ahead.[1]

Inquiry learning is based on the premise that there is indeed a "wilderness of mystery" to be explored in all fields, that every subject in school represents what can be called a *discipline of inquiry* in which all students can participate. The inquiry model, developed by Richard Suchman,[2] is based on the premise that the intellectual strategies used by scientists to solve problems and inquire into the unknown can be taught to learners. The natural curiosity of the young can be trained and disciplined in the procedures of inquiry.

The inquiry model we have selected to describe in this chapter is based on the belief that we learn best that which intrigues and puzzles us. When students ask *why* out of genuine interest, then they are much more likely to take hold of the information and retain it as their own understanding. And, more importantly, they will understand the value of working within a discipline, to participate in a way of knowing and thinking that *is* a part of every discipline.

The first step in any problem-solving process is to recognize that a problem exists and to accept the challenge of finding a satisfactory solution. Next, one must gather information through questioning and research in order to form hypotheses and test possible solutions. A final step is to posit a tentative solution that can be tested for applicability in a variety of contexts. Throughout the process, a combination of both individual and cooperative efforts will lead to the most satisfactory solution.

## Steps in the Suchman Inquiry Model

1. The teacher selects and researches a puzzling situation.
2. The teacher explains the process to the class and presents the problem.
3. Students ask questions for the purpose of gathering and verifying data.
4. Students test various hypotheses and formulate a theory.
5. The class discusses the rules or effects related to the theory and considers how the theory can be verified.
6. The inquiry process is reviewed and the class discusses the steps in solving the problem.

### ■ Step 1—Select and Research the Problem

The Suchman model begins with the teacher selecting a puzzling situation or problem. It must be a problem that is genuinely interesting and stimulating to the learner. It may be a scientific problem, such as why moisture sometimes accumulates on the outside of a glass or why sugar disappears in water. It may be a puzzling event, such as the mystery of the Lost Colony or the Bermuda Triangle. It may be a scene from a play or a story that requires the students to formulate an outcome. It may be a problem requiring mathematical skills, a problem in health, a situation to be resolved in the athletic program. Here are some example of problems that might be given to students to begin the inquiry process.

I. In 1692 there was a surge in the number of witches put to death, marking the worst outbreak of the persecution of witches in America. Strangely, this outbreak occurred 47 years after the previous epidemic of witch persecution. No one has been able to prove why this happened in 1692 in Essex County, Massachusetts, and Fairfield County, Connecticut, and not in other counties; however, there are several theories regarding this phenomena, and one in particular that seems very plausible.

II. Jefferson Davis, the president of the Confederacy, was considered to be an outstanding leader and more capable than Lincoln at the beginning of the Civil War. Yet, by the end he was totally ineffectual. What might account for this?

III. It was the final 5 seconds of the basketball game and the coach was choosing a player to send in for the crucial shot. Fred had been to the foul line four times in the game and had missed three out of the four shots. Tom had been to the foul line three times and had made all three of his shots. The coach sent in Fred. What information did the coach have about the averages of the players that caused him to make this decision?

IV. In *The Secret Garden*, by Frances Hodgson Burnett, a young girl finds a key to a secret door that leads to a garden that has not been cared for in many years. The girl lives with her uncle and his crippled son. The uncle stays away from home on business and avoids his son. What could be the secret in the garden?

V. Two plants growing in the classroom receive the same amount of water and are planted in the same soil, yet one of the plants is much larger than the other. The plants were replanted from seedlings that were exactly the same size. What might cause this difference in plant growth?

VI. Rock strata in the eastern United States are very similar. In the state of Florida, however, the rock strata are entirely different from that of any other area. What could account for this dramatic difference?

Any subject lends itself to inquiry since the process begins with a puzzling situation and ends with the students finding a logical and reasonable solution. For many students, especially those accustomed to the process of inquiry, the best and most realistic problem situations are those for which there may be more than one answer or for which no final answers have been determined.

Once a problem has been selected, the teacher completes the necessary research on the problem and prepares data sheets for quick reference during the questioning periods. The teacher also determines how much information should be provided to the students at the beginning of the inquiry process and what additional information could be supplied if the class has difficulty.

### ■ Step 2—Introduce the Process to the Class

Before beginning the inquiry lesson, the teacher explains the process to the class; in this model, the entire class can participate. The teacher is the main source of data and will only respond to questions that can be answered *yes* or *no*, thus placing the burden of framing the question on the learner. The teacher may choose to add additional information or guide the questioning, but the responsibility for hypothesizing must remain with the students, thus the teacher is in control of the process but not in control of the outcome. Students must understand that they may ask questions only when called upon and that they can talk with each other only during caucus periods, times given to group discussion and cooperative work among individual students.

Read the problem aloud to the class and/or distribute problem statement sheets. If the students are nonreaders, provide them with the problem orally and use pictures to illustrate the problem if possible. Encourage students to ask for explanations of any terms that are not clear.

### ■ Step 3—Gather Data Relevant to the Problem

In most classroom situations, students ask questions that require the teacher to do the thinking. In this model, each question must be asked as a tentative hypothesis. The student cannot ask "What makes the plant lean towards the sun?" because it would require the teacher to give the information. Rather, the question must be phrased so that the teacher can respond with a yes or no answer: "Does the plant lean toward the sun because of a magnetic force?"

The teacher may decide to add information or expand on the problem at any time; however, it is important to let the students experience some frustration as they question. There is a temptation for the teacher to rephrase the question and say, "Is this what you mean?" It is better to say, "Can you restate that question?" or "Can you state the question more clearly?" or "Can you state the question so that I can answer it either yes or no?" A teacher might also say, "Yes, that is a part of the answer, but why don't you consider this additional piece of information in light of what you already have discovered."

The data should be recorded on the board or on data sheets kept by each student. The teacher may ask a student to record the data—on the board, an overhead projector, or flip charts—in order to maintain eye contact with the class.

### ■ Step 4—Develop a Theory and Describe Causal Relationships

When a student poses a theoretical question that seems to be an answer to the problem, the question is stated as a theory and written on the board. Now, all data gathering relates directly to proving or disproving this one theory. In the problem regarding the different rates of plant growth, once the students have posed a theory that the amount of light received by plants affected the rate of growth, all questions are now focused on either accepting or rejecting this theory.

Students may ask for a caucus to discuss the information and frame hypothetical questions which they will ask of the teacher. (Some teachers assign caucus groups and leaders prior to instruction, thus saving time and reducing confusion.) Depending on the nature of the problem, the teacher directs the students to other sources of information or to actual experimentation in the laboratory. Students are encouraged to ask hypothetical questions at this point, such as, "If both plants are positioned in the same part of the room, will their growth be the same?" As before, the teacher's response is either yes or no.

If the students reach a point where the theory they have posed seems to be verified, then the class accepts the theory as a solution and moves on to the next step of the model. If the theory is not acceptable and does not satisfy the class as plausible, it is rejected and the general data gathering begins again. At any point the class may be allowed to caucus, but only with the teacher's permission.

Other theories may have been posed in the process of testing one particular theory, so the next step may be to test another theory, backtracking to Steps 2 and 3 if necessary until a theory has been accepted by the group.

### ■ Step 5—State the Rules and Explain the Theory

In this step, students are asked to explain the theory that has been accepted as a tentative solution to the problem and state the rules associated with that theory. In addition, they must determine how the theory could be tested to see if the rules can be generalized to other situations. Sometimes, students will discover essential flaws in their theory at this stage, forcing them to return to data gathering and experimentation.

In terms of the problem of plant growth and sunlight, for instance, the teacher would have the students, in their own words, state the rule based on their theory that the sun was the factor, such as, "Plants need sunlight in order to grow strong and healthy." The class would then discuss whether all plants need the same amount of sun and decide how to test for that generalization.

### ■ Step 6—Analyze the Process

Students are asked to review the process they have just used to arrive at acceptance of the theory. It is particularly important at this step for the students to consider how they could have improved the process or expedited it. Students should analyze the type of questions they asked and determine how they could have formulated more effective questioning techniques. As students become more efficient in using the steps of inquiry, the teacher may consider relinquishing some control over the situation and allowing the students to set up their own inquiry processes. However, in the beginning it is important for the teacher to control the process and to make certain all of the students are participating.

## Summary of Steps in the Suchman Inquiry Model

1. *Selection of the problem and research:* Choose a puzzling situation or an event that will create an interest on the part of the students to discover the answer, and then research the problem for possible solutions.

2. *Introduce the process to the class:* Carefully explain and post the rules that the students will follow for the inquiry. Present the puzzling situation to the students in writing and provide them with a means for recording data.

3. *Gather relevant data:* Respond to questions posed by the students for the purpose of gathering and verifying data. Guide the students to ask questions more clearly or to ask questions more completely, but avoid answering the questions for them. Encourage the students to call for a caucus when they need to talk with each other, but do not permit students to talk to each other during the questioning periods. Reinforce the idea that this is a group process, and the attention and participation of the entire class is needed.

4. *Develop a theory and describe causal relationships:* When a student poses a theory, stop the questioning and write the theory on the board. The class will examine this particular theory and decide to accept or reject it. Emphasize that at this stage the questioning is directed toward experimenting with one particular theory. If other theories are posed, write them on the board and tell the class that they will be explored later if the theory under examination does not prove adequate. Encourage the students to consider all possible types of questions. If they are focusing on events, encourage them to consider conditions that might cause that event. Questions are valuable tools at this point in the model. Students may be encouraged to go to reference sources or to experiment in the laboratory during this phase as they seek to verify a particular theory.

5. *State the rules and explain the theory:* Once a theory or a theoretical answer has been verified by the group, the teacher leads them into an explanation and application of the theory. The rules or effects of the theory are discussed and the predictive value which the theory may have for other events is also discussed.

6. *Analyze the process:* Finally, the teacher and the class discuss the inquiry process. They examine how they arrived at an acceptable theory to explain the problem and determine how the process could be improved. As the class gains confidence in the inquiry process, they may assume more responsibility for the process.

## Exercise 9.1

Which of the following would be appropriate problems for an inquiry model?

1. What is the answer to 3 × 8?
2. Who was president of the United States during the Civil War?
3. The changes of the tides on earth seem to be related to the earth's position relative to the moon. What factors might explain this relationship?
4. We have learned how plants make food through photosynthesis. Here are pictures of certain plants that can grow in the dark. How are these plants able to survive?

Answers to Exercise 9.1

The first two questions require one right answer. Such problems are taught more effectively by other means. The third problem describes a scientific conundrum for which there is no definitive answer, and the fourth presents a situation that requires students to reexamine a hypothesis when presented with new data. Either of the last two problems could be effectively used for inquiry.

## Basis for the Suchman Inquiry Model

Too often children are taught in school as though the answers to all important questions are to be found in textbooks. In reality, most of the problems faced by individuals have no easy answers. There are no reference books in which one can find the solution to life's perplexing problems. Though it is true that those who succeed in school are often those who can remember the "correct" answer, those who succeed in life are usually those who are willing to ask questions and search for solutions.

Robert Sternberg has made a persuasive argument that the problems presented by real life and those that children are taught to deal with in school are alarmingly different, so different that the training for thinking one receives in schools may be irrelevant to the thinking required in life. Sternberg discusses the differences between problems posed in school and the problems posed by life, which will be a help in understanding the Suchman inquiry model. The following summary (with parenthetical statements for transition) is meant to convey the essence of Sternberg's argument:

> In the everyday world, the first and sometimes most difficult step in problem solving is the recognition that a problem exists, . . . . [Especially as] in everyday problem solving, it is often harder to figure out just what the problem is than to figure out how to solve it. . . . [Often the difficulty in solving everyday problems is that] everyday problems tend to be ill-structured. . . . In everyday problem solving, it is not usually clear just what information

will be needed to solve a given problem, nor is it always clear where the requisite information can be found. . . . The solutions to everyday problems depend on and interact with the contexts in which the problems are presented. . . . Everyday problems generally have no one *right* solution, and even the criteria for what constitutes a *best* solution are often not clear. . . . [To further aggravate the matter] the solutions to everyday problems depend at least as much on informal knowledge as on formal knowledge. . . . [One of the biggest differences between problems encountered in school and those encountered in real life is that] solutions to important everyday problems have consequences that matter. . . . [Unlike in school where individuality is prized and competition rewarded] everyday problem solving often occurs in groups. . . . Everyday problems can be complicated, messy, and stubbornly persistent.[3]

Sternberg goes on to point out in a subsequent article that there are a number of approaches one might take in trying to create a more satisfactory congruence between problems children learn to solve in school and those they must solve in real life.[4] Many of the thinking skills needed to solve life's problems are included in the Suchman inquiry model, and the model provides a way out of most all the difficulties of teaching problem solving that Sternberg raises. The basis of inquiry teaching is derived from fundamentals of problem solving.

If students learn that all questions they are given have already been answered, then they may conclude that there is really no reason for them to learn how to think—they need only remember the answers they are given. But as we have said before, it is more practical to teach students that there are many unresolved questions in real life, and many of the answers available are open to question. One of the major purposes of schooling is so students will learn the means of answering questions and questioning answers.

Jerome Bruner has described four benefits to be derived from the experience of learning through the process of discovering answers to problems:[5]

**1.** *An increase in intellectual potency.* Bruner hypothesizes that in the process of discovery, the learner learns how to problem solve and learns the fundamentals of "the task of learning." He suggests that learners who engage in discovering possible answers for themselves learn to recognize constraints in hypothesizing solutions, which reduces what he calls pot-shotting or stringing out random hypotheses one after the other. They also learn to connect previously obtained information to new information in solving problems and to develop persistence in sticking to a problem until it is satisfactorily resolved.

**2.** *The shift from extrinsic to intrinsic rewards.* Rather than striving for rewards gained primarily from giving back the right answer, students achieve rewards from the satisfaction of manipulating the environment and from solving problems. The learner develops an ability to delay gratification in seeking the solution to a problem rather than depending on the immediate reward of giving back to the teacher what was expected.

**3.** *Learning the heuristics of discovery.* Bruner points out that the process of inquiry involves learning how to pose a problem in such a form that it can be worked on and solved. He believes that only by practice and by being involved in the process of inquiry can one learn how best to go about solving problems. The more practice the learner has in the process of inquiry, the more that process can be generalized to other tasks and problems to be solved.

**4.** *Aid to memory processing.* The primary problem of memory is the retrieval of what is to be remembered, according to Bruner. He believes that material that is figured out by the learner is more readily available to memory than that stored on demand. In addition, the learner who is a good problem solver also discovers techniques for remembering information.

In the inquiry model, strategies used by scientists for solving problems are presented as a systematic mode for processing data and learning to approach puzzling situations in all fields of study. In teaching through inquiry, the teacher must be aware that there are both convergent and divergent ways of conducting the process. If the answer to a problem is one which the teacher already knows and intends the students to discover, then the process is *convergent*. If the information presented to the students can lead to a number of legitimate responses, then the process is more *divergent*.

In working with the Suchman model, the initial problems one chooses to focus on may be primarily convergent in that the answer is known and the teacher leads the students to arrive at the right answer through the information given. But the students should gradually be introduced to more divergent situations in which the answer is not known and in which they must practice a heuristic process in learning to solve problems and deal with ambiguity, as described by Bruner.

## Scenario

In a tenth-grade biology class, Ms. Smith is beginning a unit on communicable diseases. To initiate the problem-solving exercise, she reads aloud the following problem statement describing a situation in Peru in the 1950s:

> The public health service in Peru attempts to introduce innovations to villagers to improve their health and lengthen their lives. The health service encourages people to burn garbage daily, control houseflies, report suspected cases of communicable disease, and boil drinking water. Boiling water is a necessary method of preventive medicine for these people. Unless they boil drinking water, patients who are cured of infectious diseases in village medical clinics often return within the month to be treated for the same disease.
>
> A two-year water-boiling campaign was conducted in Los Molinos, a peasant village of 200 families in the coastal region of Peru. Nelida, the local hygiene worker, attempted to persuade the housewives—key decision makers in the families—to boil water. A medical doctor gave public talks on the virtues of water-boiling. Fifteen housewives, most of whom were new to the village, were already boiling water before the campaign.

Nelida paid several visits to every home in the village and devoted especially intensive efforts to 21 families. She visited each of these selected families between 15 and 25 times; 11 of these families now boil their water regularly. No other housewives were persuaded to boil their water.[6]

The task is to determine why this campaign failed. Why was the public health service so unsuccessful in persuading the housewives to boil their water?

The teacher explains to the class that the answer to this puzzling situation has not been agreed on even by the experts, but that they are going to try to agree on a possible reason for this situation. She carefully explains the process they will follow in trying to find a possible solution. She provides each student with a copy of the problem statement that was read aloud and makes certain that the students understand the vocabulary and the basic problem. She explains that they may ask her questions for more information, but she will be able to answer only yes or no; if they ask her a question that she cannot answer in such a fashion, she will probably ask them to restate the question.

A recorder is appointed to write the facts on the board as they are affirmed by the teacher's answers to questions. The teacher explains that only one person may ask questions at a time, and each person may continue to question until finished. Students may call for a caucus at any time, but they may not talk among themselves except during a caucus period. If a student states a theory or what seems to be a possible answer to the problem, that theory will be written on the board and the class will attempt to prove or disprove that particular theory before moving on.

Ms. Smith urges the students to imagine that they are investigators at the scene and to ask questions as though they were actually doing research: "If I could test the drinking water in the village would I find that there were different levels of contamination at different sites?" This type of question, she points out, provides a great deal of information and replicates the type of activity that a researcher would use.

Ms. Smith also has a fact sheet to use in answering the questions posed by the students (see Figure 9.1). If at any time she chooses to supply some of the information to the students she may do so. For the most part, however, she encourages the students to discover the information for themselves through the inquiry process.

At one point during the initial data-gathering process, the teacher encourages the students to consider why some villagers were already boiling their drinking water. Since this is a problem with many possibilities, it helped to focus the questions on a vital point and led to the following interaction:

> Student: Had these villagers been trained by another health worker?
> Teacher: No.
> Student: Did it have something to do with their religion?
> Teacher: Yes.

**1.** Peruvian villagers have little knowledge of the relationship between sanitation and illness.

**2.** Most resident of Los Molinos are peasants who work as field hands on local plantations.

**3.** Water is carried from stream or well by can, pail, gourd, or cask.

**4.** Children are the usual water carriers; it is not considered appropriate for teenagers of courtship age or for adult men to carry water.

**5.** The three sources of water in Los Molinos include a seasonal irrigation ditch close by the village, a spring more than a mile from the village, and a public well whose water the villagers dislike.

**6.** All three sources of water are subject to pollution at all times and show contamination whenever tested.

**7.** Of the three sources, the irrigation ditch is most commonly used. It is closer to most homes and children can be sent to fetch the water. Its water is running, rather than stagnant, and the villagers like the taste of the ditch water.

**8.** Although it is not feasible for the village to install a sanitary water system, the incidence of typhoid and other water-borne diseases could be reduced by boiling the water before consumption.

**9.** The villagers believe in a complex system of hot and cold distinctions – this is a local custom. The basic principle of this belief system is that all foods, liquids, medicines, and other objects are inherently hot or cold, quite apart from their actual temperature. In essence hot-cold distinctions are the basis of avoidance and approach in customary behavior associated with pregnancy and child rearing, food habits, and the entire health-illness system.

**10.** Boiled water and illness are closely linked in the folkways of Los Molinos. By custom, only the ill use cooked, or hot, water. Once an individual becomes ill, it is unthinkable for that person to eat pork (very, very cold) or to drink brandy (very hot). Extremes of hot and cold must be avoided by the sick. Raw water, which is perceived to be very cold, must be boiled for the sick to overcome the extreme temperature.

**11.** Villagers learn from childhood to dislike boiled water. Most can tolerate cooked water only if flavoring, such as sugar, cinnamon, lemon, or herbs, is added. Boiling water is aimed at eliminating the innate "cold" quality of unboiled water for those who are ill.

**FIGURE 9.1**    **Fact sheet used for inquiry process. To be used by the teacher when responding to student questions.**

Student: Was boiling water part of a sacrifice?

Teacher: No.

Student: Did they believe that there was something in the water that made it holy?

Teacher: Can you clarify that question? What do you mean by holy?

Student: Well, did boiling the water make the person who drank it sacred?

Teacher: No, but you should pursue this line of questioning in regard to the effects of the water.

Student: Did it heal people in some way?

Teacher: Yes, it did have something to do with illness and healing.

Student: Was hot water in some way holy?

Teacher: In a way you could say that, but remember that we determined already that it had something to do with illness.

Student: Did the villagers only boil water for people when they were sick?

Teacher: Yes. Now why do you suppose that would be the case?

Student: Did they think that hot water would cure illness?

Teacher: In a way. You are very close to this point. The villagers believed that all things, including foods, are either hot or cold and that when one is ill, cold should be avoided.

Student: Maybe that is the answer. Maybe they would only boil water when there was illness in the family.

Teacher: Let us examine this as a possible answer to the problem. What facts would we have to know in order to prove this theory? Why don't you caucus and discuss what information you will need to test this theory.

Student to student
(during caucus): Well, we would have to determine that Mrs. B., who was an example of a person who learned to boil water, had illness in the family.

Student: Why not ask if there was illness in the home of all those who changed their drinking habits?

Student to teacher
(after caucus): If we visited the homes of those who learned to boil water would we find that there was illness in the family?

Teacher: No.

Student: It looks as though we will need to gather more information.

The teacher is providing some direction to the students during this question and answer segment of the process. The experience of the students and the difficulty of the problem determines how much help the teacher offers. A certain level of frustration helps to stimulate the inquiry process; too much frustration, however, can cause the students to lose interest or to avoid the process. The teacher must guide without interfering with the process.

Although the teacher was prepared with several possible solutions to this problem, the students arrived at one that seemed very plausible.

Student: Didn't you say that boiling the water was associated with illness?

Teacher: Yes.

Student: Well, if the social worker just kept talking about how the un-boiled water would make them sick, she was still connecting the boiling of water with illness.

Teacher: Do you want to suggest that as a possible cause of the problem?

Student: Yes.

Teacher: How would you state this as a theory that would apply in a more general sense?

Student: How about . . . The people wouldn't change their habit unless the bad idea of boiled water could be replaced with a good idea.

Teacher: How could you test this theory?

Student: Did the villagers like the taste of boiled water when it had some kind of flavoring in it?

Teacher: There is some evidence that they did.

Student: Is it possible that the people who were new to the region had drinks that were made with hot water like hot teas and broths?

Teacher: I think that is possible. Assuming that you can accept this theory as possible, how would you test it with the villagers?

Student: What if you had a celebration and invited the villagers and served a lot of good tasting hot drinks? Or better yet, what if the social worker invited the women and children to her home and served them drinks made from boiled water?

Teacher: You know, I think that you have hit upon a very interesting possibility. The experts suggest that the reason may have been that the villagers associated the hot water with illness. Another reason suggested is that the women never accepted the social worker as a part of the community. Your theory that she reinforced the negative aspects of the boiled water by insisting on the danger rather than by concentrating on replacing these negative associations with positive ones seems very reasonable to me.

The teacher then had the students state the rules for the theory they had postulated. Included in these were that (1) people do not readily change a habit when the change is associated with something unpleasant, and (2) people do not change their habits unless they feel positive about the change agent.

The class considered the importance of this observation in dealing with people and persuading them to change or to follow a leader. One student pointed out that there was a negative side to this knowledge. A person who was charismatic could also use these techniques regardless of the legitimacy of their cause.

The students also discussed how they had arrived at their theory and what steps were most helpful in coming to a decision. They noted that it was effective to have a person record the data as it was affirmed so that they had access to it as they proceeded.

### Activity 9.1

Select one of the problems mentioned in Step 1 in the first part of this chapter. Research the problem to determine the possible solutions or answers. Develop a lesson plan using this puzzling situation. ■

## ■ SUMMARY

The inquiry model presented in this chapter is based, primarily, on the work of Richard Suchman. The model utilizes the steps used in scientific inquiry to approach problems in general.

The inquiry model is appropriate whenever the learning that is to take place requires students to be actively involved with information while challenging and questioning solutions to determine if they are acceptable. Used in conjunction with other models in a design process, the inquiry model provides a stimulating option for solving problems and teaching thinking skills.

## ■ NOTES

**1.** Lewis Thomas, "The Art of Teaching Science," in N. R. Comley et al., *Fields of Writing* (New York: St. Martin's Press, 1984), 559–564.

**2.** J. R. Suchman, "The Elementary School Training Program in Scientific Inquiry." Report to the U. S. Office of Education, Project Title VII (Urbana: University of Illinois Press, 1962).

**3.** Robert Sternberg, "Teaching Critical Thinking, Part I: Are We Making Critical Mistakes?" *Phi Delta Kappan* 67, no. 3 (November 1985): 194–198.

**4.** Robert Sternberg, "Teaching Critical Thinking, Part II: Possible Solutions," *Phi Delta Kappan* 67, no. 4 (December 1985): 277–280.

**5.** Jerome Bruner, "Act of Discovery," *Harvard Educational Review* 31, no. 1 (Winter 1961): 21–32.

**6.** Taken from Edward Wellin, "Water Boiling in a Peruvian Town," in Benjamin D. Paul, ed., *Health, Culture and Community* (New York: Russell Sage Foundation, 1955). Adapted for this text by Beth Stroebel. This problem situation is drawn from *Communication of Innovations: A Cross-Cultural Approach* by Rogers and Shoemaker.

# Chapter 10

# The Classroom Discussion Model

## Conducting Classroom Discussions Based on the Preparation of Factual, Interpretive, and Evaluative Questions

An 11-year-old girl named Abby, making a guest appearance on the television program, "The Jeffersons," was asked what school was like. She replied, "School is taking in what the teachers dish out and then just . . . spitting it back!" How often teachers hear comments akin to this one. Questions like "Will this be on the next test?" or "Do we have to remember this for the final exam?" have a common implication—learning in school can be very temporary. School learning is borrowing information, to be given back at a later date as proof the learner was able to hold onto it for at least a little while in approximately the same form it was given.

Here's an experiment to test for yourself the difference between learning by borrowing and learning by owning. Think of some of the things you remember learning in school. For example, you can probably remember learning the Pythagorean theorem, the quadratic equation, Wilson's fourteen points, the date of the Battle of Hastings, the atomic weights of the inert elements, the causes for seasonal changes on earth, an interpretation of Robert Frost's "Stopping by Woods on a Snowy Evening," and many other details both important and trivial. Try to list a dozen or so remembrances of school learnings. For each, rate your present understanding on a 1–5 scale, 1 for low, 5 for high. See if you don't agree that the things you remember only vaguely or understand imperfectly now are the things you merely borrowed to give back on a test. And, by contrast, aren't the things you remember very well or understand perfectly now (after what may be years) the learnings of which you took *ownership*? What was the difference, if you recall any, between the way you were taught or learned these different things? What, for you, distinguishes learning by borrowing and learning by owning?

Many of the models we discuss in this book are designed for learning by taking ownership, to give students a way to generate their own ideas and thus to possess them, to make them their own once and forever. Also, many of the instructional approaches we suggest involve elaboration and discussion between teachers and students. Often, it is the quality of those discussions that determines the extent and quality of students' learning. The better the discussion with respect to its intellectual demand and objective, the better the thinking of students and the more permanent the learning.

Because discussion has such a central place in good classroom teaching, in this chapter we offer a model focused directly on the idea of discussion, the kind of discussion where teachers, through a process of thoughtful questioning, stimulate students to arrive at exciting insights of their own. We suggest this model as a most broadly applicable guide to the conduct of classroom discussion in all grades, kindergarten through twelfth, and in all disciplines, where the teacher wants to expose the students to the areas of ambiguity and complexity, indeed to the areas of deepest meaning. We owe much to the Great Books Foundation, an independent, nonprofit educational corporation in Chicago, for many of the ideas presented in this chapter.[1] We believe, however, that the method of discussion proposed here is applicable to any work of fiction or nonfiction, indeed to any topic, that is rich in ideas. The more substantive the work is, the more fruitful the discussion is likely to be.

## Steps in the Classroom Discussion Model

1. Reading the material and preparing the questions
2. Planning and clustering the questions
3. Introducing the model to students
4. Conducting the discussion
5. Reviewing the process and summarizing student observations

### ■ Step 1—Reading the Material and Preparing the Questions

The caliber of a discussion is directly dependent upon the caliber of the questions asked. Being able to generate thoughtful, productive questions is one of the most valuable skills a teacher can possess. The Great Books Foundation distinguishes between three types of questions: *factual, interpretive,* and *evaluative.*[2] Understanding the distinctions between these three types of questions makes it much easier to generate provocative questions.

#### *Types of Questions*

Factual Questions.    Questions that can be answered directly by the actual words of the text under scrutiny are factual questions. Facts are defined as everything stated in the text. Even if the text asserts things that have been refuted or that run counter to one's personal conception of reality, these assertions are considered facts in the discussion. For example, the existence of rabbit holes through which humans can fall for miles is a fact in *Alice in Wonderland*. On the other hand, the personal experiences of the participants are not a source of facts. The participants must learn to step into another world and to perceive reality from the author's perspective. This allows everyone to check the correctness of the supporting data offered. A manual formerly distributed by the Great Books Foundation recommended:

> A good rule of thumb to use to determine whether a question is one of fact is to ask yourself whether it could be answered satisfactorily by the participant holding his hand over his mouth and pointing to a passage in the book.[3]

Here are some examples of factual questions:

1. From "Little Boy Blue":

   a. Where is Little Boy Blue?
   b. Where are the cows?

2. From *Antigone:*

   a. Who is Creon?
   b. What reasons does Creon state for refusing to bury Polynices?

3. From science:

   a. What is the geocentric theory?
   b. Who first proposed the heliocentric theory?

4. From social studies:

   a. What is an indentured servant?
   b. When did the women's suffrage movement begin?

Interpretive Questions.   These are questions that explore not only what the author says but what the text means. All speakers and writers would like to think that they say precisely what they mean, but all are limited by their particular perspectives, by the meanings they attach to certain words, by the personal experiences that have formed the concepts and generalizations by which they live, by the limits of their ability to translate thoughts and feelings into words, and by the gap between their personal experiences and those of the reader. Interpretive questions are framed to explore these areas of ambiguity in order to attain successful communication. The ultimate justification for interpretation is the text itself; the ultimate burden of interpretation is on readers. Interpretive questions are meant to tease out all possible interpretations.

Examples of interpretive questions:

1. From "Little Boy Blue":

   a. Why are the sheep in the meadow and the cows in the corn?
   b. Why doesn't the "I" in the poem want to wake Little Boy Blue?

2. From *Antigone:*

   **a.** Why does Antigone attempt to bury Polynices twice?
   **b.** What reasons does Creon have for refusing to bury Polynices?

3. From science:

   **a.** Why did Ptolemy think that the earth was the center of the universe?
   **b.** What would Copernicus have said to an outraged supporter of the Ptolemaic system?

4. From social studies:

   **a.** Why would an indentured servant not spend money or time to fix up his or her house?
   **b.** How would John Adams have answered his wife's letter supporting women's suffrage?

**Evaluative Questions.**    Evaluative questions probe the relevance of the text for its readers. Before they can judge relevance, however, readers must have gained a clear understanding of the ideas presented. Evaluative questions, therefore, should not be asked until readers can demonstrate their understanding of the text. With these questions the reader is asked to make value judgments. Evaluative questions ask to what extent the ideas in the text square with the reader's own perception of life. They require the reader to

> relate ideas in the book to his personal experiences and to his own (often latent) standards of value (of truth, beauty, happiness, goodness, etc.). . . . Questions of fact are verified by turning to the book; questions of evaluation by turning to those facts of experience all participants can reasonably be expected to have in common.[5]

Examples of evaluative questions:

1. From "Little Boy Blue":

   **a.** Would you wake Little Boy Blue?
   **b.** What else might you do to get his attention?

2. From *Antigone:*

   **a.** Would you have buried Polynices the second time if you had been in Antigone's position?
   **b.** Would Creon's actions be considered just in today's world? Why? Why not?

3. From science:

   **a.** If you were creating a universe, would you make it geocentric or heliocentric? Why?
   **b.** Do you see the possibility of life in outer space as an advantage or a disadvantage to earthlings? Why?

**4.** From social studies:

    **a.** If you had been an indentured servant in England in the seventeenth century, would you have come to the New World? Why? Why not?

    **b.** If you had lived in 1778, would you have supported women's suffrage? Why? Why not?

### *Guidelines to Framing Good Discussion Questions*

Precision in wording questions is very important in asking good questions. For example, the question "What reasons did Creon state for refusing to bury Polynices?" is factual because it can be answered by turning to a passage in the book; "What reasons did Creon have for refusing to bury Polynices?" is interpretive because Creon may have had many unstated reasons. A question such as, "Why is there a moral at the end of Aesop's fables?" sounds straightforward, but could be ambiguous. A student could think it is evaluative, that it is asking why he or she thinks there is a moral in that particular part of the fable or what value morals have. It could also be interpretive, asking the student why Aesop put a moral at the end and what Aesop saw. One must be careful to make the intent of the question clear.

Just as precision in wording questions is important, so is precision in reading the author's words. Studying how an author says what he or she says yields clues to that author's intention. For this reason, textual questions make excellent interpretive questions. The meaning of one word can become the subject for an entire cluster of questions. What does the word "jealous" mean in a short story, or "inalienable" in a political document? Read the sentence where the word first appears and ask different students to venture a definition. Then read other passages where the word appears. Which definition seems most applicable? Why? Does the definition need revision?

Discussion questions should not be too broad. A discussion needs to be focused, and the questions act as a lens, singling out particular areas. For example, in discussing the short story "Charles," by Shirley Jackson, asking why the boy in the story, Laurie, invented Charles is too broad. But questions such as What does the first sentence tell us about Laurie? What is Laurie's attitude toward school? What is Laurie's mother's attitude toward him? Why do Laurie's parents encourage him to talk about Charles? serve to narrow the discussion and give it direction.

Finally, the most important rule regarding good questions is that they must reflect real doubt. It is these questions that lead the discussion into the realm of author's intent. Students must sense that you are truly searching, that their ideas are valuable.

> Young persons can handle the same questions you would ask adults. Never dilute the ideas involved in your question; the group will immediately sense it if you are talking down to them. . . . Any particular discussion by a Junior group may equal or surpass any particular discussion of the same Great Book by an adult group. Experience is a two-edged sword; it can broaden our understanding and strengthen our rational convictions; but it can also narrow our interests and shore up our prejudices.[6]

There are many systems for classifying questions. The approach described here seems particularly effective because most people, particularly students, tend to ask and to think in terms of factual questions or evaluative questions. Because factual questions have one right answer and evaluative questions are matters of opinion, they rarely lead to discussions as provocative as those produced by interpretive questions. Learning to classify questions can help teachers ask more thought-provoking questions in the classroom.

## Exercise 10.1

Identify the following questions by type:

1. In the prologue of *Romeo and Juliet*, what does the chorus tell us about the play?
2. How does the chorus help to prepare us for the story that follows?
3. How does Juliet feel about marriage before she meets Romeo?
4. Did Romeo believe his fate was in his own hands?
5. What would you have done in Juliet's place when her father ordered her to marry Paris?

Answers to Exercise 10.1

1. Factual (depending upon your interpretation of the word "tell") – The words of the chorus are clearly delineated in the prologue.
2. Interpretive – Unlike the first question, this calls for an interpretation of the facts given in the prologue and their effect on us.
3. Factual – In spite of the fact that this asks for feelings, Juliet is very definite in proclaiming that marriage is an honor she dreams not of.
4. Interpretive – Many of Romeo's words indicate a belief in fate; yet, his actions indicate a sense of being able to control events to some degree. As one could argue that Romeo is or is not a fatalist, the question is interpretive.
5. Evaluative – This question asks the participants to evaluate their own responses to the situation.

Read carefully the material you are going to discuss several days ahead. With pencil in hand, keeping in mind the categories of questions, jot down ideas, reactions, and questions. Mark words, phrases, or paragraphs that are of particular interest. Three or four days later, read the material again, or, if you are dealing with a work that is too long, read the noted parts again and write down questions as you proceed. The aspects that puzzle you may make you feel insecure, but these make the best questions. Having a good grasp of rich material does not lead to final answers, it leads to better questions. Remember too that you are not providing *any* answers, just provocative questions. In this sense you are renouncing control in an attempt to allow students to take control of their own learning.

### ■ Step 2—Planning with a Co-Leader and Clustering Questions

The Great Books Foundation highly recommends co-leaders rather than single leaders for its discussion groups. This arrangement is very desirable for classroom discussions as well. A discussion co-leader can be a willing parent, a guidance counselor, a friend, another teacher, or a student from the class. After students become familiar with the process of discussion, we suggest you teach students (middle school and older) the types of questions. With experience, students can pair up and take the role of discussion leaders themselves. The only preparation necessary is that they have read the material carefully and thoughtfully, planned a session with you, and care about the issues raised in the questions.

Talk about the material in advance with your co-leader. Compare ideas, reactions, and questions. After you have both jotted down questions that puzzle you, marked passages that seem significant, and shared reactions that interest you, combine your ideas. Just as a group discussion generates deeper insights than one can generate alone, so planning with someone generates better questions than planning alone.

Next, *cluster* the questions you come up with. This is a process that involves identifying *basic* questions and *follow-up* questions.[7] A basic question is an "umbrella" question, an interpretive question that raises an issue and is fairly broad in scope. Follow-up questions are those questions, usually interpretive, that develop that issue. Together they make up a cluster. A cluster, as illustrated in Figure 10.1, consists of one basic question and eight or ten follow-up questions.

Clustering, as part of the discussion planning process, is a way to focus discussion, providing a system for developing a line of thought. Introducing the subject of the basic question from several different vantage points (i.e., follow-up questions) affords different entrances to the issue being discussed. This allows participants to go beyond their initial reactions to the basic question and to look at a broad spectrum of information before settling upon an answer.

Clustering, therefore, allows the answers to the basic interpretive questions to become predicated upon data supplied by the answers to the follow-up questions. It must be remembered that basic questions may be answered in several different ways, the strength of supporting data from the text determining the validity of individual answers. If a question points to only one answer, it is not a basic question. The essence of an issue is that one may marshal valid reasons on more than one side. Basic questions trigger extended discussion. Basic questions are exciting; "you *care* about finding an answer."[8]

Two or three clusters should provide ample questions for a discussion, unless the participants are very young (first or second grade) or are unfamiliar with

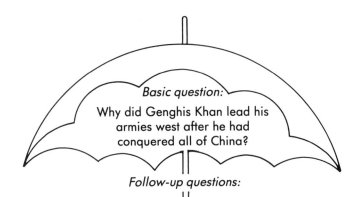

Basic question:

Why did Genghis Khan lead his armies west after he had conquered all of China?

Follow-up questions:

1. What was Genghis Khan's birthright?

2. What puzzled Genghis Khan about the trading in the Mongolian camp he visited?

3. What happened to Genghis Khan's father?

4. What effect did Genghis Khan's father's death have on the family?

5. What made the people want to follow Genghis Khan after he escaped his captors?

6. What made Genghis Khan such an effective leader?

7. What advantages did Genghis Khan's men have over the soldiers they fought?

8. Why was Genghis Khan not satisfied with his conquest of China?

9. What might have happened if Genghis Khan had stopped his conquests in 1215?

(Repeat basic question)

**FIGURE 10.1**   Subject: Genghis Khan

discussion techniques. However, the more frequently a class engages in discussion stemming from clustered questions, the fewer questions they will cover; the tendency will be to go into each question in more depth. Some high school classes will often productively discuss one cluster for an entire class period. If the group, through individual contributions, touches on pertinent areas of the text on their own, there is no need to interrupt this flow with more follow-up questions. If, on the other hand, the group strays from the original topic, a follow-up question will refocus the discussion.

One of the issues in planning a discussion is sequence. You may want to begin the discussion with a few factual questions to ground the students in the material. Then, introduce the first cluster by posing a basic question to focus the discussion and to air initial reactions. Depending upon the flow of discussion, begin to raise follow-up questions. When these have been discussed thoroughly, with responses from several students to each question, reintroduce the basic question. The students' subsequent responses to the basic question are usually far more thoughtful than their initial responses. Because they are based on a pattern of data, responses become more persuasive.

Planning for discussions follows the same format. Discussion leaders should prepare a few factual questions, depending upon how much review students or participants need. Next, decide which clusters of questions you care most about, and in what order they should be presented. Always begin and end each cluster with your basic or broadest question. Finally, end each cluster (or the entire discussion) with some evaluative questions; you do not want to neglect the area of the students' own experiences and value judgments.

In spite of the fact that your planning follows a particular sequence, you should be prepared to deviate from that sequence in the discussion. A good discussion leader is flexible, because student responses should dictate the direction of the discussion. This is not easy and can make a teacher feel insecure. There are so many implicit and explicit messages in education that teachers must maintain control in a behavioral sense, that it spills over into every facet of teaching. It takes courage and experience to let go of the control of ideas. Even here, by virtue of the fact that you are asking the questions, you are not really relinquishing complete control.

Your goal, however, should be to listen, really listen, to the students, and not to steer the discussion to a preconceived view of the material. If you find that, in following the students' leads, you are discussing something you had planned to discuss later, that is perfectly all right. When you get to the subject later you can simply skip that question, or, if you forget and ask the question, you may get more thoughtful answers. Do not be afraid of repetition. Even repeating a question *just* asked is encouraged, because it allows different responses to emerge. A thoughtful discussion proceeds slowly and carefully, with pauses for reassessment.

## Activity 10.1

Using a story or a textbook chapter, form one basic question and several follow-up questions that you think might be useful in guiding a discussion of the text with a group of your students. The main criterion for judging the quality of your questions is whether they focus on an interpretable issue. Do your questions establish a line of reason about the text and then follow through in some clear, successive way? Make sure that your basic question is at a higher level of generality than the follow-up questions and that the follow-up questions lead back to the basic question. ■

### ■ Step 3—Introducing the Classroom Discussion Model

Students learn more when they are told not only what they are going to do but why they are going to do it. As an introduction to these discussions, we suggest you ask the students what they would like school to do for them. What, specifically, do they want to learn? What should they know? Do they think it is important to learn any skills? If so, which ones? Do they think that thinking is a skill? If so, can this skill be improved by practice? What *is* thinking? When do they do it? How do they do it? What happens when they do it? You might show them a picture of Rodin's sculpture, *The Thinker*, portraying the solitary nature of the thinking process. This is a kind of thinking, but only one kind. Good thinking also occurs when people have a chance to express their ideas, to hear the ideas of others, and to react to them. Let students know that one of the major purposes of classroom discussions is to help them learn to think for themselves in intellectual interaction with others.

Ask students to read the material to be discussed for homework, or read it aloud in class, and have each student write three questions about the material that he or she would like to have the class discuss. Their questions can be an excellent source in developing your questions.

After a few discussions, we recommend that you teach students in middle school or high school the three types of questions. Being able to generate interpretive questions is an excellent tool for students in writing critical papers. The answers to their own questions become hypotheses, supported by evidence from the text.

Once students have learned the questioning process, we have found it useful to divide the students into pairs and to allow each pair to lead a discussion. Their performances have borne out the hope that young people can frame and answer the same kinds of questions one would ask adults. Allowing students to take control of discussions gives them a sense of ownership and pride, a feeling that they can manipulate information and ideas.

Give students time in class for a *second* reading before the discussion. They may think this unnecessary, that there is nothing more to be learned, but they need to begin to see the value of second readings.

### ■ Step 4—Conducting the Discussion

Ask students to put their chairs or desks in a circle. This allows you to assume the role of participant rather than authority figure. Tell the students that the questions you will ask are questions about which you have real doubt, and you want them to feel free to share their own concerns about the reading as well. For many of the questions that will arise, there will be no one right answer. For most, there are several good answers.

Next, let the students know that they are to respond to each other's ideas as well as to your questions. You might suggest that they keep a pencil and paper handy so they can jot down an idea when it occurs. This allows them to

follow the discussion without risk of forgetting their idea until you have an opportunity to call on them. Tell the students that there is just one rule that *must*
be followed: they must not talk or contribute until they have been recognized.
It is very important that they listen–truly listen–to the discussion and to each
other.

In leading the discussion, frequently ask questions that force students to
reason aloud, to show their work so to speak. The tone of your probing should
be encouraging: Tell me what you think? Why do you think so? Can you support that from the text? Could you expand on that? Could you explain that
idea? Could you rephrase that? I'm not sure I understand fully. Can you develop
that further? Jamie, do you agree with Peter? Ann, what do you think?

Allow sufficient time to elapse after asking a question before eliciting an
answer. Wait until many hands are up and do not always call on the same people
or on those whose hands went up first. The students will begin to understand
that you prefer that they take time to consider a response.

Ask for several students' opinions before going on to another question.
*This is very important.* They will learn that this does not imply dissatisfaction with
the opinion given, but that there may be several acceptable responses. It is the
richness of varying perspectives that makes the insights so penetrating.

If you feel a student's comment is not valid, you should ask the student to
support it from the text. If, however, neither she nor the other students see that
the inference may be unsupported, you should not step in and point that out,
except to ask further questions. Most students have very little confidence in
their own abilities to solve problems or make decisions. If you step in and provide answers when they are floundering, they may learn more about the specific
point you are discussing, but does that knowledge outweigh the imperceptible
loss of confidence in themselves? When faced with the next tough question, will
they defer to you? The need for a pattern of supporting evidence for an idea will
become clear through repeated discussions, and self-confidence will be built in
the process.

This runs counter to most teachers' training, and it is, of course, a matter
for your judgment. Remember, however, that these are supposed to be open-
ended questions, not questions that have specific answers. One of the most important purposes of this model–if not *the* most important–is to increase
students' confidence in their own ideas. You are asserting *their* individual ability
to generate important ideas, and the ability of the group to discern valid and
invalid assertions. There are many times when answers are appropriate, when
direct instruction is the best way to approach material, but when using this particular model, we think that holding back may pay long-term dividends. Unfortunately, there is much in the structure of daily classroom teaching that
inadvertently undermines student opinion.

One further word of caution: it is only natural to question less stringently
those answers you agree with. Try to guard against this and ask for supporting
evidence for comments that seem to you to ring true but that have not been
adequately supported.

Since this model stresses the *process* of discussion rather than achievement of one specific conclusion, there is no closure in the normal sense. This seems appropriate because one characteristic that distinguishes superior writing from mediocre writing is that superior writing leads to more and more questions, ambiguities, and complexities. The idea that there is no one right conclusion is difficult for students to grasp, but it is good for them to come to grips with this concept. It is also good for them to see that disagreement can be healthy and can lead to greater insights.

### ■ Step 5—Reviewing the Process and Summarizing Student Observations

At the conclusion of the discussion, ask the students to review the main points discussed. What was said that particularly impressed them? What do they remember? Ask them to try to determine how and at what point they were able to draw certain conclusions regarding the text. Discuss the value of different points of view and encourage students to share the way in which their perceptions of the material changed.

## Summary of Steps in the Classroom Discussion Model

1. *Reading the material and preparing the questions:* The teacher selects and prepares the material for discussion by reading and rereading the text and developing factual, interpretive, and evaluative questions.

2. *Planning with a co-leader and clustering questions:* The teacher compares ideas, reactions, and questions with a co-leader (if possible). The questions are clustered and sequenced in preparation for the discussion.

3. *Introducing the classroom discussion model:* The students are introduced to the process and the reading is assigned. Students are asked to prepare questions for the discussion. (Gradually the students learn how to prepare factual, interpretive, and evaluative questions.) The students are then given time to carefully reread the material before the discussion.

4. *Conducting the discussion:* The leader(s) conduct the discussion while maintaining a nondirective role as much as possible. The students are encouraged to listen carefully to the opinions of others and to validate their own opinions by referring to the text whenever possible.

5. *Reviewing the process and summarizing students' observations:* The process is reviewed and students are encouraged to recognize, develop, and use factual, interpretive, and evaluative questions.

## Basis for the Classroom Discussion Model

The practice of teaching by holding discussions and generating thoughtful questions dates back at least as far as Socrates; however, the Great Books' method of discussion as we know it today began to evolve at Columbia University. In 1919 an English professor named John Erskine conducted discussions of this type in his General Honors Course. One participant in the discussions at Columbia was Mortimer Adler. With the backing of Robert Maynard Hutchins, president of The University of Chicago, Adler initiated discussions at that institution. It was also in Chicago that adult discussion groups were started.

In the 1972 revision of *How to Read a Book,* Adler says that one should never say, "I disagree" until one can say, "I understand."[9] This level of understanding requires looking at a text from the author's vantage point. It involves trying to infer the meaning and use of particular words in an effort to comprehend not only what is said, but how and why the author reached a certain conclusion or held a certain point of view.

To do this, discussion leaders raise questions about a text, questions in which they themselves express genuine curiosity, such as: What does the word "right" mean in the Declaration of Independence? To whom does the word 'men' refer in the opening paragraph? What is the common appeal of the Golden Mean in art, architecture, and mathematics? What might be a good analogy to express the relationships among community, conservation, harmony, and friendship? Questions like these are clustered around a specific area of inquiry so the discussion has direction. Furthermore, these kinds of questions require readers to think in order to understand and to never read passively.

How does this model alleviate the problem of overreliance on memorization and student passivity in the classroom? By presenting complex problems for the students to solve, the teacher affirms a belief in their ability to infer, to make connections, to find answers—in short, to think well and to *create* rather than memorize ideas.

By offering a method of distinguishing thoughtful questions from dead-end questions, this model increases the teacher's ability to engage students in higher level thinking. Delores Durkin's research suggests that only rarely do teachers in elementary grades ask questions of students that have any bearing on *how* to think about text;[10] John Goodlad's observations of secondary classrooms suggest that only 1 percent of teachers' questions require of students anything but the most superficial thought.[11]

The point was made in Chapter 7 that for new words to become a permanent part of a youngster's working vocabulary, a concept must be in place. Then, when the correct tag is supplied, the new word is truly acquired. Recent research by Steven Stahl and Charles Clark finds that fifth-graders who regularly engaged in discussions of science passages containing new science words were more successful at retaining the concepts and the words than students who did not engage in discussions.[12]

Based on the later Gestalt theories and the psychology of Dewey and Bole, Hunt and Metcalf made an impressive case for emphasizing "conceptualization and reflection, and insightful learning of skills and habits" over "the learning of skills, habits, and memorized relationships, according to the principle of repetitive drill."[13] They saw discussion as the most effective way to generate this reflection. Moreover, they viewed discussion as *the* tool in social studies with which to ensure democratic heritage. "Perhaps the chief difference between totalitarian cultures and our own is that in the former virtually *all* controversial fields are closed—and closed uniformly and consistently. In a culture with democratic inclinations fewer areas are closed to open discussion, and in certain places—as in the universities—there may be none closed at all."[14]

Most important, Hunt and Metcalf saw discussion as the chief tool in encouraging people to be flexible and change their ideas. "If they can independently explore a problem, feeling no authoritarian pressure from above to . . . emerge with particular conclusions, they are much more likely than otherwise to undergo real permanent changes in conceptual and behavioral patterns."[15]

In writing about how an individual's thinking changes, Roger Holmes, in the book *The Rhyme of Reason,* asserts that an individual's thinking matures as a series of steps in which one alternates between analyzing presently held beliefs and synthesizing these beliefs with new ideas.

> On the plateaus we employ the traditional deductive logic, elaborating by way of analysis an already acquired set of judgements and avoiding contradictions. These stages are static, and for most of us, complacent. But they are essential to profound thinking. The more we analyze our position the more we understand it. And the more we understand it the sooner we see the inadequacies and begin to doubt. And when we begin to doubt we are ready for another step upward. . . .
>
> The dynamic, and more humble, stage is that in which we courageously leave one plateau and work toward another. This is the process that all education in general, and all logic in particular, should emphasize. In this stage contradictions are welcome and new syntheses sought.[16]

The thinking that occurs during a class discussion encourages new syntheses; opposing views are expressed, explored, argued. Thus, richer, more advanced views emerge, forming a type of synthesis. The presence of opposing views pushes the students to take steps up in their thinking. This is not always a comfortable process, but its value in fostering intellectual growth is borne out by the astuteness of the conclusions students reach.

In a special edition of the *Harvard Educational Review* entitled *Teaching in the Eighties: A Need to Change,* the lead article by Lee Shulman asserts that teaching reform must be built "on an idea of teaching that emphasizes comprehension and reasoning, transformation and reflection."[17] Most teachers are considered effective today, Mr. Shulman says, if they manage behavior well. Too few let their teaching methods be dictated by the ideas inherent in the material. "We find few descriptions or analyses of teachers that give careful attention not only to the management of students in classrooms but also to the management of *ideas* within classroom discourse."[18]

He cites a veteran teacher who divides her approach to guiding the students' understanding of literature into four levels: literal, connotative, interpretive, and evaluative. This is, of course, very similar to the model presented in this chapter. The strength of the approach in both cases comes from allowing *what* you teach to dictate in part *how* you teach. Serious literature contains complex, subtle, and often ambiguous ideas. Unless students are allowed to approach, manipulate, and weigh these ideas in light of their own experiences, beliefs, and values, the ideas will not affect their thinking in any permanent way.

## Scenario

Mrs. Jones's class was discussing "The Ledge" by Lawrence Hall, a chilling story of death on a duck hunting trip.[19] "The Ledge" has a central character who has earned a reputation for being a first-rate hunter, always in control of himself and the situation. The following excerpt from a class discussion of this story illustrates the importance of follow-up questions. Notice how all the conversation evolves from the *one* introductory interpretive question.

Mrs. Jones: Why is the hunter so upset when he realizes he has forgotten his tobacco?

Leon: Because it spoils the plan.

Mrs. Jones: What plan? I'm not sure I understand.

Leon: The hunter has a plan; everything has to work.

Beth: I don't agree with Leon that everything has to fit or the plan's no good.

Sarah: But if unexpected things come up, then he's not in control.

Mrs. Jones: What do you mean, Sarah?

Sarah: Well, if he could forget the tobacco he could forget something important.

Mrs. Jones: Is the tobacco important?

Beth: Important, but not a matter of life and death.

Mrs. Jones: Is there something in the text that is a matter of life and death?

Andy: Yes, forgetting to pull the boat up.

Leon: Yeah, it's like it's the beginning of his losing control. I'm going back to the tobacco now.

Mrs. Jones: What do you mean?

Leon: I'm not sure, but the hunter has always had control.

Jill: That's it, he's losing control.

Mrs. Jones: By forgetting the tobacco?

Jill: Before that.

Mrs. Jones: What do you mean?

Jill: Well, I'm not sure he wanted to go that day. But he was afraid.

Mrs. Jones: Afraid? Of going?

Jill: No, afraid of not going, of losing face, of not living up to his rep.

Leon: Yeah, that's it! He had created this rep, and now it was sort of controlling him.

Sarah: Yeah, he *couldn't* say no.

Mrs. Jones's role is one of following the students' leads. She never imposes her own ideas or her own judgment. She does, however, ask the students to amplify and to expand their statements. What do you mean? I'm not sure I understand. Could you explain further? Why do you say that? These words, delivered in a proper and appropriate tone, imply, Yes, I like that. Could you expand your idea? This gentle questioning encourages students to articulate what were earlier only vaguely felt subtleties.

Inevitably, if given some reign over the direction of the discussion, students will touch on or anticipate questions you had planned to ask later. You can either skip those questions when you get to them or repeat them. Sometimes repetition is really productive.

Spurred on by other classmates' comments, the students in this discussion slowly realized that this man, who had seemed all-powerful, had become the victim of something he had created in order to gain power. His reputation as a hunter had taken on a reality and a momentum that drove him to do things against his better judgment. Mrs. Jones was excited because this irony was not just a subtlety; it cut to the core of the meaning of the story. Thus, the students were able to grasp and articulate for themselves a crucial point that Mrs. Jones herself had not fully grasped or articulated, a point that would have remained below the level of consciousness, in all probability, if the students had not had the opportunity to share their ideas, to disagree, to push each other's thinking forward.

## Activity 10.2

Almost all textbooks place questions for discussion at the ends of their chapters. Make a survey of these questions in several textbooks appropriate to your teaching specialty. What proportion of the questions do you find at a factual level? An interpretive level? An evaluative level? Do the questions seem to you to pursue a line of thought or to attempt a common focus or are they disconnected from each other? Plan how you could make the best use of these questions in conducting discussions with the students in a class. ■

## ■ SUMMARY

This model encourages more than one right answer to complex questions and welcomes opposing points of view in the hope that these will lead to newer, richer, more advanced ideas. The underlying premise of the model is that discussion, the true and honest interchange of ideas, produces ideas over and above the ideas that solitary reading and study can generate. Implicit in this premise lies a curious paradox: when students read merely to remember, they will forget; when they read to understand, they will remember.

By repeated participation in discussions that adhere to this model, students will gain confidence in their own ability to think. By confronting them with real issues and by refraining from supplying answers, the teacher is saying, I have confidence in your ability to search for understanding and in your ability to perceive the difference between valid and invalid answers. Further, I have confidence that if you fail in a line of reasoning, you will try again.

In the chapter on synectics, the juxtaposition of seemingly opposite traits (e.g., passionately cold, calmly furious) leads to a deeper, more sophisticated appreciation of the subject being explored. In this chapter something similar happens. By presenting different, even conflicting views, the students push each other forward in their thinking, thereby coming much closer to grasping the richness of the material presented than would have been possible without the conflict of varying perspectives.

## ■ NOTES

1. Established in 1947, the Great Books Foundation selects and publishes paperback sets of readings for discussion and administers training courses that prepare volunteers, teachers, and librarians to conduct Junior and Adult Great Books groups using the Foundation's reading materials. The Junior Great Books program is available for every grade from second through twelfth. Most Junior Great Books groups are part of school programs. Adult Great Books groups meet in libraries, offices, homes, churches, and community centers across the nation. Information is available from the Great Books Foundation, 40 East Huron Street, Chicago, Illinois, 60611. The Foundation has not sponsored and is not otherwise associated with this book.

2. The authors acknowledge that the phrases and terms "factual question," "interpretive question," and "evaluative question," as well as "follow-up question," "leader," "co-leader," and "clustering" were coined by the Great Books Foundation in the context of its explanation of shared inquiry and have been used consistently as central terms in Great Books courses and materials since 1947. See the Foundation's manual, *An Introduction to Shared Inquiry,* 1987, for Great Books' use and explanation of these terms.

3. The Great Books Foundation, *A Manual for Co-Leaders* (Chicago: The Great Books Foundation, 1965), 15–16.

4. Great Books Foundation, *Manual,* 16.

5. Great Books Foundation, *Manual,* 21–22.

6. Great Books Foundation, *Manual,* 93.

7. Compare the Great Books Foundation's explanation of "basic question" and "follow-up question" in *An Introduction to Shared Inquiry,* pp. 16–19 and pp. 28–31.

8. Great Books Foundation, *Manual,* 36.

9. Mortimer J. Adler and Charles Van Doren, *How to Read a Book* (New York: Simon & Schuster, 1972), 142–143.

10. Dolores Durkin, "What Classroom Observations Reveal about Reading Comprehension Instruction," *Reading Research Quarterly,* 14 (1978–1979): 481–533.

11. John Goodlad, *A Place Called School: Prospects for the Future* (New York: McGraw-Hill, 1984).

12. Steven Stahl and Charles Clark, "The Effects of Participatory Expectations in Classroom Discussion on the Learning of Science Vocabulary," *American Educational Research Journal* 24 (Winter 1987): 541–555.

13. Maurice P. Hunt and Lawrence P. Metcalf, *Teaching High School Social Studies* (New York: Harper & Row, 1955), 21.

14. Hunt and Metcalf, *Teaching*, 6.

15. Hunt and Metcalf, *Teaching*, 150.

16. Roger W. Holmes, *The Rhyme of Reason* (New York: Appleton-Century-Crofts, 1939), 419.

17. Lee S. Shulman, "Knowledge and Teaching: Foundations of the New Reform," *Harvard Educational Review* 57, no. 1 (February 1987): 1.

18. Shulman, "Knowledge and Teaching," 1.

19. "The Ledge," by Lawrence Sargent Hall, is one of the readings in Junior Great Books, Series Eight.

# Chapter 11

# Cooperative Learning Models

## *Improving Student Achievement Using Small Groups*

The descriptive phrase for education for the decade of the eighties may well be "thinking skills"; during the nineties, it may well become "cooperative learning." Early in their careers, most teachers discover the power and effectiveness of children teaching other children. One of the authors was introduced to the power inherent in this idea several years ago.

As a high school teacher and coordinator of an independent study program, she supervised three students preparing for the Advanced Placement European History test. She examined the sample history test and found that the first section examined overview knowledge. The second section required an in-depth essay but gave wide latitude in topic choice. The third section was document-based, testing the student's ability to think critically, manage material, and write clearly. "A good test," the teacher mused, "testing for in-depth knowledge as opposed to 'skimmer bug' knowledge."

The teacher wondered if there was a way to help these students benefit from each other in their study, so she called a member of the history department at a nearby college for assistance in planning the students' programs. "I know how specialized your department is, so you will probably laugh when I tell you I am proposing that a sophomore, junior, and senior study together and teach each other European history. To do this, I need the entire subject divided into nine broad topics, or questions. I also need suggested readings."

The professor was intrigued, provided the requested materials, and met with the students occasionally. Each student selected three of the broad questions for in-depth study and prepared to teach his peers. The students took their work seriously. Because the only knowledge they had on a particular topic came from their peers, they checked up on each other regularly. The students gained general knowledge of the subject as well as expertise in the three areas studied. The success of this approach was apparent the day of the test: the three students earned top scores! The teacher was struck by this almost untapped source of power in teaching, the students themselves.

The three models presented in this chapter are based on the work of other

This chapter was written by Dr. Phyllis Hotchkiss, Associate Professor at Midwestern State University in Witchita Falls, Texas. Dr. Hotchkiss, who was formerly at the University of Virginia, has worked extensively with cooperative learning programs and the other models of instruction discussed in this book.

167

educators who have had similar experiences with cooperative education. The models are not effective solely with advanced students. Student achievement improves for most students in almost all grade levels. Further, benefits go beyond academics in terms of improving socialization skills and building class unity.

## The Cooperative Revolution

Researcher Robert Slavin terms the cooperative education movement a *cooperative revolution*.[1] He asserts that:

> the age of cooperation is approaching. From Alaska to California to Florida to New York, from Australia to Britain to Norway to Israel, teachers and administrators are discovering an untapped resource for accelerating students' achievement: the students themselves. There is now substantial evidence that students working together in small cooperative groups can master material presented by the teacher better than can students working on their own.[2]

No doubt the concept of cooperative learning is as old as formal education. Team sports, group science projects, student drama productions, and school newspapers are but a few of the cooperative activities found in most public schools.

Much of the impetus for the current movement had its origins in the early 1970s when social scientists at the Center for Social Organization of Schools at The Johns Hopkins University were called on to help Baltimore public school teachers manage newly integrated classrooms. The teachers found that children from diverse ethnic groups tended to resegregate themselves in the classroom, lunchroom, and social settings. They sought ways to encourage students to get to know and accept each other. Shared learning activities were developed in which teams of learners could study together, tutor each other, and earn team rewards. When researchers evaluated team learning, they found that student interaction increased, acceptance of minority students improved, as did the self-esteem of all students.

On another important variable—student achievement—improvement was reported also. Academic achievement gains have been found to occur with such consistency that increased achievement has become one of the principal positive outcomes of cooperative learning. In a summary of 35 studies, Slavin reported positive achievement gains for students in 83 percent of the studies. In none of the studies were positive gains reported for control classrooms.[3]

In essence, students' opportunities to learn increase to the extent that increased achievement is nearly inevitable. In traditional classes, most of students' experience with content is limited to listening and notetaking. In cooperative classrooms, students listen, write, tell, paraphrase, read, illustrate, repeat, and interact. In short, increased modalities are involved so that students who are not aural learners or are poor notetakers have many opportunities to explore materials. Students are actively involved with the subject matter rather than being passive receivers of information. Consequently, engaged time tends to increase in cooperative learning classes. The positive relationship between engaged time and student achievement is well documented.[4] Because they are working in small groups, students are less reluctant, generally, to ask clarifying questions and receive corrective feedback.

Every teacher has had the experience of explaining a concept repeatedly, only to hear "I don't get it" from students; then a knowledgeable student explains and the concept is understood. At times, students find language to communicate when adults cannot. In the same vein, students are more likely to know and remember information they have taught. When students are responsible for teaching content, they have opportunities to learn during the preparation *and* presentation experiences, and retention of the information increases.

In summary, academic achievement increases with the implementation of cooperative learning strategies because students have numerous opportunities to learn new materials. If deficiencies are noted, correction tends to be nonthreatening for students.

## Preparing Students for Group Work

What social skills must we help students develop in conjunction with their knowledge base? Certainly we want to prepare students to work *independently*. Given the amount of time spent working on independent seatwork, students appear to have ample practice to acquire this skill. Working *competitively* must be considered to be important. Students in traditional classrooms often compete for grades, the teacher's attention, and help with their work. Indeed, *competition* appears to take on more importance in schools than in other social settings.

Working *cooperatively*, however, may be the most critical social skill that students learn, when one considers the importance of cooperation in the workplace, in the family, and in leisure activities. If there were no other benefits, the importance of learning to collaborate would justify building a part of the school experience around cooperative learning activities. But occasions for cooperation are relatively rare during students' academic careers.

Two prominent cooperative education advocates, David Johnson and Roger Johnson, compared traditional classrooms with cooperative classrooms.[5] Their comparison is reproduced in Table 11.1.

Johnson and Johnson have identified five elements critical to implementing cooperative learning successfully.

> The first is what we call "positive interdependence." The students really have to believe they're in it together, sink or swim. They have to care about each other's learning. Second is a lot of verbal, face-to-face interaction. Students have to explain, argue, elaborate, and tie in the material they learn today with what they had last week.

**TABLE 11.1**    Comparison of Traditional and Cooperative Learning Groups

| Cooperative Learning Groups | Traditional Learning Groups |
| --- | --- |
| Positive interdependence | No interdependence |
| Individual accountability | No individual accountability |
| Heterogeneous | Homogeneous |
| Shared leadership | One appointed leader |
| Shared responsibility for each other | Responsibility only for self |
| Task and maintenance emphasized | Only task emphasized |
| Social skills directly taught | Social skills assumed and ignored |
| Teacher observes and intervenes | Teacher ignores group function |
| Groups process their effectiveness | No group processing |

*Source:* D. W. Johnson and R. T. Johnson, *Circles of Learning* (Alexandria, VA: Association for Supervision and Curriculum Development, 1984), 10.

The third element is individual accountability. It must be clear that every member of their group has to learn, that there's no hitchhiking. . . .

The fourth element is social skills. Students need to be taught appropriate leadership, communication, trust building, and conflict resolution skills so they can operate effectively.

The fifth element is what we call "group processing." Periodically the groups have to assess how well they are working together and how they could do better.[6]

Before beginning cooperative learning, inexperienced students may benefit from simulating effective group procedures. Moving quietly into groups, alternating speakers, attending to the speaker, remaining in the group for the duration of the activity, and allowing all group members an opportunity to participate can be practiced.

Speaking and listening skills deserve attention also. Rhoads and McCabe have noted that the four communication skills—reading, writing, speaking, and listening—get uneven treatment in most schools.[7] Reading and writing are the primary focus in most classrooms; outside of school, speaking and listening are the important communication skills. In cooperative classrooms, speaking and listening acquire increased emphasis.

Initial speaking skills that must be taught include methods of getting the listener's attention by calling his or her name or saying a simple phrase such as, "May I ask you a question?" Next, a skillful speaker makes eye contact and expresses his or her message in the first person. For example, the speaker may say, "I think there are several permissible answers," rather than "They said the answer was (b)."

Effective speakers learn to state their thoughts clearly, concisely, and completely.[8] Giving adequate background information to put thoughts in context without losing the main point in detail is a skill requiring practice. For complex concepts, students should learn to rely on visual aids, notes, and outlines, following the examples of competent teachers. Periodic checks for understanding are exercised as well. Questions regarding the content or simply checking for comprehension—Are you following this?—serve this purpose.

Listening skills include giving attention to the speaker, interrupting if the message is unclear, asking clarifying questions, or paraphrasing the speaker's points. Awareness of and responsiveness to nonverbal messages require practice as well.

Constructive use of group meeting time can be encouraged in several ways. Fostering utilization of problem-solving strategies may provide the means of resolving conflict as well as affording opportunities for applying strategies learned in the academic setting to real-life situations.

The same may be said for implementing critical-thinking strategies. Students have the opportunity to share the process employed in reaching conclusions by thinking out loud; that is, verbalizing their thinking step by step as solutions to problems are sought. In short, cooperative learning groups provide an excellent chance for applying skills learned in content areas.

Jigsaw II, Teams-Games-Tournaments (TGT), and Student Teams-Academic Division (STAD) are cooperative learning models that have been well researched and are widely used in classrooms. Each is described in this chapter and, for purposes of illustration, examples or scenarios are used to help explain the steps.

## Steps in the Jigsaw II Model

1. Introduce Jigsaw II
2. Assign heterogeneously grouped students to study teams
3. Assemble expert groups
4. Experts teach their study teams
5. Evaluate and provide team recognition

Jigsaw II is used when students are assigned narrative materials to read and learn. The original Jigsaw was developed by Elliot Aronson to increase students' interdependence.[9] Instead of providing each student with all materials to study independently, Aronson assigned students to teams and gave each team member one piece of information. To have all components of the lesson, students were forced to fit their individual pieces together as if they were working a jigsaw *puzzle*. The puzzle could not be completed unless each team member shared his or her piece.

### ■ Step 1—Introduce Jigsaw II

Jigsaw II may be introduced with an explanation similar to the following:

> To help you learn the materials in our new unit, you will be studying with a small group of your classmates, which will be called your study team.

There will be four members on your team and each of you will be responsible for learning as much as you can about one topic that is important to your team. To help you learn, you will have opportunities to study with other classmates who are assigned the same topic. We call this your expert group. When you become an expert on your topic, you will teach your study team everything you have learned. You will be working for an individual grade and a team score. The team with the highest score will be announced in the school newspaper and will be first in the lunchroom for one week.

### ■ Step 2—Assign Heterogeneously Grouped Students to Study Teams

Jigsaw II is like other cooperative learning strategies in that students are assigned to heterogeneously grouped teams formed by the classroom teacher. By controlling team assignments, the teacher may ensure that teams are balanced in terms of ability, motivation, gender, race, and other factors deemed important. When students are allowed to choose teammates, friendships tend to determine team membership and many of the advantages of cooperative learning are lost.

To form study groups, students were ranked according to ability and past performance on similar materials. The teacher decided to assign her 24 students to six teams, with four students on each team. To determine team membership, she began with Mary and numbered the students from one to six. Reversing the order of numbering with each six students, groups of students (study teams) were formed by putting ones, twos, threes, fours, fives, and sixes together. Thus, each group has one high achiever, two average achievers, and one low achiever. The procedure is illustrated in Table 11.2.

After the teacher assigned students to study teams, each team met to get acquainted and select a team name. Each team constructed a display chart for the bulletin board announcing their team name and membership. Team names and membership for this example appear in Table 11.3.

After the study teams are assembled and a name is selected, the rules are announced that govern behavior during team meetings:

1. No student may leave his or her team area until all students have completed the assigned work;
2. Each team member is responsible for ascertaining that his or her teammates understand and can complete the assignment successfully; and
3. If a student has difficulty in understanding any part of the assignment, all teammates are asked for assistance before inquiries are made of the teacher.

The social studies unit for one fifth-grade class was entitled, "The Black American Experience." The study focused on the black civil rights movement of the 1950s and 1960s. Background about the topic came from "Choices about Rights and Opportunities" in the Scott, Foresman text *America Past and*

**TABLE 11.2    Study Group Formation**

| Ability Level | Class List | |
|---|---|---|
| High ability | Mary | 1 |
| | Beth | 2 |
| | Jim | 3 |
| | Bob | 4 |
| | Arlene | 5 |
| | Jake | 6 |
| High average ability | Kathy | 6 |
| | Richard | 5 |
| | Billy | 4 |
| | Martha | 3 |
| | Joanne | 2 |
| | Jackson | 1 |
| Low average ability | Martin | 1 |
| | Simone | 2 |
| | Paul | 3 |
| | Sonny | 4 |
| | Laurie | 5 |
| | Wayne | 6 |
| Low ability | Dionne | 6 |
| | Taylor | 5 |
| | Sammie | 4 |
| | Gus | 3 |
| | David | 2 |
| | Sandra | 1 |

**TABLE 11.3    Study Teams**

| 1 Warriors | 2 Scholars | 3 Moguls | 4 Superstars | 5 Winners | 6 Tigers |
|---|---|---|---|---|---|
| Mary | Beth | Jim | Bob | Arlene | Jake |
| Jackson | Joanne | Martha | Billy | Richard | Kathy |
| Martin | Simone | Paul | Sonny | Laurie | Wayne |
| Sandra | David | Gus | Sammie | Taylor | Dionne |

*Present.*[10] In preparation for Jigsaw II, *Martin Luther King, Jr.: The Man Who Climbed the Mountain*[11] was read to the students, and news videos from the era were viewed. Terms and phrases, such as *civil rights, separate but equal, integrate, segregate,* and *discriminate* were also discussed. Study teams read the appropriate text chapter, assisting each other in reading as necessary.

### ■ Step 3—Assemble Expert Groups

After completing the reading, each student in a study team is assigned an expert topic. Mary, a member of the Warriors, received the expert sheet, "Working Against Discrimination." Mary had the following four questions, provided by her teacher, to research and learn:

1. What was the subject of the 1954 decision, *Brown* v. *Board of Education of Topeka?* Why did the case go to the Supreme Court?
2. In what ways did segregation affect the lives of southern blacks and whites?
3. What protest strategies did opponents to segregation use? What were the results?
4. What roles did the federal government play in ending segregation? How were federal actions enforced?

Jackson, Martin, and Sandra were given expert sheets with three different sets of questions pertaining to three other topics discussed in the chapter. Jackson's topic was "The Contributions of Rosa Parks," Martin's was "Participation of Other Minority Groups," and Sandra's topic was "The Women's Movement."

The same four expert topics were assigned to team members in the remaining study teams. All students with the same topic to research met to devise the best possible answers to their questions. Mary, Beth, Martha, Sonny, Taylor, and Wayne researched "Working Against Discrimination" together. When the experts had a clear understanding of their topic, they planned teaching strategies for presenting the information to study team members.

### ■ Step 4—Experts Teach Their Study Teams

When all students master their expert topics, study teams are reassembled and the experts teach their topics in turn. Each expert is responsible for teaching his or her topic, checking for understanding, and assisting teammates in learning the material.

### ■ Step 5—Evaluate and Provide Team Recognition

On completion of Jigsaw II, students are tested

1. to identify what, if anything, must be retaught
2. to assign grades, and
3. to calculate team scores.

Prior to beginning Jigsaw II, a *base score* is established for each student by averaging past grades. The base scores for the *Warriors* were:

| Student | Base Score |
|---------|------------|
| Mary | 89 |
| Jackson | 82 |
| Martin | 100 |
| Sandra | 73 |

Slavin developed the scale shown in Table 11.4 to determine improvement points, which are figured by computing the difference between base scores and Jigsaw II quiz results.

The team score is determined by adding the improvement points for each team member and averaging. Team recognition is based on the team improvement score. The Warrior's team improvement score was 20, as shown in Table 11.5. As promised, the team with the highest improvement score was announced in the school newspaper and led the lunch line for one week.

**TABLE 11.4    Improvement Points Scale**

| Quiz Score | Improvement Points |
|------------|--------------------|
| More that 10 points below base score | 0 |
| 10 points below to base score | 10 |
| Base score to 10 points above base score | 20 |
| More than 10 points above base score | 30 |
| Perfect paper (regardless of base score) | 30 |

*Source:* Robert Slavin, *Using Student Team Learning,* rev. ed. (Baltimore: Center for Social Organization of Schools, Johns Hopkins University, 1980), 19.

**TABLE 11.5    Warrior's Team Improvement Scoring**

| Student | Base score | Jigsaw II score | Improvement | Improvement Score |
|---------|-----------|-----------------|-------------|-------------------|
| Mary | 89 | 94 | 5 | 20 |
| Jackson | 82 | 71 | −11 | 0 |
| Martin | 83 | 100 | perfect | 30 |
| Sandra | 73 | 88 | 15 | 30 |
| Total Team Improvement Points | | | | 80 |
| Number of Team Members | | | | 4 |
| Team Score | | | | 20 |

## Steps in the Teams-Games-Tournaments (TGT) Model

1. Present a new concept
2. Form heterogeneously grouped study teams and practice
3. Participate in academic competition
4. Recognize winning teams

Originated by David Devries and Keith Edwards, TGT was the first cooperative learning method devised by researchers in social sciences at The Johns Hopkins University.[12] According to Slavin, TGT "is most appropriate for teaching well-defined objectives with single right answers, such as mathematical computations and applications, language usage and mechanics, geography and map skills, and science concepts."[13] When all students have had the opportunity to study cooperatively, academic tournaments are held where students compete for team points and recognition. The tournaments offer a refreshing change of pace from normal class routines.

The steps of this model are presented using an example of students learning to solve equations without grouping symbols.

### ■ Step 1—Present a New Concept

Having completed lessons on using grouping symbols (i.e., parentheses and brackets) to indicate the order in which mathematical operations are performed, students are taught to solve equations when no grouping symbols are used. Using the direct instruction model, the rule for order of operations is presented:

*Rule for Order of Operations (when there are no grouping symbols)*

1. Perform all multiplications and divisions in order from left to right.
2. Perform all additions and subtractions in order from left to right.

Numerous examples are used to illustrate the rule, such as:

- $2 + 6 \times 3 = 20$ (6 is multiplied by 3, and then the product is added to two.)
- $18 - 12 \div 3 + 1 = 15$ (12 is divided by 3, then the answer, 4, is subtracted from 18, with the result, 14. To that, 1 is added with the net of 15.)

During guided practice, students work sample problems individually to demonstrate understanding of the rule.

### ■ Step 2—Form Heterogeneously Grouped Study Teams and Practice

For additional practice, the class is divided into heterogeneous study groups following the procedures described for Jigsaw II. Within a study group, each student has the opportunity to restate the rule for order of operations to a peer as she applied it to the problems. Further, each student gets immediate feedback, thereby decreasing the likelihood of incorrect practice. Each student is responsible for seeing that teammates understand and can apply the rule.

Each team is given two worksheets with math problems similar to those provided during guided practice and two answer sheets. Working together in pairs, the teammates solve the problems, explain to each other how answers were obtained, and check their work with the answer sheet.

### ■ Step 3—Participate in Academic Competition

Students have the opportunity to demonstrate how well they have learned the rule for order of operations on tournament day. Competing in newly formed groups, students play academic games to earn points for their teams during the tournament.

To keep the competition fair, students are assigned to tournament tables with three students each, based on their past performance and ability in math. The tournament table assignments are shown in Table 11.6.

At Tournament Table I, the cards are shuffled and the play begins. Mary, designated as first reader, is given the game sheet shown in Figure 11.1. She turns over the first card in the deck, reads the problem aloud, and begins working. Beth, first challenger, and Jim, second challenger, work the problem concurrently. When Mary announces her answer, Beth has the option of passing, if she believes Mary's response is correct, or challenging, if she believes it is incorrect. If Beth passes, Jim has the *pass* or *challenge* options. If Mary's response is correct, she keeps the numbered card, which will be used in tallying her final score.

Let's follow several rounds of play to illustrate game procedures. Mary turns over card #5 with the problem $54 - 42 \div 7 = $ ____. When the three students have had the opportunity to calculate the answer, Mary responds with the answer <u>48</u>. Beth passes, as does Jim who checks the answer sheet after passing. He ascertains that Mary is correct and she adds card #5 to her collection. The game sheet is passed to Beth, who turns over card #11 for the problem $6 \times 6 + 5 = $ ____. Beth's answer, <u>66</u>, is challenged by Jim who says that the correct response is <u>41</u>. Mary consults the answer sheet and finds that Jim has the right answer, and he keeps the card. The game sheet is then passed to Jim who draws #21, $9 \times 7 - 2 = $ ____. Jim's answer, <u>61</u>, is accepted by Mary, but challenged

**TABLE 11.6**  Tournament Table Assignments

| Table I | Table II | Table III | Table IV | Table V | Table VI | Table VII | Table VIII |
|---------|----------|-----------|----------|---------|----------|-----------|------------|
| Mary | Bob | Kathy | Martha | Martin | Sonny | Dionne | Gus |
| Beth | Arlene | Richard | Joanne | Paul | Laurie | Taylor | David |
| Jim | Jake | Billy | Jackson | Simone | Wayne | Sammie | Sandra |

| Game Sheet | | Answer Sheet | |
|---|---|---|---|
| 1. | $6 + 7 + 3 - 4 =$ | 1. | 12 |
| 2. | $12 \times 4 + 5 \times 2 =$ | 2. | 58 |
| 3. | $7 + 8 + 12 \div 2 =$ | 3. | 21 |
| 4. | $6 \div 2 + 5 \times 4 =$ | 4. | 23 |
| 5. | $54 - 42 \div 7 =$ | 5. | 48 |
| 6. | $21 \div 7 + 4 \times 11 =$ | 6. | 47 |
| 7. | $15 \times 15 \div 5 \times 3 =$ | 7. | 135 |
| 8. | $9 \times 16 - 30 \div 6 - 3 =$ | 8. | 136 |
| 9. | $72 \div 9 \times 4 \div 4 =$ | 9. | 8 |
| 10. | $12 - 5 + 9 - 2 =$ | 10. | 14 |
| 11. | $6 \times 6 + 5 =$ | 11. | 41 |
| 12. | $15 + 20 \div 4 - 5 =$ | 12. | 15 |
| 13. | $36 \div 9 + 7 - 6 =$ | 13. | 5 |
| 14. | $36 \div 9 \times 3 =$ | 14. | 12 |
| 15. | $6 \times 3 \div 9 - 1 =$ | 15. | 1 |
| 16. | $5 + 2 \times 2 \times 2 =$ | 16. | 13 |
| 17. | $4 \times 4 + 2 \times 2 \times 2 \times 5 =$ | 17. | 56 |
| 18. | $24 \div 6 \times 4 =$ | 18. | 16 |
| 19. | $24 \div 8 - 2 =$ | 19. | 1 |
| 20. | $96 \div 12 \times 4 \div 2 =$ | 20. | 16 |
| 21. | $9 \times 7 - 2 =$ | 21. | 61 |

**FIGURE 11.1** Sample game sheet for teaching
order of operations

by Beth who says the correct answer is 45. Finding the correct answer to be 61, Jim keeps the card and Beth forfeits a card that she had won previously by returning it to the deck.

The rules for game play may be summarized as follows:

**1.** Each tournament table has three players of equal ability.

**2.** The three players are designated as *reader*, who has the opportunity to answer the problem after turning over the card, *first challenger*, and *second challenger*.

**3.** After the reader has supplied an answer, the first and second challengers either pass or challege the reader's answer. If the reader is correct, he or she keeps the card. If one of the challengers is correct, he or she is given the card. If the challenger is incorrect, he or she must forfeit a previously won card.[14]

**4.** When the problem has been correctly answered, the game sheet and answer sheet are shifted one player to the left. Therefore, during the second round of play, the first challenger becomes the reader, the second challenger becomes the first challenger, and so forth. Play is repeated until the deck of cards is exhausted.

**TABLE 11.7**  Calculating Tournament Points for a Three-Player Game

| Player | No Ties | Tie For Top Score | Tie For Low Score | 3-Way Tie |
|---|---|---|---|---|
| Top scorer | 60 | 50 | 60 | 40 |
| Middle scorer | 40 | 50 | 30 | 40 |
| Low scorer | 20 | 20 | 30 | 40 |
| Total Points | 120 | | | |

*Note:* In the event that a tournament table has two players, 80 points are allocated between the two players—60 points for the top scorer and 20 points for the low scorer. In case of a tie, each player is awarded 40 points.

Four-player teams share 150 points.

### Scoring the Game

The total number of points allocated to the players at each tournament table is 120. Players are instructed to count their cards to determine their scores. The player with the most cards earns 60 points; the player in second place earns 40; and the player in third place wins 20 points. Points awarded in cases with ties are shown in Table 11.7.

After totaling tournament points, players return to their study teams, team scores are calculated and averaged, and the accomplishments of the various teams are recognized.

### ■ Step 4—Recognize Winning Teams

Suggested recognitions include posting the names of top-scoring team members on the bulletin board, awarding certificates, and sending notes home to parents. Extra recess time, first in lines, extra time on preferred tasks, or no weekend homework are other ways that academic accomplishment may be rewarded.

## Steps in the Student Teams-Achievement Division (STAD) Model

1. Present a new concept
2. Form teams for study and practice
3. Test students on newly learned materials
4. Recognize winning teams

Student Teams-Achievement Division (STAD) was developed in response to teachers who were uncomfortable with assigning grades on the basis of team scores earned in TGT. Consequently, the tournament phase was replaced with a quiz or test, following team study and practice.

### ■ Step 1—Present a New Concept

Like TGT, STAD is designed for meeting well-defined instructional objectives. Because of the nature of content for which STAD is appropriate, many teachers use a direct instruction model for the presentation of new materials. In this example, the objective is to teach students to apply five rules for forming plurals of nouns. Each rule is followed by examples of that rule.

**1.** Most nouns form plurals by adding *s* to the singular form.

girl, girls          tiger, tigers          toy, toys
shirt, shirts        angel, angels          willow, willows

**2.** Some nouns ending in *f* or *fe* form the plural by changing the ending to *ve* before adding *s*.

wife, wives          leaf, leaves
life, lives          self, selves

**3.** Singular nouns ending in *s, sh, ch,* or *x* form the plural by adding *es*.

fox, foxes           kiss, kisses
wish, wishes         church, churches

**4.** Nouns ending in *o* preceded by a vowel usually form the plural by adding *s*.

radio, radios        ratio, ratios
zoo, zoos            rodeo, rodeos

**5.** Nouns ending in *o* preceded by a consonant form the plural in one of two ways: for some nouns, add -s; for others, add -es. For a few nouns, either is correct. Check the dictionary when you are unsure.

hero, heros              zero, zeros
potato, potatoes         tomato, tomatoes
memento, mementos, mementoes

During guided practice the teacher asertains that the students understand how to apply the five plural rules.

### ■ Step 2—Form Teams for Study and Practice

Following the procedures outlined for TGT, divide students into homogeneously grouped study teams. Each team has one member from the high-ability, high-average-ability, low-average-ability, and low-ability groups. When the study teams are formed, worksheets and answer sheets are provided for team study.

■ **Step 3—Test Students on Newly Learned Materials**

It is in this step that STAD departs from the TGT model. Individual quizzes, rather than games, are administered following team study. Each student is required to complete his or her quiz independently and submit it to the teacher for individual scoring and team scoring. Teams are rewarded for improvement over past performance, and scoring procedures are the same as those used for TGT.

■ **Step 4—Recognize Winning Teams**

In STAD, teams are recognized just as they are following Tournament Day in TGT. Non-material, motivating rewards, such as recognition in the class newsletter or congratulations by the school principal, are recommended.

## Pointers for Using Cooperative Learning Teams Effectively

It is recommended that study teams be changed at the beginning of each new unit or every five to six weeks. Changing teams will avoid establishing cliques, allowing many students to get to know and like each other as they study together. Further, if a team appears to be weak academically, students are not penalized over a long period of time.

In Jigsaw II, students grow more sophisticated in identifying main ideas and important information for their expert sheets, thus fewer guides may be given, encouraging students to become independent learners. References other than textbooks may be incorporated, along with interviews, films, videos, and original sources.

**TABLE 11.8**  Suggested Calendar for Cooperative Learning Acitivities

|        | Monday | Tuesday | Wednesday | Thursday | Friday |
|--------|--------|---------|-----------|----------|--------|
| Jigsaw | Introduce new topic | Read new materials | Expert group study | Teach study teams | Quiz, team |
| TGT | Introduce new topic | Review, guided practice | Team study | Team study | Tournament, team rewards |
| STAD | Introduce new topic | Review, guided practice | Team study | Team study | Quiz team rewards |

Both TGT and STAD provide frequent opportunities for practice, thus increasing the probability that information will be committed to long-term memory. In addition, using these strategies motivates students to review for quizzes and tests.

## Scenario

In science class, Ms. Wright planned a unit on reptiles combining concept development and Jigsaw II. During the introduction she asked students to tell her everything they knew about snakes. Their responses were listed on the chalkboard.

| | |
|---|---|
| they're slimy | they lay eggs |
| they're cold blooded | they are poison |
| they kill people | they eat rats |
| they live in nests | they live in water or deserts |
| they can be huge – 20 feet long | some are little, green snakes |
| snakes have scales | they don't have legs |
| they hatch out of eggs | they can climb trees |
| people are afraid of them | they are mean and vicious |
| some help by killing rodents | they use their tongues to smell |
| they eat animals whole | some poison, but some squeeze |
| some have rattles | they hiss |
| forked tongues | mothers leave eggs |
| on their own when born | leathery eggs |
| fast runners | bury eggs in sand |
| poison with their tongues | they live in holes |

Next, Ms. Wright asked the children to list items that seemed to go together. They produced the following categories and labels:

| *Physical Characteristics* | *Reproduction* |
|---|---|
| slimy | hatch out of eggs |
| cold blooded | lay eggs |
| poison | bury eggs in sand |
| not all are poison | mothers leave eggs |
| huge – 20 feet long | on their own when born |
| eat animals whole | leathery eggs |
| some have rattles | |
| don't have legs | |
| some little, green | |
| use tongues to smell | |

| *Defenses* | *Habitat* |
|---|---|
| poison | live in nests |
| some squeeze | live in holes |
| hiss | live in desert |
| mean and vicious | live in water |
| kill people | climb trees |
| people are afraid of them | born in sand |
| fast runners | |

Students were ready for Jigsaw II! Each study team member was assigned one topic to study. On the Scholars team, for example, Beth was responsible for "Physical Characteristics"; Joanne was allotted "Reproduction"; Paul, "Defense"; and David, "Habitat." After receiving assignments, the experts assembled to copy the information generated during the concept formation exercise onto retrieval charts. For the following two class periods, team members researched their topics to correct misinformation and add new details to the retrieval charts. Affirming that the new information was correct and complete, experts prepared to teach their study teams.

Ms. Wright used this procedure to direct the study of lizards, turtles and tortoises, alligators and crocodiles, and tuatara so that students could understand and make generalizations regarding reptiles.

### Activity 11.1

Select a chapter from a content-area text. List four or five important subtopics presented and develop expert question sheets for each subtopic. Select an appropriate model of teaching that can be combined with Jigsaw II to provide an introduction to the chapter. ■

### ■ SUMMARY

In traditional classes, most of the students' experience with content is limited to listening and notetaking. In cooperative classrooms, students listen, write, tell, paraphrase, read, illustrate, repeat, and interact. They are given multiple learning opportunities and generally show greater achievement gains than students in traditional classes. Students are actively involved with the subject matter rather than being passive receivers of information. Because they are working in small groups, even reticent students tend to enter discussions and ask clarifying questions.

## ■ NOTES

1. Robert Slavin, "The Cooperative Revolution Catches Fire," *The School Administrator* 44 (January 1988): 9–13.

2. Robert Slavin, "Cooperative Learning and the Cooperative School," *Educational Leadership* 47 (November 1987): 7–13.

3. Robert Slavin, *Using Student Team Learning,* rev. ed. (Baltimore: Center for Social Organization of Schools, Johns Hopkins University, 1980), 11.

4. Thomas L. Good and Jere E. Brophy, *Looking in Classrooms* 3rd ed. (New York: Harper & Row, 1984), 35.

5. D. W. Johnson and R. T. Johnson, *Circles of Learning* (Alexandria, VA: Association for Supervision and Curriculum Development, 1984), 8–10.

6. Ron Brandt, "On Cooperation in Schools: A Conversation with David and Roger Johnson," *Educational Leadership* 47 (November 1987): 14–25.

7. Jacqueline Rhoades and Margaret E. McCabe, *Simple Cooperation in the Classroom* (Willits, CA: ITA Publications, 1986).

8. Rhoades and McCabe, *Simple Cooperation,* 25.

9. Elliot Aronson, *The Jigsaw Classroom* (Beverly Hills: Sage Publications, 1978).

10. Joan Schreiber et al., *America Past and Present* (Glenview, IL: Scott, Foresman, 1983).

11. Gary Paulsen and Dan Theis, *Martin Luther King, Jr.: The Man Who Climbed the Mountain* (Milwaukee, WI: Raintree, 1976).

12. See D. L. DeVries, K. J. Edwards, and R. E. Slavin, "Biracial Learning Teams and Race Relations in the Classroom: Four Field Experiments on Teams-Games-Tournaments," *Journal of Educational Psychology* 70 (1978): 356–362; D. DeVries, P. Lucasse, and S. Shackman, "Small Group Versus Individualized Instruction: A Field Test of Their Relative Effectiveness" (Paper presented at the annual meeting of the American Psychological Association, New York, 1979); and D. L. DeVries and R. E. Slavin, Teams-Games-Tournaments (TGT): Review of Ten Classroom Experiments, *Journal of Research and Development in Education* 12 (1978): 28–38.

13. Slavin, *Team Learning,* 6.

14. This is to assure that players do not challenge at random but think through the problem and have an alternate response. Notice that there is no penalty for an incorrect response from the reader, just positive reinforcement for correct responses.

# Chapter 12

# Exploration of Feelings and Resolution of Conflict Model

The Mock Turtle, the Gryphon, and Alice were discussing education. The Mock Turtle said with a sigh,

> " 'I only took the regular course.'
> 'What was that?' enquired Alice.
> 'Reeling and Writhing, of course, to begin with,' the Mock Turtle replied; 'and then the different branches of Arithmetic – Ambition, Distraction, Uglification and Derision.' "
>
> The Gryphon, who had gone to the Classical master, declared, " 'He was an old crab, HE was.'
> 'I never went to him,' the Mock Turtle said with a sigh. 'He taught Laughing and Grief. . . .' "[1]

Hilda Taba might have applauded the topics included in the education of the Mock Turtle and the Gryphon, because she believed that engaging the emotions of the learner was essential to effective learning. In the model presented in this chapter, Taba offers precise questioning techniques for the exploration and study of feelings.[2] Once again, she stresses the importance of inductive questioning (discussed in Chapter 7). She asserts that the first step toward achieving a fair stance in conflict situations involves looking at the situation from the point of view of everyone involved, particularly those whose perspectives differ from one's own.

The first of the two strategies, Exploration of Feelings, presents a step-by-step process through which students, from elementary school through high school, explore their feelings and discuss situations from several different vantage points. Then they discuss the causes and the effects of those feelings. The data here can be emotions, actions, and behavior, as well as facts, ideas, and concepts. If used regularly, this process can help students attain a greater understanding of others and a broader perspective about the events and ideas that occur around them.

The first step of this model involves choosing a conflict to discuss. This conflict may derive from a curriculum or course of study: literature, history, science, or mathematics; or from events in the immediate world of the learners. The possibilities are endless.

Discoveries in science are presenting us with very difficult dilemmas. For example, research findings, particularly in medicine, depend heavily on the use of test animals. Are we violating these animals' rights? What about the rights of human beings to new discoveries? The second strategy, resolution of conflict, will introduce students to a process of arriving at constructive resolutions.

Modern medicine is allowing people to live much longer, but the quality and dignity of that life for those who are very ill is minimal. In some instances we are prolonging life where a patient cannot think or express her- or himself. How are the family members of the patient feeling? Do they know the patient's views on situations like this? Learning to view situations from different perspectives and becoming more sensitive to others' views will be crucial if we are to arrive at more just decisions. Scientists cannot remain isolated from the moral dilemmas they create.

Literature is built upon conflict. The teacher may stop reading a short story, novel, or play immediately after the central conflict arises in order to discuss the feelings of the different characters involved in the conflict. Then the teacher could ask how the students would resolve the conflict if they were the author, given the characters involved. The students should not decide what *they* would do, but, given what they know of the characters in the story, how they think those characters will resolve the conflict.

After finishing the story, the students can compare their resolutions with the author's. If they differ, what reasons might the author have had for choosing his or her resolution? Finally, what would the students, themselves, have done if they had been characters in the story? Why would they have acted in such a manner? Encourage them to express the values that dictated their resolution.

The model is particularly relevant for social studies. History is rife with conflict, and students need to be encouraged to view those conflicts from different vantage points in order to better empathize with the persons involved. In addition, the model may be used to discuss an actual happening from current events, from school activities, or from the students' lives.

Because the model is personally relevant, it can contribute to a healthier classroom atmosphere. Looking at conflicts and talking about feelings together does much to foster camaraderie and team spirit within a class. This sense of team spirit in turn produces an environment in which students are less apt to become discipline problems, and, if students do exhibit behavior problems, the class is much less apt to support the misbehaving students. Class attention and peer support are often motives for disruptive behavior. By talking with students, by listening to them, by valuing their opinions, and by showing empathy for their point of view, you instill a respect for others and for your role as teacher. By discussing relevant conflict situations, you also help students find more appropriate ways to feel important than by being disruptive.

This model emcompasses two separate strategies: (1) *exploration of feelings* and (2) *resolution of conflict*. It was Taba's belief that constructive resolutions to conflicts can only occur when the persons involved are sensitive to and aware of the feelings of others.[3] Thus, the first strategy should be performed several times, until students become more adept at understanding and expressing how the other person feels, and why he or she feels that way.

Performed alone, the exploration of feelings strategy has great merit because students—and adults—seldom articulate their own feelings or the causes of those feelings; they simply act on them. Teachers should use the first strategy several times, until they feel comfortable with the process, before proceeding to the second strategy.

In the resolution of conflict strategy, students again discuss the feelings (Steps 1 and 2) of those involved in the conflict. Then they propose resolutions, defend those resolutions, and explore how those resolutions would make each of the persons involved feel. Frequently, students in conflict situations, caught up in the emotion of the moment, see only extreme solutions: take violent action or do nothing. The latter is usually viewed by students as a weak response.

Often milder steps are more effective than strong action in bringing about a healthy resolution or a reconciliation of opposing positions. Sometimes students are surprised to see that doing nothing can be a mature response.

## Steps in the Exploration of Feelings Strategy

After selecting the conflict (a synopsis of an actual event or a selection from literature or history, etc.) and presenting the material, have the students:

1. List all the *facts* pertinent to the conflict.
2. Make inferences about how the persons involved were feeling.
3. Hypothesize as to why these people probably felt as they did.
4. Describe similar experiences the students may have had, as well as their feelings at the time and the reasons for those feelings.
5. Compare their feelings with the feelings of the people in the situation being analyzed.[4]

The conflict examined in the following steps is an exchange between an assistant principal and a student.

> Assistant principal: James, you know the rules here . . . no fighting. Why can't you obey them?
>
> James: Ed started it.
>
> Assistant principal: The other students all say you hit Ed first.
>
> James: He started it.
>
> Assistant principal: This is the second time you've been in my office for fighting. That means I've got to suspend you. I warned you. Why did you start another fight?
>
> James: I didn't start it. He did.

Assistant principal: He started it . . . he started it. That's all you can say. Everyone else said you started it. First you start a fight, then you lie about it.

James, raising his voice: I never lie!

Assistant principal: All right. That does it. Don't you ever raise your voice at me. You're suspended for one week. When you come back, you'll have to be accompanied by a parent.

James: My Dad'll never come here!

Following are the steps in detail, adopted from Taba,[5] with focusing questions to initiate each step. When performing this strategy, repeat each question, giving several students a chance to respond. Make a habit of repeating the same probing question in different words after you have gotten an answer, even a particularly good answer. Students will catch on to the fact that the previous answers were not wrong. Motives are complex; people usually have several reasons for acting. Different students will bring different motives to light. The situation in this scenario is quite simple; most conflicts are more complicated.

### ■ Step 1—List All the Facts about What Happened

*Key Interrogative:* What?

You will need to record the students' responses to Step 1 so they are visible to all students. (An acetate transparency or an overhead projector works well for this.) The answers to this step provide the data base for the rest of the discussion, and you or the students may need to refer to it.

#### Sample Questions

**1.** What are some of the things that happened in the conversation we just heard? (story you just read? film you just saw? chapter you just finished? etc.)

**2.** What did you hear (see, read) about this situation? (Ask several students.)

**3.** What did the assistant principal say? (Ask more than one student.)

**4.** What did James say? (Repeat this line of questioning as many times as you think necessary to get a fairly complete picture. Write down only specific answers to what James *said,* not how he may have felt or why. With practice, the students will learn to name the facts about what happened. An example of irrelevant data would be inferences about how James may have felt. That will come later.)

#### Sample Data Base

Two people talking
Assistant principal thinks James started a fight

James says he did not start the fight
Assistant principal relies on word of other students
James says Ed started it
Assistant principal accuses James of lying
Assistant principal suspends James

### ■ Step 2—Students Make Inferences

*Key Interrogative:* How?

#### Sample Questions

1. How do you think the assistant principal was feeling when he talked to James? (Repeat the question after it has been answered. One student may respond that he was frustrated, another may think he was angry.)
2. How was James feeling when he talked to the assistant principal? (Repeat question.)
3. How did the assistant principal act toward James?
4. How did James act toward the assistant principal?

There are only two main characters in this situation, but you should ask how each of the main characters in any conflict was feeling.

The exchange between James and the assistant principal was very unsatisfactory. We learned little about the actual fight, but we tended to feel James was being treated unfairly, however culpable he may have been. As we read the exchange, we sensed that emotions escalated unnecessarily.

It would be helpful if the students understood, which the assistant principal should have, that there are other ways of starting a fight besides striking the first physical blow. It would be helpful, too, if they understood that an assistant principal's job is not an easy one, that he may have been tired or frustrated. Many factors could explain why he did not question James sympathetically, but jumped to conclusions. Let these observations come from the students; resist the temptation to lead them, even if the observations do not come. The danger in overdirecting is that learners will begin to look to you for answers, and their loss of confidence in their ability to understand will be more destructive than any lesson missed here.

### ■ Step 3—Students Explore Others' Feelings or Actions

*Key Interrogative:* Why?

#### Sample Questions

1. Why do you think the assistant principal was feeling angry (exasperated, frustrated)? (Use one of the words the students used in response to the previous question.)

2. (To another student) Why do you think he might have been feeling that way? (Repeat questions 1 and 2 to other students using a different word—exasperated or frustrated.)
3. Why do you think James was feeling angry (hurt, abused, frustrated)? (Use their words.)
4. (To another student) Why do you think James was feeling that way? (Repeat questions 3 and 4.)
5. Are there other reasons why James might have been feeling . . . ? (Repeat this line of questioning for each of the main characters.)

### ■ Step 4—Students Describe Similar Experiences

*Key Interrogatives:* What? How? Why?

#### Sample Questions

1. Have you ever been in a situation like James's? What happened? Can you describe it?
2. (To the same student) How did you feel?
3. (To the same student) Why did you feel that way? How do you think (someone else in the situation the student described) felt? Why? (Repeat questions 1, 2, and 3 to another student.)
4. (To all students) Have you ever been in a situation like the assistant principal's? (e.g., Have you ever been in charge of little brothers and sisters who started fighting? How did you handle it?)
5. How did you feel? Did you sometimes feel angry, frustrated, or exasperated?
6. Why did you feel that way? (It is important that students try to identify with situations they might feel unsympathetic to, like the assistant principal's.)

### ■ Step 5—Students Compare Their Feelings with the Feelings of the People Studied

*Key Interrogative:* How (did you feel)? What (conclusions can you draw)?

#### Sample Questions

1. Were your feelings similiar to those of James and the assistant principal, or did you have different feelings? (Repeat this a few times to get different reactions.)
2. Are there any conclusions we can draw about people in situations like these?

Repeat question 2 to get different reactions. Some possible conclusions are:

- If people are upset, they bring those feelings with them into a situation.
- It is difficult to be fair if one is already angry or frustrated.
- Sometimes we need to look beyond the present situation to understand why people act as they do.
- The success of a conversation usually depends upon the mood of the participants.
- Our emotions determine the degree of fairness we bring to a situation.

The overall rule of thumb for a successful discussion is to proceed s-l-o-w-l-y. For example, if Bob responds to the question "How was the assistant principal feeling?" by saying he was feeling angry, ask Bob why he was feeling angry. Bob might reply that he was angry because of James's attitude. Before leaving that topic, ask other students why the assistant principal might have been angry. Others might present different reasons: "James had been warned before." "He thought James was lying." One student might even be perceptive enough to comment that the assistant principal could have been angry about a previous fight or about something that had nothing to do with James. Follow each of these responses with, "Why would he have been angrier because James had been warned before?"

Students tend to think one reason offers sufficient explanation. They must understand that cause and effect are complex and that usually there are many causes that lead to an action. Also, students need to practice articulating complex ideas, such as "repeated offenses should be viewed more seriously than first offenses." Even though everyone knows that fighting is against school rules, students act surprised when administrators are more severe with students who have already committed that offense. James had been specifically warned about fighting, so the assistant principal knew that as James let himself be drawn into a fight he did this with the full knowledge of consequences. Students need practice articulating distinctions they sense but are not used to expressing. Just as explaining rules to small children makes them more cooperative, discussing others' infractions makes students more understanding when they have a similar problem. The practice in switching point of view helps students look at a situation in which they are personally involved from the point of view of others.

*Keep key words in mind:* How (was so-and-so feeling?) Why? Why? Why?

When you think this line of questioning has gone as far as possible, repeat the original question to another student, "Ann, how do you think the assistant principal was feeling?" Ann might say that he was feeling frustrated. Why was he feeling frustrated? Because James was belligerent, or because James was not leveling with him. Why was James belligerent? Answers to key questions often are found only at this deeper level of questioning.

A great deal of discussion can proceed from one question, if it is pursued in depth. If students get too restless, go on, but feeling pressed can be healthy. A little frustration is productive. Perhaps the students who get restless first are the students who need this form of discussion most.

There are many subtle lessons to be learned from this model. Normally, when a teacher repeats a question to another student, students think it is because the teacher did not get the response he or she desired. During this procedure, they will gradually grasp that several responses are possible, and all are equally correct. Students will begin to sense that the teacher is not after a preconceived answer, but values the direction the students choose.

## Summary of Steps in the Exploration of Feelings Strategy

After selecting the conflict (a synopsis of an actual event or a selection from literature or history) and presenting the material, have the students:

1. List all the *facts* (not inferences about feelings) pertinent to the conflict, following the question: *What are some of the things that happened in this situation?*
2. Make inferences about how the persons involved were feeling, following the question: *How was so-and-so feeling?*
3. Hypothesize as to why these people probably felt as they did, by asking: *Why do you think so-and-so was feeling that way?*
4. Describe similar experiences they may have had, as well as their feelings at the time and the reasons for those feelings by asking, *Have you ever been in a situation like this? How did you feel? Why?*
5. Compare their feelings with the feelings of the people in the situation being analyzed by asking, *Did you feel the way they did?*[6]

### Activity 12.1

Try to think of a real or fictional conflict that you would like to discuss with a class. Next, make up sample questions for the first three steps of the exploration of feelings phase. ∎

## Steps in the Resolution of Conflict Strategy

After students have performed the exploration of feelings strategy a few times and have become more adept at expressing the feelings of others, have them perform the resolution of conflict strategy. The first two steps are similar to the previous strategy, but less time is spent on feelings as students move fairly rapidly into proposing resolutions:

1. List all FACTS pertinent to the conflict. These facts form the basis for further deliberation.
2. Make inferences about how the persons involved were feeling.
3. Propose and defend their own resolutions in light of those feelings.
4. Decide which resolution is best and give reasons.
5. Describe similar experiences the students have had.
6. Describe the feelings of each of the persons in their situation.
7. Evaluate their handling of the situation. If the students are mature enough, ask them to state the bases for their evaluations.
8. Look at other ways of handling their situations.
9. Make general statements about how people act in these kinds of situations.[7]

Once again, we present a situation that will help in discussing each of the steps of this phase of the model.

> Teacher: All right class, put your homework assignment on my desk as you leave.
>
> Lucy: (Lucy is a pale, shy girl who is conscientious about her work. She approaches the teacher timidly.) Mrs. Carter, I don't have my paper.
>
> Teacher: Why not Lucy?
>
> Lucy: Someone threw my notebook out of the bus.
>
> Jill: Yeah! Someone named Teddy Pace. He's always pickin' on us.
>
> Robby: Yeah! Well, there's no excuse for not getting your work in on time. That's what Mrs. Carter told me!

### ■ Step 1—Students List All the Pertinent Facts

*Key Interrogative:* What?

#### Sample Questions

1. What did you hear (read, see) in this situation?
2. Exactly what did Lucy say? (Repeat with Robby, Jill, Mrs. Carter.)

#### Sample Data Base

Lucy does not have her homework.
Someone threw Lucy's homework out of the bus.

Jill says that the someone is Teddy Pace, and that he is always picking on them.

Robby says there is no excuse for not having your homework.

### ■ Step 2—Students Make Inferences

*Key Interrogative:* How?

#### *Sample Questions*

1. How do you think Lucy was feeling when she told Mrs. Carter that she did not have her homework?
2. Why was Lucy feeling that way? (Repeat questions 1 and 2 for Jill, Robby, and Mrs. Carter.)

### ■ Step 3—Students Propose and Defend Their Own Resolutions

*Key Word:* Could

#### *Sample Questions*

1. What are some of the things that Mrs. Carter *could* do? (List answers on board if possible.)
2. How would Lucy react if Mrs. Carter (gave Lucy a zero)? (Use their words.)
3. Why would Lucy react that way? (Repeat line of questioning for other characters.)
4. How would Lucy react if Mrs. Carter (overlooked this homework assignment)? (Use their words.)
5. Why would Lucy react that way? (Repeat questions for other characters and other solutions.)

### ■ Step 4—Students Decide on Best Resolution and Give Reasons

*Key Word:* Should

#### *Sample Questions*

1. What do you think Mrs. Carter should do? Which of the solutions would be best for all concerned?

2. Why do you think Mrs. Carter should do . . . ?
3. What would be the consequences to Lucy if Mrs. Carter did that?
4. How would Robby feel if Mrs. Carter did that? (Repeat for the other characters.)
5. How would Lucy feel if Mrs. Carter did . . . (mention another solution)? (Repeat questions 1, 2, and 3.)

You may want to stop here, at least until you and the students are used to discussing feelings, posing resolutions, and choosing the most constructive resolution. At that time, having students discuss personal experiences is very productive.

### ■ Step 5—Students Describe Similar Experiences

*Key Interrogatives:* What Happened?

#### *Sample Questions*

1. Have you had an experience like this one? What happened? (Repeat question to other students.)
2. Has anyone that you've known had an experience like this?

### ■ Step 6—Students Describe Others' Feelings

*Key Interrogative:* How?

#### *Sample Questions*

1. How did you feel in the situation you've just described?
2. Why did you feel that way?
3. How did the other people feel?

### ■ Step 7—Students Evaluate Their Handling of the Situations

*Key Interrogative:* Why?

#### *Sample Questions*

1. Why did you do what you did?
2. Why do you think the others acted as they did?

3. Looking back, how do you feel about how you handled the situation? about how the others handled it? (For example, were you angry when the teacher refused to give you credit? Were you understanding? Can you see any reason why he or she might have handled the situation that way?)

### ■ Step 8—Students Look at Alternative Solutions to Their Own Situations

*Key Interrogative:* How?

#### Sample Questions

1. How else might you have handled the situation? (For example, would talking to the teacher in private have helped? Would offering to make up the work in some way have helped?)
2. How else might the others have handled the situation?
3. What would have happened if the situation had been handled that way?
4. What would be some of the long-term effects of this solution? Describe the effects in terms of each person involved.

### ■ Step 9—Students Form Generalizations

*Key Interrogative:* How?

#### Sample Questions

1. Looking back over our discussion, how do people in general handle situations like these?
2. Why do they generally respond this way?
3. Thinking back over this whole discussion, are there things we can say about how people react in similar situations, and why they might react that way?

Repeat the last question to get different reactions. Here are some sample generalizations:

- People respond more positively to an understanding attitude.
- A situation is more apt to be settled to everyone's benefit if each person makes an effort to see the other's point of view.

When using this model, there are several important points to keep in mind:

1. Try the model in easy chunks. First try the exploration of feelings phase. When you're ready to try the resolution of conflict strategy, simply ask

students to propose possible and best resolutions before you ask for personal experiences. Be flexible. *You* are the best judge of your classes' needs.

**2.** The resolution of conflict phase breaks down into five main elements: list facts, talk about feelings, propose resolutions, pick best resolution, and generalize.

**3.** Keep a list of steps and questions in front of you. The same general questions will be used with a variety of materials.

**4.** The discussion generated by any one of these steps is very productive, but it will not be disastrous if you skip a step.

## Summary of Steps in the Resolution of Conflict Strategy

Once your students have become comfortable talking about feelings and looking at a situation from someone else's perspective, they are ready to begin to talk about resolution of conflict. After selecting the conflict and presenting the material, have students:

1. List all *facts* pertinent to the conflict. These facts form the basis for further deliberation. *What happened? What did you see? Hear?*
2. Make inferences about how the persons involved were feeling. *How was _____ feeling?*
3. Propose and defend their own resolutions in light of those feelings.
4. Decide which resolution is best and give reasons. *What should _____ do in this situation?*
5. Describe similar experiences they have had. *Have you been in a situation like this?*
6. Describe the feelings of each of the persons in their situation. *How did _____ feel?*
7. Evaluate their handling of the situation. *Do you think you handled the situation well?* (If the students are mature enough, ask them to state the bases for their evaluations.)
8. Look at other ways of handling their situations. *What else might you have done?*[8]
9. (Optional.) Make statements about how people in general act in situations like this. *What can we say in general about how people deal with situations in which a rule has been broken?*

### Exercise 12.1

Mark true or false beside the following statements. You may disagree with our answers, and your reasons in a particular situation may be perfectly sound. Some of these are judgment calls, not absolutes.

1. Teachers should fire questions rapidly to keep students from getting restless.
2. When a student has answered a question incorrectly, let him or her know right away.
3. Answers to Step 1 of the exploration of feelings phase must be factual.
4. A resolution proposing no action is incorrect.
5. A proposed resolution for conflict in a work of fiction should be a constructive resolution.

Possible Answers to Exercise 12.1
1. False – rapid discussion is frequently not thoughtful discussion. Encourage a slow, thoughtful pace.
2. False – not in this strategy. The ensuing conversation should make the point clear. Even if it does not, this is not a right-or-wrong kind of investigation.
3. True in all cases.
4. False – there may be valid reasons for taking no action. The reasons should be stated.
5. False – The resolution should be plausible, meaning what the characters would – not should – do.

## Basis for the Model

Hilda Taba's work was grounded in Piaget's theories of growth and development, particularly his idea of horizontal development. Piaget believed that the speed with which a youngster goes through each phase of cognitive development is less important in the long run than the depth of each stage; he called this horizontal development. Taba's strategies are designed to allow maximum growth in this sense.

There are three elements that Taba thought were essential to effective learning: (1) how knowledge or "human experience" is transmitted; (2) the social interaction of the classroom; and (3) the reason for learning. They are like three strands of a braid which, when woven together with a creative flair, make a whole that is greater than the sum of its parts.

1. *The "transmission of the funded capital of human experience."*[9] The "what" (content or subject matter taught) of this transmission is largely dictated by authorities in the community; the "how" is largely left to the teachers in the classroom. But the "how" is crucial. This "funded capital of human experience is more successfully transmitted through a goal-seeking type of experience than through a formally organized passing-on of information from the notes of the

instructor to the notes of the student without passing through the mind of either."[10]

**2.** *The social interaction of the classroom.* According to Taba, "a genuine learning situation . . . involves the emotions of the learner."[11] Since the deepest insights frequently occur as the result of the interaction of student contributions, trust is essential. Unless students know their inner thoughts and feelings will be valued, they will not risk revealing them. This does not necessarily connote agreement. If offered in a constructive manner, disagreement can be productive.

**3.** *The reason for the learning.* Is the knowledge being transmitted "for power or merely for social ornamentation?" Is it "an instrument for creativity or simply more material for the dead files?"[12] Is the individual teacher teaching content simply because it is what was taught last year and the year before, or is there a clear idea of exactly where the instruction is going and why? Further, does the teacher understand that *how* content is taught determines the effectiveness of teaching? "The fundamental point is that the quality of the inner subjective world, created by each individual and used by him to guide his impulses into behavior, is the heart of the educative process."[13]

We all have our own private core, that arena where thoughts and feelings merge to dictate our behavior. If learning is to be effective it must have an impact on that inner world that dictates our actions. Students live in the real world, not in the world of the textbook. Examining the world of the textbook in the same way that we examine conflicts in the real world makes that textbook seem more significant.

When you hear students initiating how and why type questions in class; when you overhear one student say to another as they leave class, "But how will she feel if you do that? How do you think she'll react?"; when students tell you they discuss things more, things that they previously kept to themselves, you will know that you have indeed touched that inner arena. In so doing you have helped your students to be more in control of their lives. You have transmitted power to them, the power to act upon their environment rather than react to it.

One of the cornerstones of Taba's philosophy is that children need to be emotionally ready to learn. For effective learning to take place, students must *want* to learn. Since the writings of the philosopher Descartes, society has tended to view the intellectual realm and the emotional realm as quite separate. This Cartesian view has created many stereotypes—the unemotional mathematician and the overemotional artist, to name just two.

This intellectual/emotional dichotomy is being questioned today. One skeptic of this separation is Israel Scheffler, who is the Victor S. Thomas Professor of Education and Philosophy and a co-director of the Philosophy of Education Research Center at Harvard. The center explores such questions as: What is thinking? Can thinking skills be taught? What implications do our findings have for education? In an article entitled "In Praise of Cognitive Emotions," Scheffler says,

The mention of cognitive emotions may well evoke emotions of perplexity and incredulity. For cognition and emotion, as everyone knows, are hostile worlds apart. Cognition is sober inspection; it is the scientist's calm apprehension of fact after fact in his relentless pursuit of Truth. Emotion, on the other hand, is commotion—an unruly inner turbulence fatal to such pursuit but finding its own constructive outlets in aesthetic experience and moral or religious commitment.

Strongly entrenched, this opposition of cognition and emotion must nevertheless be challenged, for it distorts everything it touches: Mechanizing science, it sentimentalizes art, while portraying ethics and religion as twin swamps of feeling and unreasoned commitment. Education, meanwhile—that is to say, the development of mind and attitudes in the young—is split into two grotesque parts—unfeeling knowledge and mindless arousal. My purpose here is to help overcome the breach by outlining basic aspects of emotion in the cognitive process.[14]

It has been our experience that students reach their deepest insights when they are the most excited. As Professor Scheffler said, "I never met a mathematician worth his salt who did not care passionately about mathematics."[15] Indeed, what drives intellectual pursuit through its often lonely and frustrating periods? Is it not intense curiosity and fervent caring?

## Scenario I: Elementary School

Elementary students discuss their feelings freely, but need practice in trying to understand the feelings of others. An exploration of feelings discussion after reading "Jack and the Beanstalk" can employ questions like: How were Jack and his mother feeling before the decision to sell the cow? after the cow was traded for the beans? What were the reasons for those feelings? Talk about how Jack and his mother and the ogre and the ogre's wife were feeling after Jack's first trip up the beanstalk. (Discussing the ogre's feelings is good practice in switching point of view.) Why did they have those feelings? How did those feelings affect their subsequent behavior? What feelings did Jack have that led to the second trip? The third? Why?

A resolution of conflict discussion makes an excellent follow-up to reading "The Ugly Duckling." How were the other ducks in the pond feeling before the mother duck arrived? Did they want more ducks around? Why? Why not? How did the old matriarch of the ducks feel? Why? Why did the turkey cock single out the ugly duckling? How did picking on the ugly duckling make the turkey cock feel? How might each have acted to make the ugly duckling feel better? Why didn't each one do this? Have the students had experiences with someone different, perhaps a new student in class? How did they feel? Did they feel friendly? competitive? uneasy? envious? Did they feel the new person might be a threat? that they might lose their friends? Do people who are different, as the ugly ducking was, make us feel uncomfortable? Why? Why might we have those feelings? How might those feelings affect our actions?

What follows is an excerpt from a fourth-grade discussion of the Hans Christian Andersen version of "The Ugly Duckling." The students had recapped what had happened on the pond; they had made inferences about how the queen duck, the mother duck, the baby ducklings, the turkey cock, and the ugly duckling were feeling. Then the teacher asked what each of these characters might have done to make the situation less painful for the ugly duckling.

Teacher: What are some things the old queen might have done to make the ugly duckling feel better?

Billy: If she had accepted him the other ducks would have accepted him too.

Teacher: How might she have done this?

Anne: She could have praised him for being a strong swimmer or for being big.

Teacher: Would this have changed the attitudes of the other ducks?

Billy: Yes. They really liked the old queen and wanted to please her.

Sarah: Lots of times kids copy the way older people act.

Teacher: So you think the other ducklings would have made friends with the ugly duckling if the queen duck had?

Anne: Yeah! Even the mother. She tried to stick up for him at first, but then even she stopped.

Teacher: And what about the ugly duckling? Were there things he could have done to make things easier for himself?

Billy: If he had tried to impress the old queen she might have become his friend.

Teacher: How could he do that?

Billy: He could have bowed elegantly. He could have sat up straight and proud.

Chad: Maybe he could have found her an eel's head.

Whit: Maybe he could have talked it out with her, told her how he felt and asked for her help.

Teacher: What might he have said?

Whit: Maybe he could have said that there are lots of different kinds of ducks, and maybe he was a special kind.

Pete: He should have painted himself brown.

Teacher: Would looking more like the other ducks have helped?

Billy: Yeah. Looking so different, his brothers and sisters were afraid he was making a bad impression for the family.

Teacher: Why do you think we're uncomfortable when someone is different?

Chad: Because you don't know what he might do.

Whit: Yeah, you're not used to him.

> Pete: He could have hit the other ducks.
>
> Anne: Ducks don't hit.
>
> Pete: Well, he could have bitten them and flapped his wings. After all, he was bigger.
>
> Teacher: What do you think they would have done?
>
> Anne: Maybe they would have stayed away and been afraid of him.
>
> Betty: Maybe they would have been his friend because they were afraid not to.
>
> Whit: Maybe they would have bitten him back.
>
> Teacher: Do you think it takes more courage to bite him back or not to bite him back?
>
> Whit: Not to. It's like hitting on the playground. You have such an urge—such an urge to hit back, but you know you'll be in trouble.

## Scenario II: High School

The class is an eleventh-grade American History class taught by Mr. Moore, and they have just studied the causes of the Civil War. Mr. Moore is concerned that the students, sophisticated as they are, still view President Lincoln as a stereotype and have little understanding of the man. To get beyond this superficial grasp, to get into the situation and the man, Mr. Moore has decided to use the exploration of feeling strategy (the class has used this model several times before).

To introduce this strategy, Mr. Moore reads aloud four stanzas from Vachel Lindsay's "Abraham Lincoln Walks at Midnight":

> It is portentous, and a thing of state
>     That here at midnight, in our little town
> A mourning figure walks, and will not rest
>     Near the old courthouse pacing up and down,
>
> Or by his homestead, or the shadowed yards
>     He lingers where his children used to play,
> Or through the market, on the well-worn stones
>     He stalks until the dawn-stars burn away.
>
> A bronzed, lank man! His suit of ancient black,
>     A famous high-top hat and plain worn shawl
> Make him the quaint great figure that men love,
>     The prairie-lawyer, master of us all.
>
> He cannot sleep upon his hillside now.
>     He is among us, as in times before!
> And we who toss and lie awake for long
>     Breathe deep, and start, to see him pass the door.[16]

Mr. Moore and the class have discussed the word "portentous"; the effect of the spectre in ancient black, with high-top hat; the reasons why President Lincoln might cause people to "start." Mr. Moore had also shared with the class the award-winning, beautiful book *Lincoln: A Photobiography.* [17]

In Step 1, the students had compiled a data base, which includes the following items:

1. Lincoln's admissions to Secretary Welles that he did not sign the document bearing his name that was sent to the Secretary of the Navy.
2. Lincoln's knowledge that his political support had come in great part from northern workers.
3. Lincoln's consciousness of the plight of the iron workers in Pennsylvania and the wool growers in Ohio and their inability to compete with England's merchandise because of low tariffs supported by the South.
4. Lincoln's horror of the proclamation by the delegates at the convention in South Carolina following their secession that "the United States of America is hereby dissolved."
5. Lincoln's sympathy for the suffering of the slaves rescued through the Underground Railroad.
6. Lincoln's sympathy for the South's financial dependence on slavery.
7. Lincoln's recognition of the angry and bitter mood of many of the people.

We pick up their discussion in Step 2. Mr. Moore is asking for inferences about President Lincoln's feelings and actions.

Mr. Moore: Why do you think Mr. Lincoln was pacing up and down at midnight?

Shirley: Because he was angry.

Mr. Moore: Why do you think he was angry, Shirley?

Shirley: Because he had been deceived by his own Secretary of State and others. They had substituted their own versions of Mr. Lincoln's views in critical messages, versions that would promote the actions they wanted.

Anne: I think he felt betrayed.

Mr. Moore: Why did he feel betrayed, Anne?

Anne: Because he felt he couldn't trust anyone. Remember he said, "If you can't trust your own Secretary of State, who can you trust?"

Ben: Going back to what Shirley said, I don't think he felt angry, I think he felt indecisive and powerless.

Mr. Moore: Why do you think he felt indecisive and powerless rather than angry?

Ben: If you're angry you usually take action. If you're indecisive, you pace. Remember, the *New York Times* had called him indecisive. If he had been angry, the Secretary of State and others would have been more frightened of him, less apt to cross him.

Ted: But they implied he was indecisive because he was weak. I don't think his indecision came from weakness.

Mr. Moore: Can you explain what you mean, Ted?

Ted: I'll have to think about that a minute.

Mr. Moore: Take your time. Meanwhile, the rest of you think about this: Was Mr. Lincoln's apparent indecision caused by weakness or strength or something else?

Ted: A weak man might have gone along with what all the vocal people wanted—and defended Fort Sumter knowing that meant war. It took courage to wait. Lincoln's indecision stemmed from his wisdom and his feelings, not from fear. He saw the bind the South was in. He also saw that the new nation couldn't survive secession. He saw, too, how horrible a war would be. But he felt powerless to stop events and silence the hotheads.

Jane: Yes, the message he sent to Fort Sumter backs up what Ted is saying. He tried to give the Confederacy a way of saving face.

Mr. Moore: How, Jane?

Jane: By saying he was only sending provisions, not ammunition, to the fort. By doing that he was preserving the status quo, not being aggressive.

Jerry: I think he felt all those things: anger, sadness, frustration, indecision, powerlessness, betrayal, fear. He was driven by so many conflicting emotions he couldn't sleep, he had to pace.

Gradually the students painted a picture of a man tortured and struggling, a spectre who caused people to start from fear, not of him but of a situation in which events were out of control and leading inexorably to what would be a horrible war. By trying to understand some of the feelings of the man, the students had come much closer to understanding Lincoln and the moment than if they had just stayed with the facts. They also obtained a glimpse of the loneliness and powerlessness of this man at the top.

These are only inferences; no one can know precisely what Lincoln was feeling. But actions stem from both thoughts and feelings, and Lincoln's actions appear to point to the students' conclusions. We can try to study a situation in all its complexities, and then imagine what feelings those events would engender. History examines concepts and thoughts, but feelings also play a role in the intricate realm of cause and effect. They are more obscure and less easily documented, but they may play the larger role. To ignore them because they are elusive may distort our picture of the past more than any attempts to assess them, as long as we are careful to remember we are making assumptions.

### Activity 12.2

In the first activity, you were asked to choose a conflict you would like to discuss with a class and to make up sample questions for the first three steps of this model. Using the same conflict, make up sample questions for the resolution of conflict phase. ■

### ■ SUMMARY

If used with any regularity, this model can begin to empower students to resolve conflicts with some regard for opposing views. At the very least, students express feelings and become more aware of the feelings of others. Students have commented that they had no idea other students had the same doubts, fears, hang-ups. "She looks so confident," they say, or "He seems so cool." Voicing their insecurities has made them feel less alone, more willing to share.

There is a cycle in our lives in which thoughts and feelings dictate actions. These actions cause more thoughts and feelings that dictate further actions. Suddenly, we are caught up in events dictated by an action taken long ago, often without sufficient consideration. In this complicated cycle that produces the momentum that directs our lives, exploring and examining feelings may be one key to breaking down barriers between people and allowing students to stand briefly, albeit hypothetically, in another person's shoes.

As our world becomes smaller and the population grows exponentially, it becomes more important to learn techniques for arriving at fair and amicable resolutions to conflicts. This model for exploring feelings and resolving conflicts can help individuals communicate more effectively, resolve conflicts more equitably, and exert more control over the direction of their lives.

### ■ NOTES

**1.** Lewis Carroll, *The Annotated Alice* (New York: Bramhall House, 1960), 129–130.

**2.** Hilda Taba, *Teaching Strategies Program* (Miami, FL: Institute for Staff Development, 1971), 8.

**3.** Taba, *Teaching Strategies,* 159.

**4.** Taba, *Teaching Strategies,* 8.

**5.** Taba, *Teaching Strategies,* 8.

**6.** Taba, *Teaching Strategies,* 8.

**7.** Taba, *Teaching Strategies,* 7.

**8.** Taba, *Teaching Strategies*, 7.

**9.** Taba, *Teaching Strategies*, 157.

**10.** Taba, *Teaching Strategies*, 157.

**11.** Taba, *Teaching Strategies*, 158.

**12.** Taba, *Teaching Strategies*, 160.

**13.** Taba, *Teaching Strategies*, 161.

**14.** Israel Scheffler, "In Praise of Cognitive Emotions," *Teacher's College Record* 79, no. 2 (December 1977): 171.

**15.** Scheffler, *In Praise of Cognitive Emotions*, 171.

**16.** Vachel Lindsay, "Abraham Lincoln Walks at Midnight," in *Collected Poems* (New York: Macmillan, 1923), 53.

**17.** Russell Freedman, *Lincoln, A Photobiography* (New York: Clarion Books, 1987).

# *Matching Objectives to Instruction*

In Part Two we surveyed a selection of models for teaching, ranging from the rather structured format of direct instruction to the more open-ended model for exploration of feelings and resolution of conflict. Throughout, we have tried to emphasize that models are akin to blueprints or patterns, sets of plans that describe but do not rigidly define approaches to teaching. All plans are subject to interpretation, modification, and adjustment, and models of instruction are no different. Every model must be seen as a flexible plan, subject to constant adaptation within the limits of its intended purpose.

Furthermore, models of instruction cannot be adopted in disregard of what will be taught and to whom the teaching will be directed. One does not merely say, "I think I'll use model X today. Now what is it I need to teach?" If anything, the opposite should be the case—after considering the subject matter and the particular class to be taught, the teacher then selects a model of instruction that best combines the two variables. The instructional models we have discussed are best seen as approaches to teaching that must be selected with judgment.

Though Part Two does not present an exhaustive list of models, it covers the range of types of models. We hope that our descriptions and explanations have left every reader confident that he or she can make judicious choices of models for teaching and that doing so will have a positive effect on instructional outcomes.

# Part Three

# Putting It All Together: Matching Objectives to Instructional Models

An essential activity of the professional instructor, as we emphasized in the Preface to this book, is the process of designing or *struct*uring (the root of *instruct*) that which is to be taught. We have emphasized that the planning process of setting goals and objectives, designing the units and lessons, and selecting the materials is as important as knowing the material to be presented to the learners.

In Part Three, we describe the integration of planning, instruction, evaluation, and management that takes place in an effective classroom environment. We would emphasize that each teacher must develop his or her own way of achieving this integration. There is no one way to approach the process of putting it all together in the classroom. There are, however, certain essential components of this process to which every good teacher attends. These are (1) planning, (2) instruction, (3) evaluation, and (4) classroom management.

In Parts One and Two of this text, we discussed the planning, evaluation, and instructional components. In Part Three, "Putting It All Together," we describe how teachers in classroom situations utilize the ideas presented in Parts One and Two, and we give some general suggestions for managing the classroom. Of the four chapters in this section, Chapter 13 is a case study of a kindergarten class plan, Chapter 14, a middle school case study, Chapter 15, a high school case study. Evident in these three examples are individual approaches to instructional planning, which utilize some of the processes and strategies described earlier. The teachers in these examples do not arrive at their plans by the same route nor do they incorporate exactly the same instructional steps in their indivdual plans. All of the teachers do, however, attend to the needs of their students, and they systematically determine objectives and match those objectives to instruction.

Chapter 16 describes some techniques for dealing with problems in discipline and personal interaction that can occur in the classroom. Most of the material presented in this last chapter is drawn from our personal experience;

however, we have attempted to connect this experience with research regarding effective classroom practice.

It is our belief that teachers are essentially instructional experts, not therapists or counselors. Like all good managers, they must have very keen interpersonal skills and be able to think quickly on their feet. Anyone who is responsible for managing groups of people and for the welfare of individuals under their direction should have the personality and the skills to manage the group and to give direction. But we should not ask of teachers what we do not ask of other professionals. Teachers should not be expected to prescribe and treat seriously disturbed individuals without help from other professionals, such as psychologists, social workers, and guidance counselors, nor should they be expected to teach in life-threatening situations.

Having said this, it is our belief that many students who are considered to be serious discipline problems and are sent out of the classroom, often labeled as hyperactive or emotionally disturbed, are in fact suffering because of the way they are being taught. Youngsters who are bored, whose learning style is different from the teaching style, who are asked to learn material that is too difficult or too easy can become discipline problems. Too often, teachers diagnose instructional problems as emotional, physical, or mental problems, thus failing to meet the challenge of finding an instructional solution.

In this part of the text we reemphasize the need for careful instructional planning and design and for creating a classroom environment in which students can and will learn.

# Chapter 13

# A Kindergarten Case Study

Miss Gloria Abbott, kindergarten teacher at Central Elementary School, relaxed one warm summer afternoon with a pad and a pencil and wrote down some thoughts on her chosen profession, the role of education, and what she wants for her students. She realized that some rethinking of her approach to teaching would help her to begin the new school year with a renewed energy and commitment. Miss Abbott made these notes:

> I went into teaching because I enjoy being with children and because I think that teaching is the most important profession. It has always seemed to me to have the greatest potential to make the most lasting positive difference to the largest number of people. The fate of our democracy, our very way of life, depends on the political and economic participation of all its citizens. But despite these lofty ideals and aspirations, my frustration is that I may not be able to do my part. Though I want all the students to learn, I know that many of them leave my classroom without the skills they need to succeed at the next level. Some of the children are bored because they already know what I am trying to teach. Others are frustrated because they have difficulty in learning what I am teaching.
>
> What I love most are the times when I read to the children and we talk about the characters and the story. Some of the so-called slower children have the best insights. I want them all to love ideas and to exercise their imaginations in creative use of language. I also want these students to gain respect for each other; too often I see that some children are left out of activities and ignored by the rest. I want the students to work together and to learn to cooperate with each other in the classroom. Most of all, I want them to leave kindergarten with more curiosity about learning than when they walked into school in September.

In reading what she had written, Miss Abbott circled the key words and phrases that indicated her primary concerns for the children in her classroom. Then she wrote the following goals:

1. The children will develop the skills necessary to succeed in first grade.
2. Those who have attained a certain skill level will not be bored while others are still learning those skills.
3. The children will be introduced to ideas and language that will stimulate their imaginations.

4. The students will develop confidence in their abilities to learn.
5. The students will appreciate each other and learn to work cooperatively.

"Fine," she thought to herself. "Now, how do I make this happen?"

The first step was to find out as much as possible about the children who would be coming next fall, a habit she had neglected in recent years. The school is located in a small southern city, in a neighborhood close to a university. Some of her students are the children of university faculty and others are the sons and daughters of the hourly employees—secretaries who run the offices, janitors and cooks who clean the buildings and prepare the meals. Most of the children of the faculty are white; many of the children of the support staff are black. Some of the children have traveled around the world; some have never been out of the city.

Frequently, she had walked around the neighborhoods where students in her class lived. There were some streets where maids were carefully sweeping the porches and gardeners were mowing the verdant lawns. On other streets, houses stood on lots where no grass grew in the hard-packed dirt in front of sagging stoops.

She knew that regardless of the neighborhood, there were some children who would suffer from abuse and neglect and others who would be nurtured and cared for. She realized how important it was for her to bring together these children—from different neighborhoods and family environments—and to provide a classroom atmosphere where all could succeed. Could she make each of these children feel that while they were with her and with each other they were important, safe, and competent? Could each of them feel that school was a place of happiness where they were glad to be? Could she feel that way as well?

Readiness tests had been given to all the children when they were enrolled in the system. Miss Abbott spent the next day going through the results. One of the children who would be in her classroom could have entered the second grade on the basis of the tests. More than one-third of the children, however, were more than one year below the norm. Over half of the children would be eligible for the after-school childcare program because both their parents were working or because the one parent in the home was trying to hold down two jobs. Most of the children showed some potential for problems in their readiness to learn. In the past, she would have focused on the number of children with potential learning problems and wished that they were in some other class. This time, she told herself that these children must be a part of the challenge of teaching. In the planning process, she would attend to their special needs.

The old building was not air conditioned, so she would again this year have to get the children outdoors as much as possible during the early fall months. These ventures must be tied to learning, however, and not just for cooling off. There was no money in the school budget for trips, so when they went outside it would need to be in the neighborhood of the school or on the playground. Also, if she were going to move the group around, they would need to understand the rules and to cooperate with her and with each other.

She thought about the subject matter the students needed to learn and remembered a chart prepared by the school system that listed the important skills children should master in kindergarten. One skill relating to hand/eye coordination would be developed by teaching the children to stay inside the lines as they colored with large crayons.

The word *line* caused her to think about the fact that during the first weeks of school the students would learn to line up before leaving the room and stay in line as they moved through the halls. This was important when she took the children on walking trips in the neighborhood. On the playground they were to develop gross motor skills by bouncing a ball across a line.

As she reviewed the skills chart, it occurred to her that the concept of *line* arose frequently and might be an excellent focus for the first unit; she could introduce a number of ideas about lines that could be expanded upon throughout the year. For instance, the concept of *lines* can represent a drawing in, as well as an acceptance of, limits. Lines are used to form boundaries and to represent infinity. Two ends of a curved line can be joined to form a circle. Straight lines can be assembled to form a square. Miss Abbott smiled as she realized that in her enthusiasm she could go off in twenty directions at once. There was a limit to what she could include in one unit and how much these children could absorb. "Keep in mind how many times the same concept has to be experienced before it can be understood," she reminded herself. It was time to order her own thoughts in developing the unit on lines.

## Miss Abbott's Plan

Typically, Miss Abbott planned a unit to last for two to six weeks, depending on the time of year and the content to be covered. Miss Abbott usually divided each unit into four to six lessons, with each lesson lasting three to five days. There was an organizing theme for each unit (for example, the unit on "Community Helpers" that every kindergarten teacher taught) and an organizing subtheme or idea for each lesson (e.g., Nurses and Doctors, Police and Fire Officers). The unit objectives were explained to the students at the beginning of the unit; lesson objectives were explained at the beginning of each week and cumulatively reviewed each day in oral and written form. A space on the chalkboard was reserved solely for this purpose—if they were to learn to read, the students needed to see important information in print, and this was one way to effect that. And she had always thought it important to keep the kindergartners informed as to what led to what in their study.

Her experience had taught her much about teaching. In the past, Miss Abbott had often developed daily lesson plans that were unrelated to each other and were not part of any design. Over the years, she became convinced that students did better when they could see connections in what they were learning each day. Unit planning helped her to decide what to include and in what order.

She decided that the general objectives for this first unit on lines would be as follows:

- Students will feel a part of the group and be enthusiastic about the learning process. (an affective objective)
- Students will understand the meaning of the concept "line." (a cognitive objective)
- Students will line up when asked to do so, within 30 seconds without intimidation. (a psychomotor, cognitive, and affective objective)
- Students will increase hand/eye coordination as evidenced by the ability to stay inside the lines when coloring. (a psychomotor objective)
- Students will be able to distinguish between a straight line and a curved line. (a cognitive objective)
- Students will be able to identify a circle. (a cognitive objective)
- Students will be able to identify a square. (a cognitive objective)

Then she preliminarily organized the content for the unit in the following arrangement:

### Learning a Lot about Lines

| | |
|---|---|
| Straight lines | Lines that curve |
| Lines of people/Lines on a page | Faces and flowers |
| Squares | Circles |

As she worked with the content, moving parts around and trying to decide what the children could learn and what would be appropriate, she realized that there was probably more content here than she could cover in one unit. Why not limit this introductory unit to two weeks and reserve major study of the concepts of geometric shapes—the square and the circle—for a separate, but related, unit to follow? There would then be less chance of confusion at the critical stage when the young learners would need to be clear on the fundamental notion of *line* as distinct from two- and three-dimensional shapes. Besides, by separating this first unit into two related units, she'd be able to do more with the second part  on geometric shapes.

So, the initial unit on lines would be planned in anticipation of a follow-up unit. Now her diagram of the content included squares and circles, but each of these would be the focus of a future unit of study. In other words, she could teach the unit on lines to make it the organizing concept that would tie several units of study together. Here's what her revised diagram looked like:

### Learning about Lines

| *Squares* | *Circles* |
|---|---|
| Lines that are straight | Lines that are curved |
| Soldiers in a parade/Lines in a book | Faces and flowers |
| Angles and sides | Inside and outside of lines |

As she prepared the first lesson in the unit on lines for the opening day of school, Miss Abbott was plagued again by second thoughts. After all, this was a difficult concept and these were very young children. On the other hand, she thought, they hear this word *line* all the time. Adults are always talking to them about lines: "Wait in line to get on the bus." "Make a beeline for bed." "Draw a line." Even so, she worried a little, wondering how to make this abstract concept more concrete.

It occurred to her that the children might need to have a line to hold in their hands—to touch and to feel. The kind of line that would be the most familiar to them would be a fishing line, but nylon fishing line might cut. The line she needed would have to be something strong that would not break and still would not hurt the children's hands. She visualized bright lines of yarn extending out the door of the classroom on the first morning to draw in the children. Now she felt more confident about planning the details for the unit on lines. She calculated that each lesson in the unit would occupy less than an hour each day.

## Unit: Lines That Draw Us Together

*Teaching time:* Ten days, one hour or less per day.
*Unit Objectives:* The students will

1. feel at home and wanted in the classroom (affective);
2. define the concept *line* (cognitive);
3. describe inside and outside the line (cognitive);
4. form a line in an orderly and expeditious manner (psychomotor, cognitive, affective); and
5. discriminate between lines and nonlines (cognitive).

### ■ Opening Activity—Drawing in the Students

*Objective:* The children will feel welcome and wanted in the classroom.

Just outside the classroom there will be a table. Lines of yarn will extend from the classroom and will be draped across the table. Attached at the end of each line will be a cardboard fish with a child's name on it. A parent volunteer will stand at the door, and as the children arrive they will line up. One at a time, the children will come forward, and the volunteer will give each child the string with his or her name on it and call out the name. The teacher will pull in the yarn and give each child a welcome hug. When all the children are assembled in the room, and throughout the first week, stories emphasizing lines will be read aloud to the class (e.g., *The Line Up Book,* by Marisabina Russo, and *Lines and Shapes,* by Solvig Russell). (Estimated time: Day One of unit; 30 minutes.)

*Materials:* 12-foot lengths of heavy, brightly colored yarn; cardboard name tags in the shape of fish; and appropriate books.

*Evaluation:* Ask the parent volunteer to observe the children's reactions, particularly those children who display fear or frustration with the activity. Make notes following the lesson.

## ■ Lessson One: Practicing the "Line-Up"

*Instructional model: Direct Instruction*

Estimated time: on appropriate occasions each day of first two weeks, 2–7 minutes (or faster) per occasion, depending on skill level.

*Objective:* The children will form a line in an orderly and expeditious manner.

*Rationale for choice of model:* "People moving" is one of the fundamental routines that teachers must establish at the beginning of each year. Going to lunch, to recess, to other classrooms, to the bathroom, out for a fire drill (or the real thing)—all this moving around is part of the typical day of the elementary student and his or her teacher. Precisely because lining up to move is such a basic routine, direct instruction is most suitable for its mastery. Sometimes the model is called the "training model," a terminology we have rejected as having a negative connotation, though it does get the point across. Kindergarten-age children do have to be trained to get in line with minimum confusion; in a week of short practice sessions, the students will be so accustomed to lining up on command that the procedure will be second nature to them. Such behavioral habits lend themselves perfectly to a direct instruction approach.

*Application of the model:* Lines will be taped on the floor with a place for each child marked on each line. Each child will practice taking his or her place on the different lines, on command, as appropriate to the purpose of the line-up. The children will be called to their places—by name at first, then by rows, and then by boys/girls. As each student takes a place on the line, he or she will establish a direction and a path from desk to line, depending on where the line-up is and how it is arranged. Short practice periods each day will establish the necessary behavioral patterns.

*Evaluation:* The activity of lining up will be timed repeatedly and a daily record kept of the increasing efficiency of the class in taking their place on the line.

## ■ Lesson Two: Defining a Line

*Instructional model: Concept Attainment*

Estimated time: Day Two of unit; 20 minutes.

*Objective:* The children will develop an initial definition for the concept of *line*.

*Rationale for choice of model:* A concept is a general idea derived from encounters with specific instances. Before this lesson, and the lessons and units that will build on it, can proceed, it is crucial that students have in mind a working definition of lines. There will be plenty of opportunities for them to refine their concept of line in the lessons and learning activities to follow. The intent of this concept attainment activity is to establish the general idea of *line* so that students have the groundwork on which to build successively sophisticated understandings. For example, these children eventually will learn that though two points define a line, every line extends in two directions to infinity. An infinite number of lines in a plane define that plane, which is also infinite in its single dimension. But these and many other very sophisticated concepts will be built on the initial understanding of what a line is and is not. Thus, the choice of concept attainment as the instructional model to introduce the general idea of *line*.

*Application of the model:* The children will sit in a circle on the floor. They are then presented with a number of positive and negative examples of the concept.

### Positive Examples

a clothes line
a fishing line
a line drawn on the board
a line taped to the floor
the cracks between the ceiling tiles and the floor tiles
a picture of the crosswalk in the back-to-school safety poster

### Negative Examples

a bowl
a fork
a shoe
a picture of a fish

*Evaluation:* A variety of items like those used in the lesson will be placed on a table. At different times of the day, ask each child individually to select something that can be used as a line or to represent a line, and ask the child to explain the selection. Those children who did not understand the concept can receive individual attention at this stage.

### ■ Lesson Three: Refining the Concept of Line

*Instructional model: Concept Development*
Estimated time: Day Three of unit; 30 minutes.
*Objective:* The children will discriminate between those items that are lines and those that are not.
*Rationale for choice of model:* Having acquired the basic idea of *line*, the students will now need practice in applying their idea to a variety of circumstances. It will not be enough to know, conceptually, what a line is unless the learners

can categorize things they encounter as *lines* or *not lines*. To be sure, this skill is alluded to in the previous day's lesson, but the question now is, can the children think *with* their new ideas? The development of concepts rests only superficially on definition. In order to *think with* definitions, the learners will need practice in categorization. Since categorization is the essence of concept development, concept development is the model of choice for this lesson.

*Application of the model:* Pictures of different items will be selected and prepared for the flannel board; some of the items will be lines and some will not be. Of the lines, some will be curved, some will be straight. The group will decide which items can be grouped together and talk about what these items all have in common, why they are alike in some way.

*Materials:* Pictures of lines and pictures of other items; a flannel board and material to prepare the pictures.

*Evaluation:* A parent volunteer will observe the group and note those children who are not participating or who do not seem to understand the concept of *line* well enough to apply it to the task of discrimination. In addition, students will be asked to look for lines on their way to and from school, which they will discuss in class.

### ■ Activity: The Line Game

*Objective:* The children will describe staying *inside* and *outside* of a line.

*Description of activity:* Two lines will be drawn on the playground. The students will line up just outside the lines, on each side, to begin the hokey pokey song. The first time we will practice just "I put my body in, I put my body out," and so on. The emphasis will be on going inside and outside the line as they dance, in preparation for learning to color inside the line. However, these related concepts of "inside" and "outside" will not be stressed at first. The activity will be repeated several days for fun and then used as an organizer in teaching students about "staying inside the line" (e.g., When we do the hokey pokey dance on the playground what do we say we are doing with the line?).

*Evaluation:* See if the children can follow the directions. Make a clipboard list of those children who cannot remember the words or who have coordination problems.

## Notes on Day One

The following is an anecdotal record of what happened on the first day of school when Miss Abbott started to teach her unit on lines.

The opening activity went very well except for the awkward moment when several of the children arrived at the same time and the lines got tangled. Miss Abbott decided that the next time she used this activity she would use soft clothesline rope.

Preparing the concept attainment lesson had taken more time than Miss Abbott had anticipated. Her first task was to define for herself the meaning of *line*. She wrote down that a line was something that had a beginning and an end and was connected. Then she realized that she could not tell what was the beginning and what was the end, and just what was it that connected the two. The definition of a line was not as simple as she had thought. The dictionary had 30 different definitions of the word, but the root of the word was from the Latin *linea*, for linen thread. The definition she finally settled on was: two ends connected by something that looks like a string or a rope.

After each child had been seated in a circle on the floor, Miss Abbott held up the word *line* and said, "This is a word we are going to learn all about today. This word is *line*."

Tommy said, "I can read that word."

Miss Abbott remembered the high test results for Tommy. "Good, Tommy," she said and went on. "Look at the line you followed into the room today. Tell me what it looks like."

The children said that it was made of yarn and that it went from one place to the other and that you could follow it. "Let's look at another line and see if it is like the line you followed."

This time she held up a clothesline. "Is this one made of yarn?"

"No," came a chorus of answers.

"Then a line doesn't have to be made out of yarn. How is this line like the one you followed?"

"Well, it has two ends like a snake. But it doesn't have a head and a tail," said one of the children. Several of the children began to talk about snakes and Miss Abbott had to bring them back.

"Tommy, point to the two ends of the line you followed in and to the two ends of the clothesline. That's right, Tommy. Now, everybody find the two ends of your line. Can we say that a line has two ends? What is between the two ends," Miss Abbott asked as she held up the line of yarn and the clothesline. The children were puzzled and several began to creep away from the group. Miss Abbott realized that for most of them this was too hard, but Tommy came to the rescue.

"Something that's skinny and bends," he said. This response caught the attention of the children and they got back in the circle.

Miss Abbott held up a fishing line. "Does this have two ends?"

"Yes," they chorused. "And you can catch fish on it," one of the little boys said.

"Are the two ends connected by something that is—can I use the word 'thin' Tommy?—that is thin and can bend?"

Susan said that she liked the word skinny, and so did the rest of the class. Miss Abbott decided that for the time being she would accept their word.

Next she pointed to a line that had been taped to the floor. "This is a line, too," she said. "Does it have two ends?"

"Yes," they chorused.

"Is it skinny?"

"Yeeess!" They were really into the action now.

"But," she asked, "will this line bend?"

Tommy did not want to lose his definition. "You could draw another line that would be bent," he said. "Yes, Tommy, you are right. But this line will not bend. So, in your definition, a line doesn't have to bend. Tommy, you hold up the clothesline, Susan you hold up the fishing line, and all of you look at your yarn lines. What can we see that is the same about all of them?"

"Well, they have two ends, and they have a skinny thing in between and they are floppy," said Mary.

"Don't forget the line taped to the floor," said Miss Abbott. "Is that line floppy?"

Mary liked the word "floppy," but she agreed that the line taped to the floor was not. "Our lines have two ends with something skinny in between."

Miss Abbott thought about how "skinny" seemed to please the children. It had not occurred to her when she planned the lesson, but it was a word that seemed to fit. She held up a cup. "Is this a line?" she asked.

"No," they said in unison. "Because it doesn't have two ends and it isn't skinny."

"It isn't floppy either," said Mary, attempting to get her word back in.

Tommy said, "It doesn't have to be floppy, stupid."

Miss Abbott put her hand on Tommy's shoulder and said, "No one in this class is stupid. We all work together." She made a mental note to think through why Tommy needed to say what he did and to plan for a lesson soon using the exploration of feelings model, through which they could discuss name calling.

Miss Abbott held up a long piece of string. "Is this a line?" she asked.

"Well, it has two ends with something skinny between. Yes."

A fork got a quick rejection, as did a plate and a hat.

After recess they had lesson three, using the concept development model, in which she asked the children to put together all the things that were lines and those things that were not. So far, so good, she thought. And then she realized that she was really excited about what was happening in the class. Exciting and stimulating—two words that had been missing from her classroom for some time.

## Epilogue

As the weeks progressed, Miss Abbott became more enthusiastic about the abilities of all her students. Tommy, who was often the catalyst for ideas and a source of information, gradually developed a respect for the rights and abilities of the other students. As concepts grew one upon the other, the children responded to the logic behind what they were being asked to learn. One memorable moment came one morning during the lesson on squares when they were discussing the relationship between lines and squares. Susan said, "You know, Miss Abbott, skinny isn't a very good word to describe a line." And all the class agreed.

**Activity 13.1**

Regardless of the age of students you teach or plan to teach, develop lessons that will fit into this unit for kindergarten youngsters. If you do not wish to use *line,* try *square* or *circle,* or choose some other concept that is of particular interest to you. Select a concept, however, that will be challenging to young minds and then challenge yourself to design lessons appropriate for the kindergarten class-room. Use as many of the instructional models as are appropriate in your lesson plans. ■

## ■ SUMMARY

Knowledge of the background and abilities of the students in a class is essential to planning if that knowledge is coupled with a determination to see each child's needs as a welcome challenge. Young children can be presented with content that is challenging to the teacher and interesting to the learners as long as that content is presented through appropriate instructional techniques.

# Chapter 14

# A Middle School Case Study

The interdisciplinary teaching team for the seventh grade at Mumford Middle School had a problem. Some of the teachers in the team, which covered the subjects of math, social studies, language arts, and science, were concerned that the students were fixed in their opinions. As Alice Brown, the science teacher, said one morning in frustration, "Narrow-minded! That's what they are. These kids just won't entertain a new thought about a fact or idea in the courses they take or about each other. Sometimes teaching them feels more like plowing rock than planting seeds."

So began a conversation that would extend over several days and result in one of the most exciting teaching experiences any of these teachers had known. Like many teachers, the team had lately fallen into a bit of a rut, but they were about to find a way out of it.

Sam Lopez, the math teacher, a native of the small midwestern farming community in which the school was located, came to the defense of the locals. "This may not be cosmopolitan Madison Avenue, Alice, but in place of refinement, there is good, solid common sense in this community and in these kids. Their behavior is generally very good, and you know it is. They do what they are told and what their parents expect them to do."

"Yes," replied Alice, "but they also think the way they are told, and they can be very cruel to those who are different in any way. In science, it is very important to be willing to look at ideas with an open and inquiring mind."

Mary Teague, the social studies teacher, took her usual role of conciliator. "I appreciate the fact that they are dependable and that they are motivated to do well. However, I too am concerned that we challenge their intellects and encourage them to play with ideas instead of being so concerned that they get a good grade."

Henry Martin, the English and language arts teacher, as usual the bemused observer, said, "If we decide to challenge their intellects, we better be sure that the school board doesn't decide to challenge us. Those board members may not be very enthusiastic about the kids playing around with ideas."

"I'm not thinking of turning them into radical revolutionaries," said Alice. "I just want them to have some perspective, a point of view that is broader than the one shared by the members of this community."

"Sounds radical enough to me," Henry rejoined. "Oh well, it might break the boredom for a while."

Alice went on, ignoring the subtle cynicism. "It just so happens I've been thinking lately of a unit of study based on the concept of *perspective*. My hope is that I can get our students to consider the various ways in which a problem may be approached, whether it be a problem in science or in any other subject."

"It's funny you should mention the word *perspective* this morning, Alice," said Sam. "I have been working on a unit in geometry, where perspective is all-important. My thought was that since the kids are fascinated with the design capabilities of computers, I might introduce them to linear perspective in a way that would teach them both about a new design program we have and about lines in three-dimensional space."

Alice responded with renewed enthusiasm, momentarily forgetting her frustration with the students. "You know, understanding the use of perspective marked the Renaissance. It literally changed forever the way we would describe and know the universe. I have always wanted to know more about the mathematical principles involved in the great paradigm shift of the Renaissance. I'd also like to teach the impact of perspective on our understanding of the physical world, particularly in regard to mapmaking. Could we plan this unit together?"

"The concept of *perspective* certainly fits into the unit I am preparing to teach on the westward movement," Mary interjected. "I've been trying to think how to get across the idea that historians have their own perspectives that influence the way in which they recount events. No doubt, any historical perspective differs from the perspective of those who were involved in the events of history. Think how much difference it makes if one looks at the westward movement from the perspective of a settler or from the perspective of a native American. I've heard it said that those who win the wars win the right to write the histories."

"You know, we haven't taught an interdisciplinary unit in a long time. Why don't we design a unit with a focus on the concept *perspective*?" said Mary, her excitement evident to all.

Henry abandoned his role of detached observer and enthusiastically joined in. "I have been planning a unit in literature on point of view, but perspective is really the basis for understanding the meaning of *point of view*. As I recall, the *view*point—or point of view—is the point where parallel lines converge in a painting to convey a sense of depth." Turning to his friend Alice, he said, "It was the Renaissance painters who rediscovered this technique from Greek writings and who were able to create perspective in their painting just as the mapmakers learned to do. Perspective is a much better concept to use for the focus of my unit. And I can choose material that will fit into your time frame of the westward movement," he continued, now turning to Mary. "That way we can look at historical perspective through the eyes of fictional characters as well as through the eyes of the historian."

As usual, the other team members were astonished at the wealth of information Henry could bring to a discussion when he chose to do so. Everyone was ready, without actually putting the matter to any sort of vote, to try an interdisciplinary unit based on the concept of *perspective*.

The four team members shared a common planning time and were able to schedule the students for blocks of time each day. The rooms in which they taught were traditional classrooms except that there was one movable wall that allowed them to create a larger classroom area for special purposes. In the past, their attempts at team teaching had been only partially successful, but this time they seemed to have ignited each others' interest.

At the next team meeting, Mary suggested that they brainstorm objectives for the unit. "For instance," she said, "I want the students to compare and contrast the perspectives of various groups regarding the westward movment. I want them to evaluate the perspective of the historian who is writing, as well as to identify other possible perspectives of those who were involved in the events."

"I am concerned that they be able to define the term *perspective* in a general sense and then to see how perspective relates to writing," said Henry. "In their writing I want them to use various perspectives in describing an event, as well as develop more dynamic ways to describe how others feel and act."

"I want them to be able to accept the possibility that there are various ways to look at the same phenomenon," said Alice, "and I want them to recognize and value the importance of looking beyond and questioning what appears to be obvious. I also want them to use the scientific approach in solving problems that require inquiry, particularly problems in which perspective affects how we interpret the physical world."

"I want them to use parallel lines and viewpoint to create perspective in simple designs with the use of the computer," said Sam. "Some of these kids are way ahead of me already on the computer, and I am going to really have to do my homework to keep up. That's part of the great fun we have teaching in a field that is developing faster than any of us can imagine, let alone keep up with. But in all the excitement of computers, I want the students to develop respect for the capabilities of this tool in describing three-dimensional phenomena on a two-dimensional screen."

Henry rolled his eyes as he sensed just how enthusiastic everyone was becoming, but he did so very slightly, not wishing to offend as much as to poke a little fun. But Alice wasn't going to let the seriousness of the moment pass. "And all of us are concerned that the students develop more understanding for others and increase their willingness to consider another point of view in solving problems in human relations," she said.

"We have our objectives for the unit right in front of us," said Mary. "There is *so much* content that we could incorporate into this unit! I think we should each bring to our next meeting an outline of the most important concepts that need to be covered in each discipline."

When they met again, each of them had diagrammed the main concepts they thought should be included in the unit on *perspective* (see Table 14.1).

It was obvious that *viewpoint*, so important in creating perspective, had become an essential concept as it applied to understanding events and ideas relating to perspective. The teachers then realized that the meaning of *viewpoint* was one that the art teacher, Mrs. Fisk, could best explain to the students. She agreed that a discussion on the point at which parallel lines converge in a painting, or in a design, to create the illusion of space would serve as an excellent

**TABLE 14.1**   Perspective

| Geometry | Earth Science | Literature | History |
|---|---|---|---|
| The viewpoint | The viewpoint | Point of view | Point of view |
| Geometry | Exploration/Mapmaking | Characters | Participants |
| Parallel | Scientific method/Inquiry | Plot | Events |
| Point, line, plane | | Narrator | Historian |

advance organizer for the study of perspective. It was exciting to think that one of the fundamental concepts of the art curriculum would be the focal point for study in many different disciplines simultaneously. This single concept would bring everything together, just as it had 400 years ago!

After their discussion with Mrs. Fisk, who agreed to do the keynote lesson twice—each time in the double classroom with two of the teachers and their classes present—the team members developed the chart shown in Table 14.2.

## The Mumford Plan

It was time to design the unit. The team members decided to emphasize the geometry and earth science portions during the first part of the unit, followed by the literature and history sections. The art teacher's introductory lesson would extend across two days, at which time the main concepts related to perspective would be introduced. *Viewpoint*, or physical point of view, would be tied to visual perspective and to ideas and attitudes.

Mrs. Fisk planned to teach the definition of *viewpoint* by using the concept attainment model in a way that would allow the definition to serve as an organizer and point of reference for all the teachers on the team throughout the unit. Her idea was to spend one day helping the students to capture elementary perspective in their own drawings. Then, the next day she could bring in prints of pre-Renaissance and Renaissance art to use as positive and negative examples of perspective in art. A collection of M. C. Escher's pen and ink drawings, in which the mathematician/artist plays with perspective in a variety of ways, would serve as material for a culminating reinforcement activity. She would close

**TABLE 14.2**   Perspective: Advance Organizer—Viewpoint

| Art | Geometry/Science | History/Literature |
|---|---|---|
| Space | Design | Plot/Events |
| Distance | Point, line, plane | Character |
| Relative position | Parallel | Narrator |
| | Convergent | |
| | Scientific method | |

with a brief lesson on how the students could achieve such play and deliberate ambiguity in their own drawings.

Following this lesson, all of the teachers would explain the plans for the unit as it pertained to their classes, provide an outline of assignments and activities, and answer any questions the students might have about the unit. A test of the students' understanding of the content to be covered would be given at this point. This would provide valuable information to the teachers regarding any changes or modification that might need to be made in the design of the unit. This was particularly important to Sam Lopez in setting up the teams for instruction in computer skills.

The geometry and science lessons would be taught for approximately three weeks. After the students had a basic introduction to computer-aided design (CAD), they would learn to create simple three-dimensional designs with the use of the computer. Mr. Lopez decided that a form of the Jigsaw model used in conjunction with direct instruction would be an excellent way to teach the principles of CAD. Individual students would first work through a tutorial on the basics of computer design. Then, pairs of students would be given elementary problems to solve with immediate feedback on their success. Next, teams would be formed made up of students with a range of abilities related to the computer, making it possible for students with more advanced computer skills to work with those with less skill. Each team would be able to solve a different problem set while acquiring a different set of computer skills associated with computer-aided design. Individual team members would be expert in a particular aspect of design, and they would have the responsibility of teaching other students in their study group.

Following the computer lessons, the science teacher would introduce the relationship of perspective to an understanding of the physical world, particularly in recording what is observed through the design of maps. Alice Brown would present to the students puzzling but relatively common problem situations involving perspective. The students would solve these problems with an inquiry approach using the Suchman model. For instance, one of the problems would be to describe the appearance of a ship on the horizon and explain why it seems to grow larger as it draws near. Another problem would be to explain the fact that the moon seems to be very large on the horizon, but appears to grow smaller as it rises in the sky. The third and most difficult problem the students would be asked to solve by inquiry would be that of how to transfer the surface of a sphere (like a globe of Earth) onto a flat surface without distorting the relative sizes of land masses.

With these introductions to the concept of *perspective* as a foundation, Mary Teague and Henry Martin would work with the students toward an understanding of the way in which individuals interpret events in literature and in history, stressing that interpretation often depends on the individual's point of view. They decided that concept development, direct instruction, and Jigsaw models would be effective in meeting their objectives. (This part of the unit is described in more detail in the next section.)

The concluding lesson in the unit would be a discussion of how an under-standing of perspective applies in human relations. Using the exploration of feelings/resolution of conflict model, each of the four teachers on the team would lead groups of students in applying what they had learned regarding per-spective to the exploration of feelings and the possible resolution of conflict in a particular situation.

To illustrate how the models approach to teaching would work in this situation, we present the detailed lesson design from the portion of the unit that focused on the concept of *perspective* in history and literature.

## Unit: Perspective—It All Depends on Where You Were When

*Teaching time:* Two weeks
> *Objectives:* The students will

1. compare the meaning of perspective in geometry and science to the use of the concept in literature and history.
2. relate the concept *perspective* to literature and history by recognizing how individuals both real and fictional perceive events.
3. identify various perspectives in a situation, explain the point of view of each participant, and explain how the point of view determines the per-spective.
4. describe how previous experiences and preconceptions affect the percep-tion of events.
5. be willing to describe a perspective other than their own in relation to a situation.

> *Advance Organizer:* Relate the meaning of *viewpoint* as it has been discussed in art, geometry, and science to the application of the term in literature, history, and human relations. Introduce the idea that it is the point of view that deter-mines perspective.

### ■ Lesson One: Toward a Perspective on Point of View

*Instructional Model: Concept Development*
> Estimated time: 2 hours
> *Objectives:* The students will

1. generalize that a variety of points of view can exist on a single subject.
2. relate the meaning of *point of view* and *perspective* in art, science, and math to attitudes and beliefs.
3. define *bias* and *preconceptions* and relate these terms to their own experience.

*Rationale for choice of model:* It has been said that there are three kinds of thinkers—those who think what they think is the only way to think, those who think others who think like they do are the best thinkers, and those who can think in several ways about the same thing. The psychologist Jean Piaget termed the first thinker *egocentric*, the second thinker *concrete*, the last and best thinker *formal*. But the great contribution Jean Piaget made to psychology was in proving that the child learns from experience by constructing a model of how the world is. Concept development will provide these students the opportunity to see that different points of view (of possibly equal validity) can be held by reasonable thinkers on the same topic. As they have the chance to discriminate between different points of view on a similar topic, they will see that each thinker is at once a concrete thinker, who sees the world through one set of eyes, and a formal thinker, who can recognize the reasonableness of alternative views of the same facts and ideas. The move from egocentric thought to higher level thought is stimulated by experience with alternative ways of thinking, and concept development activities will allow that experience.

*Application of the model:* Students will be given a series of quotations representing points of view that are both alike and different in various ways. For instance, some will represent the same bias, some will be about the same event, some will be spoken by the same person. The students will be asked to group and categorize these quotations and then to explain the reason for their decisions. The students will work in pairs and then come together as a large group to discuss their decisions and the reasons for their decisions.

*Evaluation:* At the conclusion of this model, the students will discuss what they learned earlier in the unit during the math and science portions and how that material will relate to the new learning that will occur in this lesson. This discussion will also serve as a midpoint evaluation of the students' progress.

■ **Lesson Two: Perception—It Depends on Where You're Coming From**

*Instructional model: Direct Instruction*
Estimated time: 3 hours
*Objective:* The students will describe how preconceptions and experience affect the perception of an event.
*Rationale for choice of model:* In the present instance, instruction will be both indirect and direct in that the teachers will set up a circumstance that gives rise to questions, which will be answered by direct instruction. (As this example demonstrates, direct instruction does not equate with passive learning.) Basically, the questions the teachers will pose and the activities in which the students will engage center on the issue of perception—what one is predisposed to see, what one sees. But predisposition is always governed by three factors, and those factors are the point of this instruction. By setting up a series of experiences for the students whereby they see that the relation between where they are (figuratively and liter-

ally) and what they are observing determines what they see, the stage is set for presenting the three factors that define "where the observer is coming from."

*Application of the model:* The lesson will begin with the reading of a description of a house. The description includes the setting of the house, the number of windows, doors, rooms, the present furnishings and decorations, where the occupants keep their valuables, and so on. Half the class will be asked to read the account as if they were a professional burglar, the other half will read the account as if they were a prospective buyer of the house. (Since directions will be written, rather than given orally, each half of the class will be unaware of the alternative perspective taken by the other half.) Following a silent reading of the passage, students will retell what they recall. (Research by Goetz, Schallert, Reynolds, and Radin has shown that readers will focus their attention on the aspects of the information that bear on their interest.[1]) This initial experience will provide dramatic proof that the same experience for different people is a different experience. When perception is different, experience is different.

Next, the teachers will present a roleplay in which an armed robbery occurs. The students will be asked to write down what they perceived to have happened. Then the teachers will reenact the roleplay after having the students change their seats in the room and after giving them some additional information. The students will then be asked to reevaluate their original observation based on a different perspective and with different information.

Using this activity as an organizer, the teachers will present the three factors that influence the perspective of those who witness events:

1. the viewpoint of the perceiver
2. previous experience of the observer
3. preconceptions

After these have been explained, with many examples, students will be questioned and asked to give examples themselves, to check for understanding. More guided practice will take place when students are asked to view a filmstrip of an accident and then identify the various perspectives of the witnesses as these relate to point of view, possible previous experiences, and preconceptions. For independent practice, the students will be given an assignment to describe an event depicted on a television sitcom from the point of view, previous experience, and preconceptions of the different characters involved. They will then be asked to retell the event using another point of view, experience, and preconception.

*Evaluation:* Students will be given a worksheet to take home that will ask them to answer specific questions relating to the television program. Those students who choose to write their own essay may do so, but those who have more difficulty in writing may follow the format of the worksheet. These worksheets will be evaluated to determine if the class understood the assignment.

### ■ Lesson Three: Relating Point of View to Perspective

*Instructional model: Jigsaw*

Estimated time: 3 hours class time plus outside work in preparation.

*Objectives:* The students will

1. relate the concept of *perspective* to literature and history by recognizing how individuals, both real and fictional, perceive events.
2. identify various perspectives in a writing, explain the point of view of each author, and explain how the point of view determines perspective.

*Rationale for choice of model:* Jigsaw is both an instructional model and an instructional activity, with the great virtue of accommodating a wide range of student abilities in a single classroom and allowing for great efficiency of effort on the part of the group. In the present instance, the students can, collectively, read many selections and thus encounter many perspectives and points of view, historically and fictionally. By cooperating in their learning and sharing in their understandings, they will cover much ground quickly, reading, literally, hundreds of pages of material and experiencing the same ideas through many different eyes. Jigsaw thus allows each learner to come to the insights of many different learners merely by sharing his or her own insights.

*Application of the model:* The students will be assigned to teams of four, with a range of ability in each group. Each individual in the team will be given a reading assignment related to the westward movement; assignments will be selected to match the reading abilities of different team members. The teams will be given different sets of readings—some short stories, some selections from novels, some drawn from original source documents, some taken from textbook chapters on the westward expansion. The students have three days to study the material and will be encouraged to discuss their selections with those on other teams who have been assigned readings similar to their own. They are to identify the perspective of the author and of the major characters or persons in the story or essay and then to explain this perspective to the other members of their team. Following team discussions, the class as a whole will discuss the selections and the various perspectives presented in the material.

*Evaluation:* The class discussion will be audio- or videotaped for the teachers to review and determine if the students have reached the objectives of the lesson.

## Epilogue

At the end of the actual unit of study, the team had dinner together one evening to discuss and evaluate their experience in teaching the unit. Although there were some instances when an activity had proven unsuccessful, everyone wholeheartedly agreed that the unit had been a great success. The evaluations of how well the students had met the cognitive objectives indicated a high rate of success, and attitudinal surveys, designed to insure anonymity, indicated that most of the students had enjoyed the unit and had an increased awareness of different perspectives.

The team remembered the final discussions with particular pleasure. The students had been presented with a situation that involved a person entering the school who was from another country with an entirely different culture. The discussion centered on the various problems the students would encounter and how that individual's perspective would differ from others. The teachers had taped and were able to compare the various discussions. All of them agreed that the students had gained insights into how others might feel about a particular situation. The teachers had also learned that these young people had the capacity to deal with complicated ideas and respond to material that challenged their preconceptions. "My perception is that these really are a great bunch of kids," said Henry Martin. And to that, there was agreement all around.

### Activity 14.1

Regardless of the age of the students whom you teach or plan to teach, become a part of this interdisciplinary team. Design lessons that can be used in this unit or in a unit that focuses on an interdisciplinary study of another concept. ■

### ■ SUMMARY

Cooperative planning by teachers across disciplines can provide a rewarding professional experience. In addition, such cooperation enriches the learning experience for students, particularly young adolescents, who enjoy seeing the way in which a concept threads meaning through a variety of disciplines, enriching the understanding of each.

### ■ NOTE

1. E. T., Goetz, D. L. Schallert, R. E. Reynolds, and D. I. Radin, "Reading in Perspective: What Real Cops and Pretend Burglars Look for in a Story," *Journal of Educational Psychology* 75 (1983): 500–510.

# Chapter 15

# A High School Case Study

As the pungent scent of Rudy's Dry Cleaners greeted Jake Samuels, an unfamiliar voice said, "Hi, Mr. Samuels."

"Hi," responded Mr. Samuels, trying to place the friendly face.

"I'm Chris Pezzoli. I go to Madison High School. May I help you?"

"My cleaning, please," came the request, as he handed Chris the laundry ticket, still curious about where he'd seen this young man. Just a face in a sea of faces in the halls at Madison.

"Yes, sir. Coming right up." Chris started the line of clothes moving around. As Mr. Samuels's suit appeared, Chris handed it to him, saying, "I always wanted to have you for English, but I'm in a general class. I've heard what a good teacher you are, but you teach only the advanced classes." He hesitated, feeling a little embarrassed at his own boldness.

"Thanks for the vote of confidence. I'm sorry I'm not teaching you, Chris. I'd like to."

"So long." Chris shrugged and smiled. "See you around."

Jake Samuels thought about Chris as he put his car in reverse. He thought about his own schedule. Now that he was chairperson of the department he taught only three classes; and Chris was right, they were all top-track classes. The encounter reminded him, though, that he missed the general classes he used to teach. Those students struck a special chord for him, possibly because his was the last English class they might take. He remembered how he always wanted to give it all to them—everything he loved about English—served up on a silver platter, so invitingly they would surely seek more.

He began to think aloud. "Instead we water it down, trying to make it more palatable. But there's a contradiction in that. Shouldn't it be just the reverse? Shouldn't we enrich the content of classes for general students?"

As he turned onto Madison Avenue his mind was whirling. Sure, there had been problems for him when he taught regular and remedial classes. His teaching style of lecture and discussion did not work for students who had difficulty taking notes and paying attention for long periods of time. But he had learned so much in the past few years as department chairperson, observing other teachers and attending workshops and inservices on instructional strategies. In his advanced classes he had learned to use a variety of instructional models, and he was certain that these would work well with all students. The idea he was playing with would give him an opportunity to put his theory to the test. He wanted to give it a try.

At four o'clock the following Monday afternoon, Jake Samuels poked his head into the classroom next to his.

"Liz, do you have a minute?"

"Sure, come on in. I'm always too drained to get anything done this time of day. Good to see you. How do you manage to look so chipper at the end of a long day?"

"Thanks, I don't always feel chipper—it's just a facade I put on. I need to talk to you, though. I met a student of yours the other day, Chris Pezzoli. Tell me about him."

"Well, Chris is a very nice young man—imaginative and hard working, very likable. He's in my fourth-period class. I see his parents around town now and again. His Dad was laid off when the woolen mill closed. He does odd jobs—forced self-employment, he calls it—but he hasn't been able to pick up anything steady. Chris's Mom works, but they really need what Chris brings in from his job at a dry cleaner's. I know he's going to work there full time after graduation. I'm trying to talk him into taking community college courses at night, but I think it's futile. Of course, if his Dad does find something steady . . ." she trailed off without much hope in her voice.

Jake interrupted, "I've been thinking about these kids in the general classes and about how much I miss teaching them. I had an idea. How would you like to try switching classes fourth period for about four weeks, as a kind of experiment? I have some ideas I'd sure like to try with them. I thought I'd try to teach them *Macbeth*." After a pause, he grinned. "Think I'm crazy? You'd be teaching the poetry of the romantics, not one of my favorite units, but just your cup of tea, I know."

Liz looked at him for a minute as the suggestion he was making took shape in her mind. "Do I think you're crazy? Yes. Do I think it's a good idea? It just might be an excellent idea. I'd love to see how they would respond . . . and I'd love to have crack at your kids. Nineteenth-century poetry is my first love."

## Jake Samuels's Plan

That night Jake Samuels put aside the mountain of papers he was planning to grade. He thought about Chris and the large, probably slightly jaded group he would face. But the challenge of it was energizing—he was more excited than he had been for some time. He began making notes on what he wanted to accomplish.

First, he wanted them to enjoy the play. He pondered a minute, then crossed out "enjoy" and replaced it with an overworked word he seldom used in such a context; the word was "love." Yes, he wanted them to *love* this play, maybe the finest piece of literature ever written. He starred that goal. It would guide everything he did those four weeks. Next, he wanted them to appreciate how shrewd the Bard was and how relevant his thinking remains today.

He wanted them to examine the concept *ambition* and how it can be a constructive force in moderation, a dangerous force in excess. To do this they must understand the complexity of Macbeth's and Lady Macbeth's characters. They must not see them as all bad or they would miss a great deal of the play's wisdom. He wanted them to grasp the power of suggestion, and of what it could mean to plant an idea in an all too fertile mind. Further, he wanted them to be stirred by the beauty, subtlety, and bawdiness of the language. He hoped to draw them into this Elizabethan world much as Shakespeare had drawn his audiences into his plays.

Where did these goals come from? Jake Samuels is an expert teacher with years of experience that have taught him much, and because of that he is willing to rely intuitively on his judgment as a teacher, his expertise in *Macbeth*, his convictions about these students' needs, and his knowledge of his community's expectations. Thus, with some confidence he translated his vaguely defined goals into a specific list:

The students would

1. *love* the play;
2. gain confidence in their own intellects by partially mastering very difficult material;
3. appreciate the power and relevance of Shakespeare's work;
4. grasp some of the complexities related to the concept "ambition";
5. understand the dimensionality of the characters in *Macbeth*;
6. recognize the effect of the power of suggestion;
7. become attuned to the richness of iambic pentameter; and
8. become acquainted with the major distinguishing characteristics of Elizabethan England.

This was the point at which, in the not so distant past, he might have stopped his general planning and begun to think in terms of daily lessons. He had recently come upon the realization that he needed to be far more precise in his planning. This meant listing specific student needs after doing some research on their backgrounds. It meant selecting specific objectives and the models that would help him reach those objectives. It also meant devising means of evaluating how well he had achieved those objectives. It sounded complicated but it was becoming second nature, and it saved time and effort in the end. Most of all it increased his sense of satisfaction.

During the next week he did a lot of data gathering: he talked to Liz; he looked at records and test scores; he casually, unobtrusively, observed the class he was to teach; and he carefully reread the play and outlined the content for essential concepts. He remembered Chris's shrug. It had been eloquent; it had said, "We don't deserve the best."

He believed the students needed to be given challenging material, and implicit in his choice of *Macbeth* was the statement, "You can do it. I will not teach down to you." But that, in turn, implied a commitment to give the students the support they needed to become independent. The thought seemed almost contradictory, but what it implied was that he must not fail them or allow them to fail themselves. He knew they wouldn't, but if the unit was to build their confidence, then they would first have to commit themselves to the challenge, to like what they were doing well enough *not* to fail in it. He listed what the students would need:

1. To be presented with challenging material
2. To know that someone thought they could grasp difficult material
3. To be taken seriously, to have their opinions sought and valued
4. To gain confidence in their own abilities
5. To talk about important issues and real feelings
6. To gain a sense of accomplishment *because* they had mastered difficult material successfully

Based on a combination of goals and needs, he wrote general objectives for the unit on *Macbeth* and considered how he might evaluate the success of the unit. After all, if he could not demonstrate to himself that the students had learned and profited from this unit, then he might better stay with the advanced classes and leave well enough alone. Jake wrote out his objectives, including methods to evaluate each objective.

1. Students will *love* the play *Macbeth* and be interested in learning more. This will be evaluated by using a pre- and post-unit questionnaire in which the students can check their reactions without fear of being identified.

2. Students can relate themes in the play to their daily lives. The evaluation of this will be in skits developed by the students to place scenes from *Macbeth* in contemporary settings.

3. Students will demonstrate appreciation for the elegance of iambic pentameter, for how sound can augment meaning and humor. This will be evaluated by having them present a piece of their favorite music and having them explain how beat and lyrics work together.

4. Students will analyze the main characters and identify the elements that create complexity. A writing assignment will be used to evaluate this objective. However, pictures could also be used to illustrate these elements; these pictures could be drawn or created from a collage of pictures cut from magazines. (He knew that in the past he had sometimes failed to realize that a student had understood a concept that had been taught because that student had been unable to express the concept in written terms. The student could, however, sometimes express that concept if given another medium. Writing would not be neglected, but he wanted to be sure that he measured what he was teaching and not just the students' reading and writing skills.)

5. Students will demonstrate familiarity with Elizabethan England by teaching some aspects of that society to small groups (here using a cooperative learning model). Evaluation will be based on the students' performance in this activity.

6. Students will exhibit understanding of the power of suggestion and the idea of a self-fulfilling prophecy by giving examples from their daily lives. This will be evaluated through discussions and brief taped oral presentations.

With these objectives in mind, he began to think about the possible models he would use to achieve them, in what sequence he would use them, and how much time he would allot for each part of the unit plan.

**1.** He would start with a concept attainment lesson on classics . . . no, he would use the term *bestsellers*, because that had more drawing power and was much more appropriate. Shakespeare, after all, was very conscious of box-office appeal. (After the play they would talk about the distinction between a classic and a bestseller and about how some works of art are both.) He would use positive examples of bestsellers, such as *The Bible, Gone with the Wind* (the movie version), an Elvis record, and a Beatles tape. His negative examples would consist of one of the lesser-known short stories from their text, a poem he had written, a record called *Comin' Home* that a friend had cut, a favorite painting from home by a little-known Quaker artist. Once they could define the concept of *bestseller*, he would ask what ingredients they would include if they were trying to write a play that would be a bestseller. He would make a list of their ideas (he predicted they would mention things like suspense, violence, maybe a little romance), and then as a group they would try to derive a set of standards of excellence from this list.

They would try to apply their standards to the play *Macbeth,* considered in the time of its first appearance in the Globe theatre. How many of the same standards did Shakespeare seem to apply? What standards did he employ that they did not? What ingredients did they think of that Shakespeare did not attend to (for example, the medium of delivery)? How would the passage of 350 years alter the standards of literature? All of these questions and others of the sort which would arise would cast a new light on the play for these young readers.

**2.** Next, he would use direct instruction with lectures, monologues, filmstrips, and artwork to give them background information on Shakespeare's life and times. He would emphasize the tricks Shakespeare used to capture the vocal and critical groundlings in the opening scenes. He would show the ghost in the opening scene of *Hamlet,* the fight in the opening scene of *Romeo and Juliet,* and make them guess what ploy would be used to open *Macbeth.*

**3.** He would also use a cooperative learning model for background information. He would divide the class into five groups. They would do research in preparation for teaching each other, in a variety of ways, about daily life (food, fashion, sports, sanitation, etc.), government, art and architecture, social class structure, education, and, finally, agriculture and industry.

**4.** He would open the play with the movie version of the first two acts of *Macbeth,* allowing the students to track the play in their books as they watched it. With a basic understanding of the plot firmly established, they would read Act Three together, dramatizing various scenes and speeches, closely examining words, connotations, and concepts.

**5.** He would utilize a concept development model in a lesson on *ambition*.

**6.** If the reading went well, they would read Act Four together rather than viewing the film. He would use cooperative learning again for Act Five. In groups, they would prepare a scene to present to the class.

**7.** While they were working on their scenes, he would interject a lesson on Lady Macbeth using the synectics model. This would be a powerful and effective tool for showing them the contradictions and opposing forces within a character.

**8.** When they had finished the play, he would use the exploration of feelings model in a discussion. In order to gain a more sympathetic view of the main characters they would look at events through the eyes of the characters and try to assess their feelings.

**9.** Finally, he would build on these insights by using an inquiry model to explore how the tragedy came about. At the beginning of the play Macbeth is not such a villain. He had had many good qualities, but in a very brief time he had caused the downfall of most of his country's leadership. How had this happened? Was so much violence plausible? This was the puzzle he hoped to get them to consider. He suspected they would see the cause of the tragedy purely in terms of too much ambition, and he wanted them to look further, to delve into other causes. To understand the answer to the questions posed, they would have to go outside the play, to inquire about conditions in Scotland in the eleventh century. What about the isolation of life in eleventh-century Scotland, near the height of the Dark Ages? Perhaps it is easier to plot against someone you seldom see. It was a violent time, with frequent attacks from unknown sources, and a street gang mentality had developed in response to the constant threat against the territory. Macbeth had gained his reputation by warring successfully. Jake Samuels wanted the students to search for these explanations themselves; he did not want to spoon-feed them.

He drew a chart of the sequence of lessons within the unit that he had developed (see Table 15.1). One of Mr. Samuels's detailed lessons—the concept

**TABLE 15.1**    Macbeth: A Study in Ambition Turned to Avarice

| The Stage of Anticipation (Before the Play) | The Stage of Realization (During the Play) | The Stage of Contemplation (After the Play) |
|---|---|---|
| Concept Attainment on bestsellers (1 day) | Synectics on Lady Macbeth (2 days) | Exploration of Feelings on characters (1–2 days) |
| Direct Instruction on background (1 day) | Concept Development and Classroom Discussion on ambition/suggestion (5+ days) | Suchman Inquiry (1 day) |
| Cooperative Learning—research on background (4 days) | Cooperative Learning for skits on Act Five (3 days) | |

development and classroom discussion on ambition/suggestion—held an important key, he felt, for understanding the play. His first thought had been to focus solely on the concept *ambition*, but the more he thought about this, the more he felt his two primary concepts—*ambition* and the *power of suggestion*—were inextricably woven together in the play.

## Unit: *Macbeth*—A Study in Ambition Turned to Avarice

### ■ Lesson Five: Ambition and the Power of Suggestion

*Teaching time:* 6–8 days, on approximately the following schedule:

> *Monday and Tuesday:* Concept development lesson on the witches, culminating with a paragraph by each student on one group of items in concept development lesson. The group's label will be the topic sentence, the categorized items the supporting evidence.
>
> *Wednesday:* Classroom discussion of the dual concepts of ambition and suggestion in *Macbeth*.
>
> *Thursday:* Classroom discussion to continue, with emphasis on contemporary examples.
>
> *Friday:* Students to find expression (e.g., a formal paper, a collage, a tape recording, a drawing, or a dialogue) for the single idea from the discussion that they found most interesting.
>
> *Monday:* Students share their work in groups of three to get feedback, reactions, and suggestions.
>
> *Tuesday:* Students share their final products with the class.

*Lesson Objectives* (objectives are cross-referenced to the list on pp. 235–236): The students will

1. express in one of several artistic media their comprehension of the meaning of the word *ambition* in its best sense; (1, 2)
2. state orally their understanding of the danger of a trait possessed in excess; (2, 4)
3. demonstrate in writing how the concept of *ambition* relates to their daily lives; (2, 4)
4. infer from discussions about the causes of Macbeth's and Lady Macbeth's ambition; (2, 4)
5. describe in writing the power of suggestion by using examples from their daily lives; (2, 6)
6. give examples of the connection between the two concepts; (4, 6)
7. hypothesize orally about what form the witches might take in contemporary life. (6)

*Instructional models: Concept Development and Classroom Discussion*

*Rationale for choice of models:* The students in this class will be likely to see things in rather concrete terms and to cast things in black and white. By verbalizing all the impressions they have of the witches in this play, they should see collectively what they may not see individually, namely that the witches are symbolic of the fate which plays in every man's or woman's life. The students also need to see that the witches are Shakespeare's ploy for speaking directly to his audience about what is going on in Macbeth's mind and how strong the power of suggestion is. The classroom discussion model will extend the ideas generated by the class in the concept development activity. In addition, the discussion model will provide factual, interpretive, and evaluative questions regarding the *power of suggestion* and *ambition*.

### Application of the Concept Development Model

In effect, these two sophisticated concepts, the *power of suggestion* leading to *unbridled ambition*, will be approached through the witches.

Specific learning activities will have the students

1. list everything they remember about the witches (including inferences about their purpose);
2. group these details;
3. label these groups, showing their understanding and agreement on the reason for connecting the items;
4. rethink these connections, and new ones, by forming new groups;[1] and
5. demonstrate their grasp of the witches' role by synthesizing the items and forming generalizations.

The following questions will direct this concept development lesson. (The parenthetic instructions are reminders to himself.)

1. What specific things does the word *witches* bring to mind in the play *Macbeth?* or Name everything you can think of that is connected with the witches. (Don't stop until you have a comprehensive list.)
2. Look carefully at this list. Are there items that belong together or are alike in some way? (Group items where they are visible.)
3. Why do you think *cauldron* and *smoke* go together? (Don't label the group until the students have agreed on the reason for the grouping.)
4. Let's look at the original list again. Are there other groups we could put together? (Move slowly here. Give them time to rethink. List groups.)
5. Looking over the entire chalkboard, what can we say in general about witches?

*Evaluation of the concept development model:* The students will express their enriched understanding of the role of the witches by developing one of the groups into a paragraph where the label becomes the topic sentence and the items become supporting evidence.

### *Application of the Classroom Discussion Model*

A follow-up discussion to the concept development activity. Estimated time: 2 days.

First Cluster: Role of the Witches.   The discussion will begin with a few factual questions. The majority of questions will be interpretive. The basic question with which this cluster will begin and end: *Would Macbeth have killed Duncan if he had never heard the witches' prophecies?*

1. Where were the witches seen?
2. Under what conditions were the witches seen?
3. What did the witches look like? (Discuss implication of beards)
4. What did the witches do?
5. Were there limits to their powers?
6. What could be the meaning of "Fair is foul and foul is fair"[2]?
7. Is there a logical way they could have obtained their information?
8. Why do you think they appeared three times?
9. Do we have anything like the witches in our lives? (One class called them the voices of ambition within us, another the voices of temptation, another the voices of family or friends who want us to do things that are wrong.)
10. What does Banquo mean when he says, "the instruments of darkness tell us truth. . . ."[3]?

Second Cluster: The Power of Suggestion/Ambition.   In this section, most of the questions will be evaluative. The purpose will be to build on the ideas generated by exploring the role of the witches and to help the students connect these to *ambition* both in the play and in their own lives. Some sample questions follow. The basic question for this cluster is: *What forces shape our goals in life?*

1. Was Lady Macbeth ambitious? In what sense? What form did her ambition take?
2. Are the concepts of *ambition* and the *power of suggestion* related in the play? If so, in what way?
3. Have you seen examples of the power of suggestion in your own lives (e.g., horoscopes, fortune tellers, tarot cards)?
4. Have you seen examples of ambition in the classroom? on the athletic field? in your family? with your friends? in politics?

Mr. Samuels always prepared more questions than he could use. He gauged when to move on to the next question by the content and caliber of the discussion. He moved very slowly so as to give several students time to respond to each question.

*Evaluation of the Classroom Discussion Model:* The discussions would give an excellent idea of how well the students were grasping these concepts. But their knowledge would be taken one step further. They needed practice in writing, because this was a weak area, and it was necessary to know, on an individual basis, how well they had grasped these sophisticated concepts. He would ask them to do two of the following:

1. Represent through pictures modern versions of the witches.
2. Choose one of the concepts and, in a one-page paper, give an example of how that concept has affected you in your daily life.
3. Write a one- to two-page paper on your goals in life and what forces shaped them.

The students were to write a first draft of their papers, share them with small groups of students to get *positive* suggestions, and then write a final draft.

# Epilogue

When the four weeks were complete, Mr. Samuels was pleased with the outcome of his experiment. By and large the students had responded to his vote of confidence in their ability, and, as he had suspected, they had been capable of talking about far more sophisticated ideas than they had been able to get on paper. He was disappointed that they hadn't been able to read more of the text together. As he had anticipated, it had been very difficult for them, and they had gotten discouraged and a bit defensive. The reading would have gone much better if they had seen the entire movie version first, so they would have known what to expect.

The instructional models had allowed the students to be active participants in the learning process. As a result, they had fidgeted less and had seemed to take pride in participating. One of the highlights of the unit had been the synectics lesson. The following is an abbreviated description of that lesson.

*Step 1:* Students worked in groups of three to discuss Lady Macbeth and to brainstorm ideas and impressions of her. As follow-up, each student had written a short paragraph about the Lady. From these paragraphs, the students compiled a list of their strongest specific descriptive words—*shrill, shrew, iceberg, obsessed, conspirator, vixen, acid-tongued, murderous, two-faced, treacherous, sly, wily, conniving.*

*Step 2:* The students were asked to look at what they had written, to see if those words suggested an animal or a machine. Here are some examples of their answers:

> tiger (stalks its prey secretly)
> spider (lures its prey within its clutches)
> stiletto (looks delicate, is deadly)

*Step 3:* Next, the students were asked to pick one item from the list, to pretend they were that object, and to describe how that object felt. They picked the stiletto. Here are some of the feelings individual students described:

I feel *dainty:* I am slender, small, tapering, fancy, swift, (and deadly).
I feel *proud:* I am slim and fancy and quite beautiful.
I feel *sly:* I can be easily hidden and I fly quickly, silently.
I feel *powerful:* I can hurt enemies before they even know it.
I feel *sneaky:* I can be concealed and used on someone unsuspecting.
I feel *lonely:* I have no friends; I sit alone in my case.
I feel *imprisoned:* I am kept covered and hidden.
I feel *helpless:* I have no control over when and how I am used.
I feel *deadly:* I am small and quiet, but razor sharp.

*Step 4:* The students then were asked to look at their list of feelings and pick out words that seemed to contradict or fight with each other. They picked

proud and sneaky
dainty and powerful
imprisoned and powerful
dainty and deadly

*Step 5:* The class chose "imprisoned and powerful" to pursue. They were asked to name things that are both imprisoned and powerful. They named

nuclear power
a submarine captain
a boxer against the ropes
a wounded bear
a gladiator performing for an emperor

*Step 6:* Returning to the subject of Lady Macbeth, Mr. Samuels asked them to choose one of the above and compare it to her. Most chose a "gladiator performing for an emperor." They described her as powerful and deadly, but a puppet of her ambition as a gladiator is a puppet of his emperor.

## Activity 15.1

Consider one of your general or average classes. Design a lesson for teaching a topic that will be challenging to these students but that is generally considered to be reserved for advanced students. Plan specific steps for using at least two different instructional models. ■

## ■ SUMMARY

Teaching strategies that work for advanced classes are generally effective in average and remedial classes. The combination of careful planning and instructional variety allows students to become engaged in learning challenging material too often withheld because it is thought too difficult. Students who may not go on to college have a particular need to encounter such content in primary and secondary school, for if not here, they may never have the chance.

The teachers we have described in this chapter and the two preceding are all individuals with different backgrounds, interests, and teaching experiences. Like those of you reading this text, they have a variety of concerns and they approach instruction in different ways. They all share, however, a respect for their profession and a desire to improve, to find better ways to reach students and to be successful in the classroom. They are all seeking answers.

None of these professionals is willing to follow prescriptive formulas in a mindless fashion, but all attend to essential concerns in their planning. The focus of these teachers is on the learners. They give careful thought to what will be the outcome of instruction and assume the responsibility of evaluating to determine if what was taught was also learned.

It is our hope that these three chapters raise more questions than answers in the minds of our readers. We believe that teaching is an adventure for life and that no day is like another. No one can tell you exactly how to teach. We have suggested directions; you must chart the course.

## ■ NOTES

**1.** Hilda Taba, *Hilda Taba Teaching Strategies Program* (Miami, FL: Institute for Staff Development, 1971).

**2.** William Shakespeare, *Macbeth*, In *The Works of William Shakespeare* (New York: Oxford University Press, 1938), 859.

**3.** Shakespeare, *Macbeth*, 860.

# Chapter 16

# The Wisdom of Practice

## Creating a Positive Learning Environment

The difference between the expert and the novice in any profession is something more than years of service. There are professionals with 20 year service pins that should read "one year service, twenty times." Teaching is not exempt from this phenomenon—some teachers are novices forever, some are experts when they put their foot in the door. Eliot Wigginton, creator of *Foxfire* and author of *Sometimes a Shining Moment: The Foxfire Experience—Twenty Years Teaching in a High School Classroom,* is an example of the latter, an inspiration to all teachers. Why? What difference is there between ordinary and excellent teachers?

One big difference is that the expert teacher, no matter how many years' experience, has a greater repertoire of alternative instructional strategies to fall back on when things don't go exactly as expected. Which, we might add, they usually don't. The corollary to this difference between novice and expert is that the expert knows how to arrange matters in advance so that the chances of success are greater than average. It is the expert teachers, or those who are called gifted, who often beat the odds of failure, to the amazement of the naive observer. How does this happen? What does the expert teacher know that all good teachers should know?

Before we try to answer that question, we would point out that there is no formula for becoming a good teacher. Models of instruction are not formulas, like "one part oxygen plus two parts hydrogen equals water." Rather, models of instruction are more akin to recipes that have to be adapted to the needs and tastes of the cook and to the available ingredients. Teaching, like cooking, is a deliberative activity in the sense that through conscious reflection, or deliberation, the process can always be improved. Its quality always depends on the judgment of the teacher. Part of that judgment centers on the students and their changing needs, part centers on the process of teaching. But in any case, good teachers are never satisfied merely to teach; their teaching must also be appropriate and successful.

To say there is no formula for good teaching is not to say, however, that an accumulated wisdom about the practice of teaching does not exist. On the contrary, there is a large body of experience in and research on effective schools and instructional practices that provide the basis for many generalizations about teaching. And each of these generalizations must be continually tested by teachers. In this chapter, we would like to share some of those generalizations under the rubric "The Wisdom of Practice." The basis of these generalizations lies in our own experience and that of countless other teachers whom we have asked, "What makes you a good teacher?" Where appropriate, we have cited research findings that support these generalizations.

It was of particular interest to us to note recently that of the 25 different characteristics and behaviors a group of teachers mentioned in answer to our question "What makes you a good teacher?" only one mentioned knowledge of subject matter. That gave us pause at first; certainly teachers must be expert in the content they wish to teach. But when we stopped to reflect, we realized that good teachers likely take knowledge of their subject matter as a given, a necessary but not sufficient condition for good teaching. Most teachers would probably say, in other words, that knowing what you are trying to teach is essential to good teaching, but knowing how to teach it is what distinguishes good teachers from mere experts on content. The answers to our question, as we had hoped, address the issue of what insights good teachers have that make them good teachers. We want to share 11 of these insights.

## Good Teachers Are in Charge of Their Classrooms

We have asked students of elementary and high school age the same question—"What changes would you make in the instruction you have received thus far in school?" We prefaced the question by explaining that the administration had asked us to make recommendations on how to improve instruction in the school, but that we didn't feel capable of framing those recommendations without trying to see the present instructional program from the eyes of those learners who had experienced it, some of them for many years.

In general, the learners had only three things to say, though they said them in many different ways. Notice that in every case, their proposed changes were under the teacher's control.

- I'd like teachers to stick to the point.
- I'd like a classroom in which kids didn't get away with fooling around.
- I'd like to know that whatever I'm to be tested on, I have been taught.

Whether teaching 6-year-olds or 60-year-olds, the teacher is the person in charge of the classroom and everyone will feel better if that fact is clearly established from the start. The teacher is not a buddy or a chum, but neither is the teacher a warden or a tyrant. The teacher is the professional responsible for keeping the class focused on what is being taught, for maintaining discipline in a fair and consistent manner, and for insuring the reliability and validity of evaluation.[1] While much of that responsibility can and should be shared with learners, the teacher must retain the right of ultimate authority in the interest of the safety and well-being of the children—their physical, emotional, personal, and intellectual well-being.

The teacher's bearing, voice, appearance, and approach to the class should emphasize professionalism and careful preparation for the job. All of us are reassured when we feel that those persons responsible in controlled situations know what they are doing and will do it responsibly. Students of all ages depend on their teachers for that reassurance.

Research on classroom management is quite clear on the fact that good teachers establish a system of control as soon as possible in organizing each new class of students. "The effective teacher at the beginning of the year has an objective of setting up an efficient and smoothly running classroom where instruction, not management, is the major thrust."[2] Expert teachers agree that the first few days of school are critical in establishing and practicing instructional and managerial routines for the smooth operation of the classroom. A substantial line of research supports this insight.[3] The classroom is a social context in which everyone benefits if each member of the group feels a personal responsibility for the accomplishment of shared goals. Furthermore, each student in the classroom must understand that certain routines make those goals attainable. Leinhardt, Weidman, and Hammond label three basic kinds of routines that need to be established. These are

1. management routines for housekeeping, discipline, maintenance, and people moving;
2. support routines for the teacher and the students to keep lessons running smoothly; and
3. exchange routines for the give and take of instruction.[4]

To make these routines automatic, good teachers tell their students what they expect, they demonstrate it for the students, they guide the students in practicing expected moves, and they accept no less than mastery execution of the routines necessary for successful learning and instruction. It is important to note that demonstration and guidance aimed at correct routine is more effective than later correction of errors in routine. An ounce of prevention is the watchword in classroom management.

## Good Teachers Create a Pleasant Physical Environment for Learning

In his landmark study *A Place Called School,* John Goodlad paints a picture of the typical American school and classroom—aesthetically drab and emotionally flat.[5] But adequate workspace and a pleasant environment for learning are undoubtedly associated with student motivation and achievement.[6] There is little the individual teacher can do to create an attractive school building, but the tone of the individual classroom is very often under the control of the teacher and the students who share the room. There are many things teachers can do to create a pleasant setting for students to learn. At the very least, displays, physical environment, announcements, and seating can be effectively manipulated.

## ■ Displays

Insofar as possible, the room in which learning is to take place should be an attractive, inviting place to be. Colors and design can make the environment of a classroom more interesting and more exciting, for example, displays of students' artistic efforts–mobiles, dioramas, models, diagrams, and charts. Bulletin boards and visual display areas can be used to reinforce the essential concepts of a lesson or unit. For example, devote one section of your bulletin board to a display of words and concepts being encountered in the current unit of study. Arrange the words, with the help of the students, to reflect the relationships among the concepts you are teaching. Leave the words in place even when students are doing writing exercises and being tested on the material; it provides easy access to the words and concepts you are teaching.

Put students' work up for all to see, in a manner that reinforces all the students and not just a few. Pictures of class members and examples of student hobbies or collections can make the classroom reflect positively on individual students and groups. At the beginning of the year, perhaps as an introduction to the process of history, ask each student to bring to class some object of future memorabilia by which archaeologists a thousand years hence will know of the student's family, interests, hobbies, or style of living. Display these items together with a picture of the student and a brief biographical sketch.

## ■ Physical Environment

Although it is not absolutely essential to provide bulletin boards and displays, it is essential to attend to lighting, air, and room temperature. Many excellent lessons have been ruined because the temperature in the classroom was so hot or so cold that the students could not concentrate.

If the room in which you teach is too crowded, if it is too hot or too cold, if the air is stale, try to find another space. Talk with the principal about the physical conditions that are creating a problem. As an instructional specialist, you will be the person most aware of the effects of the physical environment on the learners.

## ■ Announcements

More than any other problem, teachers mention the intrusive presence of the sound system in their classrooms. If classes are continually interrupted by announcements or by students being called to the office, try to work out a plan for improving the situation. Administrators usually respond better to a plan than to a complaint.

One teacher developed a plan in which each week a different student sat by the door and received any messages sent to the room by the office. If the message was for another student, the message was handed to the student and that student quietly left the classroom. If the message was for the teacher, it was placed on the teacher's desk.

## ■ Seating

Few classrooms today have seats that are permanently fixed in one spot, but many teachers behave as though the chairs were immovable objects. Seating arrangements can do a great deal to enhance the success of instruction, and it is essential to plan for the orderly rearrangement of seating as class activities change.

Unless the class is very crowded or particularly difficult to manage, row seating in which most of the students are looking at the back of the person in front of them, is an undesirable arrangement. Circles and semicircles are generally more effective for sharing information and for discussion. Clusters of two, three, or four desks create a setting for small-group, cooperative work among students.

Students need instruction in how to efficiently change seating patterns in the classroom. For instance, if after a presentation, the students are to work in small groups, it is necessary to explain carefully in advance how the seats will be arranged and where each group is to be located. Classrooms can also be set up in such a way that individual and group work can go on at the same time. Plan in advance for the type of seating arrangement that you'll need so that sound and sight disturbances can be minimized. Procedures for furniture arrangement should be routine.

## Good Teachers Manage Human Relations Effectively

There are those who believe that teachers are in classrooms just to teach and that control of disruptive behavior in the classroom should be the responsibility of parents or administrators, not the teacher. While it is certainly true that violent and threatening behavior in the classroom should not be the sole responsibility

of the teacher, most discipline problems in the classroom need to be resolved by the teacher and the student.

### ■ Discipline as a Human Relations Problem

The problem of discipline is a human relations problem, and as the responsible adult in the situation, the teacher is the expert who must set up circumstances to resolve the conflict. (See Chapter 12 for guidelines in conflict resolution.)

Lashley has suggested four generalizations about classroom and behavior management, which he finds justified by the research. According to his extensive review of the literature on the issue of classroom management, the effective teacher

1. develops and implements a workable set of classroom rules;
2. structures and monitors the classroom in a manner that minimizes disruptive behavior;
3. clearly defines and quickly and consistently responds to inappropriate behavior; and
4. couches the response to inappropriate behavior in a tone that does not denigrate the students to whom the response is directed.[7]

### ■ Models for Discipline

Just as there are models for instruction, there are models for discipline available to the teacher. Wolfgang and Glickman, in a book entitled *Solving Discipline Problems: Strategies for Classroom Teachers*, have summarized these models. They point out that the teacher as a professional should be familiar with the strengths and weaknesses of various models for solving discipline problems and be able to utilize a variety of approaches in managing problems. They have identified eight models for discipline, but "teachers will be most effective by diversifying and individualizing their approaches."[8] Thus, the approach used to reach a depressed youngster who is unable to participate in classroom activities will be very different from the approach used to stop a fight or to defuse aggressive behavior. Effective teachers know what their options are in dealing with problems and are able to make appropriate choices.

One of the most constructive pieces of advice for dealing with human relations in the classroom comes from William Glasser. He advises teachers to pay personal attention to problem students when they are *not* in trouble. "The importance of personal contact in teaching has been receiving less attention in recent years as the emphasis on methods, objective testing, and classification of students has increased," writes Dr. Glasser.[9] Getting to know students as individuals may seem too time-consuming to a busy teacher, but "it takes less of a teacher's time to give the child the personal human touch coupled with firm disciplinary limits that will lead to change rather than to struggle endlessly to discipline a child with whom the teacher has no contact."[10]

### ■ The Importance of Knowing Your Students

A teacher recounted to us an experience that led her to realize the importance of knowing her students personally. A young man in her advanced English class had been uncooperative and even disruptive in classroom discussions and activities. A call to his parents had yielded only the response that English was his favorite subject, that they didn't know what was the problem.

When the student became seriously ill, the teacher visited him in the hospital, and they had a pleasant discussion in which, for the first time, the student revealed his intense enthusiasm for literature and language. He told her that he had been uncooperative (a troublemaker, he called himself) in her classroom because she usually read aloud the poems or passages of literature to be discussed. He said, "You read very well, but when you read you put your own interpretation on the writing. You put your voice into the words of the author and it bothers me. I hear a different voice and a different interpretation." This teacher had learned the importance of finding out what is causing a problem with a student.

Sometimes the conflict is between a student and teacher, sometimes between a student and other students in the class, sometimes it is a problem unrelated to the classroom. Regardless, it is usually worth the effort to seek out the student and listen to him or her to determine what is causing the disruptive behavior.

Finding the root cause of problems that arise can be crucially important. Teachers may need to consult not only the students in their classes, but other teachers, administrators, parents, and support staff before some problems can be solved. Management and human relations skills must be among the skills that teachers value and continue to develop throughout their professional lives.

## Good Teachers Engage Learners in the Process of Their Own Learning

Eleanor Duckworth tells her undergraduate classes in education that there are two important principles they must always keep in mind as they teach.[11] First, she says, always put learners in as direct contact as possible with whatever you want them to learn. That is usually the purpose of field trips and other hands-on activities in schools. But there are many ways students can be given direct contact with their learning. They can model the formation and movements of the solar system. They can keep diaries of their observations of animals who share their community. They can construct models, engage in mock and simulated experiences, and conduct interviews.

Second, and this is related to the first principle, Duckworth admonishes her teachers-to-be to provide frequent opportunities for learners to explain what they understand—both to the teacher and to other students. Anytime teachers are tempted to tell students something they want them to know, they should start by asking students to explain what they already know.

We'd suppose that if a beginning teacher had only these insights about teaching–provide direct contact and allow learners to explain their own understandings–Duckworth's advice would be critical to the teacher's instructional effectiveness. We know that learners will learn more in proportion to how engaged they are with what they are trying to learn. This is the *law of meaningful engagement,* though it is a law violated all too often. Not all students have the same time for learning in school,[12] and it is sadly the case that the students who need the most time to learn may be given the least. For example, Brady and his colleagues found that the times of engagement vary from 90 percent to 4 percent of classtime for different students in different classes throughout the day.[13] Benjamin Bloom has suggested that the academically lowest 10 percent of students might need five to six times the amount of time to learn the same thing as the academically highest 10 percent.[14] Our experience tells us this: providing direct contact with what is to be learned and giving students frequent opportunities to explain what they know are corollaries to the law of meaningful engagement. Implicit in these principles is that teaching is more akin to drawing out than to putting in.

None of this is meant to suggest that in the context of the instructional models we have advocated, teachers should not provide learners with information or sources for that information. On the contrary, good information presented in a variety of forms is essential to learning. But models of instruction are powerful when they serve not as rules for teaching and learning but as signposts to understanding.

The learner's understanding and insight must be the goal of instruction. One of the great paradoxes of education, which few laypersons but every good teacher will sooner or later discover, is that understanding cannot be given to the learner directly anymore than a parent can teach a child to tie her shoes by merely telling her how. Give her a shoe to practice on (or, better, let her practice on her own shoe), and have her explain to you or another person what she is doing as she practices. And if that advice is good for learning to tie shoes, how much better is it for learning all the complicated things students are expected to know in school?

# Good Teachers Teach Up

### ■ The Pygmalion Effect

The Pygmalion effect in education was made famous by Rosentahl and Jacobson in the late 1960s.[15] Essentially, their research asserts that a teacher's expectation that a student will do well can have a positive effect on the academic success of that student. The other side of the coin, namely that teachers do treat high- and low-achieving students differently to the detriment of the low-achieving student, has been brought to light as well by research.[16] Good lists the ways in which teachers most often discriminate in their treatment of high- and low-achievers:[17]

- by seating low-achieving students farther away from the teacher;
- by paying less attention to low-achieving students;
- by calling on low-achieving students less frequently to answer questions;
- by giving low-achieving students less time to answer questions when they are called on;
- by not providing cues or asking follow-up questions to help low-achieving students answer questions;
- by criticizing low-achieving students more frequently for incorrect answers;
- by giving low-achieving students less praise for correct or marginal responses;
- by giving low-achieving students less feedback and less detail in the feedback they are given;
- by interrupting the performance of low-achieving students more often that that of high-achieving students; and
- by demanding less effort and less work from low-achieving students than from high-achieving students.

A first-grade teacher said to one of us recently, "All of my students think they are good readers." And we know why—their teacher makes them feel that way. But how do teachers do that, honestly, without glossing over problems or saying things that aren't really true? After all, it would be a mistake to hold the same expectation of all students. How do teachers achieve the optimum expectation for all students? There is no easy answer to that question, but there are some behaviors that will help teachers encourage *all* students to reach their full potential.

### ■ Capitalize on What Students Know

Teachers should find something in what students already know to establish a basis for new understandings. Students often feel as if they know nothing of what's taught in school and could not care less—it all seems so irrelevant. But good teachers help learners see that they already know much about what they are trying to learn, and *what they already know is the single most important factor influencing what they will learn*. Learners are crucially important to their own learning and teaching should make them feel that way.

### ■ Celebrate Differences among Students

There's an old adage that says, "None of us is as smart as all of us." That's true in a classroom, too. If teachers make it quite clear that what each one knows or learns is of value to everyone, then they make it safe for everyone to share whatever they know and thus to value their own understanding, no matter how meager. Half of what we're talking about here is polite behavior–respect–and the other half of it is intellectual honesty–no one knows everything about anything, not even the teacher, and that's OK. It just means two heads are always better than one.

### ■ There Is More Than One Right Answer to Important Questions

Every teachers' manual includes suggestions about what to say to students and what to expect them to say in return. In elementary school, the manuals for teaching reading will often go so far as to put what the teacher is to say in one color print and what the students are to say in another color print. But a lesson script can only be an approximation. In fact, the one certainty is that *answers will vary.* The trick is to take advantage of the variance.

### ■ Recognize Achievement and Minimize the Importance of Error

Remember learning to drive a car? If you were lucky, the person teaching you kept affirming that you could do it and praising you for all you were doing right. When difficulties arose, your instructor helped you focus on what to do rather than berated you for your shortcomings. But if you were unlucky, the person teaching you continually harped on everything you were doing wrong. To what effect? To shake your confidence, whether or not that was the intent.

The road to understanding is paved with errors, but the errors are not the point. Just as surely, the road is striped with success, and stripes are always brighter than pavement. Use them as your guide and help learners to see them.

## A Good Teacher Is a Good Learner

### ■ The Teacher as a Model for Learning

We're tempted to say that the teacher should be the best learner in the class, except we know how stiff the competition for that honor will always be. Anyway, we wouldn't want to set it up as a competition. What we're after here is the idea that the teacher must be an eager learner, willing to share the process of learning with other learners–the class. Good teachers learn from their own study, and they share that study with their students. Frequently, even daily, they bring a new idea to class from something they've read or seen. They are scholars and they share the process and the product of their scholarship. Teachers learn from their students, both about teaching and about the content they are studying together. Having the chance to teach someone else is one of the best ways to learn, and it is always a favor to both the learner and the teacher to reverse their roles from time to time. Teachers learn from teaching, and not just about their teaching but about their students and what they are studying.

It is a serious mistake for any teacher to project the image of the person who knows it all and is here to tell everyone. In the first place, such an attitude conveys an erroneous impression of the nature of knowledge, as if it were a once and for all matter. It has been said that the half-life of human knowledge in any field is about six years, and even that duration is slipping.[18] This does not mean that everything we know has to be replaced every five years because it is no longer true. But the knowledge humankind possesses is expanding so rapidly that the infrastructure of knowledge has to continually accommodate new insights and understandings. Thus teachers, like their students, are faced with the necessity of constantly learning just to keep abreast. The exciting result for the teacher who realizes this is that there is always a ready audience with which to share new insights and understandings. By contrast, a know-all, tell-all attitude treats knowledge as a fixed entity, excluding learners from the process of learning and dooming them to focus on the acquisition of information that may be obsolete even before their school days have passed. The more appropriate image of teacher as learner invites students to join with others (the teacher included) in the joy and thrill of coming to know. The long-term effect is that students will learn well, learn more, and be learners for life.

## ■ The Importance of Professional Knowledge

There are professional organizations for every branch and subject of teaching and for the field of education in general. The major function of these bodies is to provide a comprehensive literature to assist teachers and administrators in their mission to educate the children and adults of the nation. This literature consists mainly of professional journals, books, audio- and videotapes, and research and technical reports available in microfiche and laser disc form. Each professional organization also acts as host for regional, state, national, and international meetings and forums in which teachers come together to share and discuss common problems and ideas. Taken together, these sources form the basis of professional study in education.

We mentioned earlier that the half-life of human knowledge is about six years. This is as true in education as it is in the sciences, as the sheer volume of what we know about what we teach and how to teach it increases exponentially. (It's probably no coincidence that most school systems adopt new textbooks every five years.) The teacher who doesn't continue to study the education profession may soon be as outdated as yesterday's newspaper. The antidote is continuous staff development, available to virtually all teachers.

Little identifies four factors that encourage teachers to pursue their professional development:[19]

1. mutuality, respect, and collaboration among teachers;
2. multiple administrative mechanisms for cooperative planning among teachers;

3. opportunities for continuous learning by teachers, opportunities that are problem-centered, involve experiential application, and are properly sequenced; and

4. mutually conducted evaluation of program effectiveness.

### ■ The Teacher as Researcher

In addition to an attempt to keep abreast of the professional literature (as any professional must), teachers are in a position to be their own directors of research and development. It is no exaggeration to say that the observed result of every teaching experience forms the basis for refinements and improvements in teaching. A simplified model of the action research we have in mind, called the IPO model, is found in Figure 16.1.

If the observed outcome of the teaching/learning process (what the teacher and students do) is what was expected, then the input and the process must have been appropriate. But if there is any discrepancy between the expected outcome, formed on the basis of the instructional objectives, and the observed outcome, such discrepancy is to be explained by a shortcoming in either the input or the process or both. The IPO model will apply in virtually all teaching situations where the teacher has some degree of control over input (what to teach and what to teach with) and process (how to teach) and can make appropriate changes in either or both factors. Using the IPO model makes the teacher a student of his or her own experience.

## Good Teachers Develop Instructional Objectives with Learners

### ■ Vesting Students with an Interest in Learning

The quality of instruction in a classroom will be determined largely by whether the students have a vested interest in the instruction and in their own learning. In other words, they have to care about what's going on in the class and be

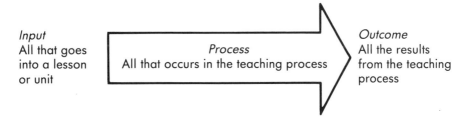

**FIGURE 16.1**   IPO Model

willing to cooperate to reach shared objectives. Instructional objectives, from the point of view of the learners, are learning objectives. Whether the objectives are achieved or not will depend on the learners' willingness to adopt the teacher's instructional objectives as their own learning objectives.

We are not advocating that teachers plan their instruction on the basis of what students say they want to learn, even though that can often be taken into account. What we do advocate is that teachers share the process of their own planning for instruction with their students. How can teachers do this? Initiate a unit of study with an exploration of what students have already studied on the topic, followed by a listing of what they think they want to know in addition. Many studies of effective instructional practices make clear that teaching that builds on what learners already know leads to higher achievement.[20]

### ■ Guides to Planning Instruction

Plan instruction by asking students to create a hypothetical outline of a chapter they are going to read. Then check to see that the chapter does indeed address the topic in the anticipated way; if there are shortcomings, involve the students in deciding what to do to augment the available information. Plan instruction by providing students with many different means and sources to learn the same thing and to accomplish the same objectives. Plan instruction by giving learners opportunities to help each other in achieving shared objectives.

## Good Teachers Find Out Why a Plan Isn't Working

L. W. Anderson has summarized the major conclusions to be drawn from the vast body of literature on effective teaching.[21] Effective teachers, he suggests,

- know their students;
- assign appropriate tasks to their students;
- orient their students to the learning task;
- monitor the learning progress of their students;
- relate teaching and testing, testing what they teach;
- promote student involvement and engagement in the learning process;
- provide continuity for their students so that learning tasks and objectives build on one another; and
- correct student errors and misunderstandings.

If these effective teaching behaviors are to be a reality, it is important that teachers be aware of options. If one approach or technique is not working with a class, analyze the problem and redesign the instructional plan. For instance, some classes are not ready for group work. Many times, teachers will attempt a group activity and, when chaos develops, they swear they will never try it again. Students must be prepared for group activities, and the procedures involved in setting up those activities must be carefully planned and directed. The models in this book for Jigsaw and for Teams, Games, Tournaments are only two of a number of effective group-process models. With some instructional models, the students may need to have more preparation time. It may be that certain steps in the model have not been adequately explained.

Sometimes the instructional plan is too ambitious, content to be covered is too extensive, or the students do not have the necessary readiness and predisposition for learning. Evaluate the situation and consider what options you have to correct the difficulty. Treat problems as a challenge rather than as a threat.

## Good Teachers Strive to Make Their Teaching Interesting

The relationship between interest and curiosity is no accident—learners are interested in learning those things about which they feel the greatest curiosity. Therefore, if teachers can pique the curiosity of learners, they will make what they teach interesting to learners. For example, if the topic of study were the Civil War, rather than rely on a textbook presentation of the major events of that great conflict, the instruction could draw upon the vast literature that focuses on it: the short stories of Ambrose Bierce; the children's novel, *Across Five Aprils*, by Irene Hunt; and excerpts from the diaries of slaves contained in *To Be a Slave*, by Julius Lester, to name a few selections. For every major topic of the curriculum, there is a vast literature to draw on in teaching. The effect is to open windows on scholarship for young learners.

Curiosity must be nurtured if it is to flourish. John Dewey once remarked that "curiosity is not an accidental isolated possession; it is a necessary consequence of the fact that an experience is a moving, changing thing, involving all kinds of connections with other things."[22] The key to curiosity rests in the idea of connections. Teaching in ways that make information interesting to learners helps them see the connections between what they are learning and what they know, between what they are learning in school and the world, and between the same information in different disciplines.

## Learners Must Have Access to Information and Opportunity to Practice

Research on effective schools unequivocally supports the idea that learning is most likely to occur when learners have access to information and the opportunity to practice using that information.[23] But what kind of information and practice are appropriate? Most obviously, students need whatever information is necessary to accomplish the learning objective at hand—accurate information presented in a palatable form. And students need practice in applying or recalling the new information in the solution of problems that require it. In the case of a learning objective that called for students to compare and contrast the causes of the French and Indian War with the War of 1812, the students would need information about these two wars and guidance and feedback on their attempts to make appropriate comparisons and contrasts.

The information needed by students is more than facts, data, and algorithms, however. Paraphrasing from a research report by Yinger, we can identify these other sorts of information as (1) knowledge of what to do with information gained and of how to use it in practice, (2) knowledge of when the information will apply and of how to apply it, and (3) knowledge of whether the uses of the information have been successful or not.[24]

Likewise, the practice students need is not solely of those behaviors implicit in the specific learning objective they have been given. In addition to applying or recalling information, Perkins and Salomon state that learners need practice in "low road" and "high road" transfer.

> When teachers introduce a literary classic with reference to the related experiences of their students, they are creating conditions for "low road" transfer. When teachers point out parallels between the elements of content, such as the points of comparison between the treatment of blacks in the United States before the Civil War and in South Africa today, they are facilitating "high road" transfer.[25]

Low road transfer is direct application of information to contexts and problems like those in which the information was first encountered. For example, students might practice application of the Pythagorean theorem by calculating the diagonals of their classroom and a football field, given the distance of the lengths and widths. High road transfer is indirect application of information to contexts and problems unlike those in which the information was first encountered. For example, students might compare the events and political alignments of the French and Indian War with the alignments of loyalties in the play *Romeo and Juliet*.

It is always important to keep in mind that long-term, meaningful learning depends on the access students have to good information and the opportunity to transfer and apply that information in ways that make it both meaningful and memorable.

## Good Teachers Teach for Two Kinds of Knowledge

It is impossible that students could learn in school all they would ever need to know in their lives. They must, therefore, learn how to learn. In every course of study in school, students are given access to a portion of the accumulated knowledge and wisdom of mankind—the facts, ideas, algorithms, events, and implications of history, literature, science, math, health, and so on. But *knowing that* will not stand the learner in good stead in the future if he or she doesn't also acquire a complimentary kind of knowledge—the skills of reading, writing, study, and thinking necessary for continued growth and life-long scholarship—*knowing how*.

Thus, teaching in the kind of classroom we have in mind here would give learners access to information to be learned and to a conscious knowledge of how to learn it. In this classroom, the teacher creates an environment in which

students are responsible for knowing and for knowing how they know, for taking control of the processes of their own learning and thinking. The intended result is an improvement of the learning and thinking necessary for participation in the discipline under study. We would want teachers at all grade levels and in all content areas to believe that the most important thing they have to teach students is the process of learning. This thought reminds us of an old expression: "Give a man a fish, and he'll eat for a day; teach a man to fish, and he'll eat for a lifetime." Consider the analogy: "Teach students only the information you want them to have and they'll pass the test tomorrow; teach students how to learn and they'll pass the test for the rest of their lives."

## ■ SUMMARY

There is more to managing a classroom of learners than just keeping the lid on. In fact, the necessity for most of that kind of management is preempted when the teacher takes control of the learning in the classroom and, in effect, turns the responsibility for learning over to the learners. Good teachers manage their instruction with that objective in mind, and they are able to do so because they operate out of a sound knowledge base and as intuition feeds their good judgment. In this chapter and throughout this book, we have tried to share with you the idea that there are always options the good teacher can draw on, even though most of the time good teaching, like any skilled performance, looks completely spontaneous. We hope that the suggestions we have offered will become part of your instructional repertoire.

## ■ NOTES

1. J. S. Kounin, *Discipline and Group Management in Classrooms* (New York: Holt, Rinehart, & Winston, 1970).

2. G. Leinhardt, C. Weidman, and K. M. Hammond, "Introduction and Integration of Classroom Routines by Expert Teachers," *Curriculum Inquiry 17* (1987): 137.

3. E. T. Emmer and C. M. Evertson, *Effective Management at the Beginning of the School Year in Junior High Classes,* Report No. 6107 (Austin, TX: Research and Development Center for Teacher Education, University of Texas at Austin, 1980); and D. L.

Duke, ed., *Helping Teachers Manage Classrooms* (Alexandria, VA: Association for Supervision and Curriculum Development, 1982).

**4.** Leinhardt, Weidman, and Hammond, "Classroom Routines," 143–144.

**5.** J. L. Goodlad, *A Place Called School: Prospects for the Future* (New York: McGraw-Hill, 1984).

**6.** M. Rutter, B. Maughan, P. Mortimore, J. Ouston, and A. Smith, *Fifteen Thousand Hours: Secondary Schools and Their Effects on Children* (Cambridge, MA: Harvard University Press, 1979).

**7.** T. J. Lashley, "Research Perspectives on Classroom Management," *Journal of Teacher Education* 32, no. 2 (1981): 14–17.

**8.** C. H. Wolfgang and C. D. Glickman, *Solving Discipline Problems: Strategies for Classroom Teachers,* 2nd ed. (Boston: Allyn and Bacon, 1986), 317.

**9.** W. Glasser, *Reality Therapy: A New Approach to Psychiatry* (New York: Harper and Row, 1965), 158.

**10.** Glasser, *Reality Therapy*, 159.

**11.** E. Duckworth, "Teaching as Research," *Harvard Educational Review* 56 (1986): 481–495.

**12.** D. A. Squires, W. G. Huitt, and J. K. Segars, *Effective Schools and Classrooms: A Research-Based Perspective* (Alexandria, VA: Association for Supervision and Curriculum Development, 1983).

**13.** M. P. Brady and P. L. Gunter, *Integrating Moderately and Severely Handicapped Learners: Strategies that Work* (Springfield, IL: Charles C. Thomas, 1985).

**14.** B. S. Bloom, *Human Characteristics and School Learning* (New York: McGraw-Hill, 1976).

**15.** R. Rosentahl, and L. Jacobson, *Pygmalion in the Classroom: Teacher Expectation and Pupils' Intellectual Development* (New York: Holt, Rinehart, & Winston, 1968).

**16.** J. E. Brophy and T. L. Good, "Teacher Expectations: Beyond the Pygmalion Effect," *Phi Delta Kappan* 54 (1972): 276–278.

**17.** T. L. Good, "Teacher Expectations and Student Perceptions: A Decade of Research," *Educational Leadership* 38 (1981): 415–421.

**18.** J. McTigue, and J. Schollenberger, "Why Teach Thinking: A Statement of Rationale," in *Developing Minds: A Resource Book for Teaching,* ed. A. L. Costa (Alexandria, VA: Association for Supervision and Curriculum Development, 1985).

**19.** J. Little, *School Success and Staff Development: The Role of Staff Development in Urban Desegregated Schools*, final report: National Institute of Education (Boulder, CO: Center for Action Research, 1981).

**20.** L. M. Anderson, *Student Responses to Classroom Instruction* (East Lansing, MI: Institute for Research on Teaching, Michigan State University, 1981).

**21.** L. W. Anderson, *Teachers, Teaching, and Educational Effectiveness* (Columbia, SC: College of Education, University of South Carolina, 1982).

**22.** J. Dewey, *Democracy and Education* (New York: Free Press, 1916), 209.

**23.** C. Fisher, R. Marliave, and N. Filby, "Improving Teaching by Increasing Academic Learning Time," *Educational Leadership* 37 (1979): 52–54.

**24.** R. J. Yinger, "Learning the Language of Practice," *Curriculum Inquiry* 17 (1987): 293–318.

**25.** D. N. Perkins, and G. Salomon, "Teaching for Transfer," *Educational Leadership* 46 (1988): 22–32.

# Summary of Part Three

# *Putting It All Together*

In Part Three we have tried to be specific in exemplifying the principles and practices advocated in the first two parts of this book. We have drawn our examples from various grade levels and then made a more general list of attitudes and practices that make a good teacher. Every teacher wishes to improve in the science and the art of instructional practice, and the case studies presented here, set against our general suggestions for creating a positive learning environment, are intended to assist in that improvement.

In our presentation of these three case studies, we intentionally varied the manner in which the steps were followed, precisely because there is no one prescribed formula to reach a successful instructional plan. One might rigidly follow a set of prescribed procedures and, without a spirit of creativity and enthusiasm, have a very negative teaching experience.

It has been our intention through this book to suggest procedures for planning, selecting, and utilizing instructional models, and behaviors for interacting with learners in the classroom. In our many years of experience working with teachers and prospective teachers, we have found the spirit of adventure, the intellectual excitement, and the creative innovations that they bring to the task are what make any set of procedures work in the classroom.

# Index